THE
Feminization
OF
POVERTY

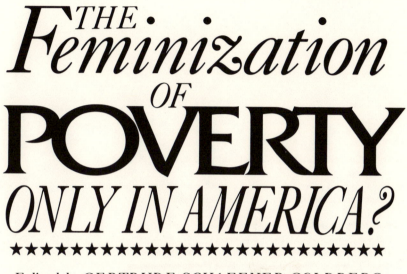

THE Feminization OF POVERTY

ONLY IN AMERICA?

★★★★★★★★★★★★★★★★★★★★★★★★★★★★★★

Edited by GERTRUDE SCHAFFNER GOLDBERG

& ELEANOR KREMEN

New York
Westport, Connecticut
London

Library of Congress Cataloging-in-Publication Data

The Feminization of poverty : only in America? / edited by Gertrude Schaffner
 Goldberg and Eleanor Kremen.
     p. cm.
   Includes bibliographical references and index.
   ISBN 0–275–93691–0 (pbk. : alk. paper)
   1. Poor women—Cross-cultural studies. 2. Poor women—United
States.   3. Women heads of households—Cross-cultural studies.
4. Women heads of households—United States. I. Goldberg, Gertrude
Schaffner. II. Kremen, Eleanor.
[HQ1154.F4493 1990]
305.4′0973—dc20   90–7424

A hardcover edition of *The Feminization of Poverty* is available from the Greenwood Press
imprint of Greenwood Publishing Group, Inc. (ISBN 0–313–26421–X)

Library of Congress Catalog Card Number: 90–7424
ISBN: 0–275–93691–0

First published in 1990

Praeger Publishers, One Madison Avenue, New York, NY 10010
An imprint of Greenwood Publishing Group, Inc.

Printed in the United States of America

The paper used in this book complies with the
Permanent Paper Standard issued by the National
Information Standards Organization (Z39.48–1984).

10 9 8 7 6 5 4 3 2 1

To our dear colleague
Ruth Kantrow

Contents

    Gertrude Schaffner Goldberg and Eleanor Kremen

    Index   219

    About the Editors and Contributors   229

Tables

Acknowledgments

We owe thanks to many for helping us to write a book that touches on the important themes in our lives and work: to those who taught us about social justice; to those who helped shape our thoughts about gender, race, and class; to those who encouraged us to look beyond the narrow confines of nationalism, professionalism, and parochialism. The time we live in with its ferment of ideas and events must also be acknowledged.

To begin, we name those who directly contributed to the research and writing of this book. Our colleagues Ruth Kantrow, Marguerite Rosenthal, and Sophie Wojciechowski helped us to plan the research, and each wrote or coauthored a chapter of the book. Former dean of the Adelphi University School of Social Work, Joseph L. Vigilante, encouraged us to do research on the condition of women and provided time and other resources to support this study. Helen Ginsburg offered boundless enthusiasm for this project, provided her own solid example of crossnational research, and generously introduced us to her network of scholars in several countries. Sumner Rosen was a source of encouragement and of relevant materials from several of the countries studied. Frank Riessman helped the project by recognizing early the value of our work and publishing a feature article based on it in the journal *Social Policy*. Seymour Martin Lipset kindly shared a chapter from his unpublished book and pointed the way toward a basic understanding of Canada. Patricia Daenzer shared her knowledge of Canadian labor-market policy and equal-opportunity policy.

Study in Sweden and France was aided by the Swedish Information Service and by Jean-Claude Delaunay and Frederique LePrince of the Commissariat General du Plan.

The following individuals read and commented on chapter drafts: June Axinn, Louise Dulude, Helen Ginsburg, Siv Gustafsson, Jane Jenson, Seymour Martin Lipset, Maureen Moore, Marguerite Rosenthal, Colette Shulman, Lynn Turgeon, Janice Wood Wetzel, Sophie Wojciechowski, and Narayan Viswanathan.

Our special thanks go to Susan Levien who typed parts of the manuscript, set up tables, and raised helpful questions about the text. Hilda Brady also provided much help with preparation of the manuscript. Florence Bolatin secured reports and information about current legislation and ferreted out other material for several chapters.

We, of course, have final responsibility for what we have written. May it help to stir women's and men's thoughts about the need for greater equality.

THE
Feminization
OF
POVERTY

1

The Feminization of Poverty: Discovered in America

GERTRUDE SCHAFFNER GOLDBERG
AND ELEANOR KREMEN

Writing more than a century and a half ago, Alexis de Tocqueville remarked on the relative equality that he had witnessed in the world's first modern democracy: "Men are there seen on a greater equality in point of fortune and intellect, or in other words, more equal in their strength, than in any other country of the world, or in any age of which history has preserved the remembrance" (1945, Vol. I, p. 55). Nonetheless, this great French observer of the American republic was not oblivious to inequality and oppression in the New World—to the bondage of blacks, the gradual extinction of the Indian tribes, and the subjugation of married women. Yet, the implicit standard of his age—indeed of much of re-corded history—was that of white men. Into the late twentieth century the very groups observed as subordinate by Tocqueville have remained economically disadvantaged, and women, particularly, are figuring in a form of inequality that has only recently been "discovered" in America.

The relatively brief span of years from 1960 to the mid–1970s witnessed not only the resurgence of American feminism but the feminization of American poverty. Despite a new movement for the liberation of women and an unprec-edented increase in the labor-force participation of women, poverty was "rapidly becoming a female problem" (Pearce, 1978, p. 28). In 1960, families with a female householder and no husband present constituted less than one-fourth of poor families; in little more than fifteen years, this proportion had doubled.[1] By the late 1980s the trend was even more pronounced. Women and their families were a clear majority of the American poor (U.S. Bureau of the Census, 1989, p. 11).[2]

Despite the persisting and substantial economic inequality in the United States, the disadvantaged condition of women is not uniquely American; indeed it is a worldwide phenomenon. Ruth Leger Sivard, who conducted a survey of 140 countries, drew a sad, if not surprising, conclusion: "What women have found to bind them together is a single thread that winds through all cultures. They share a sense of inequality of opportunity, the injustice of a traditionally imposed second place whether in the family, social, economic or political setting" (1985, p. 7). Also writing from a global perspective, Margaret Leahy commented similarly: "Evidence . . . indicates that in no nation do women presently have equality with men; in no nation is women's political position, economic position or social status equal to that of men" (1986, p. 4). These writers, however, have not specifically discussed the feminization of poverty in industrialized societies. Our task here is to determine whether the trend toward the feminization of poverty—the tendency for women and their families to predominate among the poor—is a peculiarly American phenomenon or whether it is developing in other industrialized nations as well.

CONCEPTUALIZING THE FEMINIZATION OF POVERTY

The term "feminization of poverty" has two meanings. In the stricter sense it refers to the fact that women who support themselves or their families are becoming the majority of the poor. In the United States this is now the case; single-mother families constitute about three-fifths of all poor families with children (U.S. Bureau of the Census, 1989, p. 11). We will be using this definition in making crossnational comparisons, and poverty will be measured by the poverty standard or social minimum, as it is termed in socialist countries, in each of the nations studied. We are cognizant that the level at which the minimum standard is set varies from country to country and that this can introduce some error into international comparisons.

The primary subjects for this study are women without male economic support—women who are "poor in their own right" (Pearce, 1978, p. 28). In the apt phrasing of Mark Granovetter and Charles Tilly, "the two events most likely to cast a household from relative prosperity into poverty are a major wage earner's loss of job and the loss of a major wage earner through divorce, separation or death" (1988, p. 178). Regardless of family structure, women as a group are economically disadvantaged, but when they must support themselves and their children, their economic disadvantages are highlighted. Typically, the earnings of a married woman, even if low, can supplement family income and may even have become the primary means of lifting families out of poverty. For the single woman the same low earnings are a path to poverty.

While this book focuses on spouseless women and on those living below the poverty standard, we nonetheless believe it is also important to think of the definition of the feminization of poverty in broader terms. Hilda Scott proposes that the feminization of poverty include the women who would be poor if they had to support themselves. In her view the official definition of poverty is "only the most obvious manifestation of the threat that hangs over the majority of women" (1986, pp. 3–4). To Scott, the "displaced homemaker," whose previous work has largely been confined to the domestic sphere, epitomizes the woman who is unable to escape poverty when she loses her husband to death, divorce, separation, or desertion. Scott has estimated that between two-thirds and three-fourths of working-age women would be poor if they were obliged to support themselves and just one dependent. Although two wages have become increasingly necessary for many families, U.S. Census Bureau data suggest that many fewer men would be impoverished in similar circumstances (1988, p. 23).

While elderly poverty is highly feminized, this study focuses on women of working and reproductive age. One reason for this is that the economic circumstances of elderly women are derived primarily from their earlier experiences in the family and in the labor market.

The feminization of poverty stems from a complex set of circumstances. It is important, first of all, to recognize that although women are increasingly part of the labor force, much of the work that they do is unpaid. As Granovetter and Tilly state: "the largest differences in returns to male and female labor . . . result from the fact that many women, including all housewives, receive no wages for their work" (1988, p. 178).

Women's position in the labor market is another key factor. As a result of a long and persisting tradition of occupational segregation and discrimination in the workplace, women earn low wages. Contributing to their secondary position in the labor market is the nature of the dual role that women in industrialized societies have assumed. Because they have continued to perform unpaid domestic work in the home, particularly to retain primary responsibility for the care of children, women have not been able to participate in work outside the home on an equal footing with men. Their careers are interrupted, they lose opportunities for promotion, and the strain of their domestic responsibilities causes them to modify their aspirations and to accept positions that mesh with their work at home. Women's dual role is linked to their low wages and thus indirectly related to the feminization of poverty. Indeed Wendy Sarvasy and Judith Van Allen attribute women's poverty to what they term the "unjust dual role . . . whereby many women combine unpaid domestic labor with underpaid wage labor" (1984, 92).

In the United States women have assumed a dual role almost unnoticed, combining work outside the home with their domestic and child care responsibilities. Public discussion has been limited to whether the woman's work outside the home will have a negative impact on the rearing of children. There has been little recognition that this has become a widespread and stable phenomenon requiring social intervention. The consequences of the dual role on women themselves, such as the impact on their health, their careers, and their lifetime earnings, have not been addressed by public policy. We are interested in how the other industrialized nations studied in this book have addressed this issue.

The concept of a family wage paid to the male breadwinner for the support of himself and his dependent wife and children has provided a rationale for the payment of low wages to women. Simone de Beauvoir recognized early that because the working woman was assumed to be economically dependent on her husband she was "led to accept remuneration far below what a man required" (1952, p. 107). The belief that women are supported by their spouses has persisted despite the fact that most women now support themselves or share the breadwinner role with their husbands. This concept of a family wage that has justified the payment of low wages to women is another indirect factor contributing to the feminization of poverty (Ehrenreich and Piven, 1984).

Demographic factors such as divorce, separation, and unmarried motherhood also contribute to the feminization of poverty. Since women have the primary responsibility for the care of children, they become the custodial or single parents when marriages break up or fail to form at all. Often with little or no financial support from the fathers of their children, mothers struggle to support their families on a single, low wage. As single motherhood becomes prevalent, as it has in the United States, poverty is likely to become feminized.

Efforts to reduce women's inequality in the labor market have been undertaken in all of the industrialized countries. In the United States, for example, legislation has been enacted that forbids sex discrimination in hiring, promotion, and training opportunities, and employers have been required to hire women in occupations traditionally held by men. In addition to these efforts to reduce occupational segregation, there have been laws to equalize pay for the same jobs or those of comparable worth. Such efforts, directed at long-standing sexist traditions in the workplace, have been limited in duration and scope. While showing promise, these policies have not substantially reduced inequities in the labor market and the resultant low wages that women receive.

The adequacy of the social welfare system or the social wage that is derived from it stands alongside the low wage as a significant factor in determining whether the feminization of poverty will occur.[3] The social welfare system can facilitate women's entry and participation in the workforce through such mechanisms as subsidized child care and transportation. It can substitute for lost earnings or supplement low wages. The social wage can compensate for the costs of parenthood through paid maternity or parental leave and family or children's allowances. In the absence of adequate paternal support, the system can provide or assure a minimum level of income for single mothers and their families. There are, of course, women who are outside the labor force, either temporarily or permanently, often because of child care responsibilities. To these women, clearly the social welfare system is of critical importance.

Social policy analysts in the United States differ in their views regarding the capacity of the social welfare system to inhibit the feminization of poverty. Diane Pearce (1978), who first identified the trend, pointed out that women in the United States are underrepresented among the beneficiaries of the more generous, work-related social insurance benefits and overrepresented as recipients of public assistance, a far less generous, means-tested program. This is particularly the case for women of color in the United States.

Sarvasy and Van Allen (1984) hold that the social welfare system in the United

States actually contributes to the feminization of poverty because it reinforces a traditional family ideology in which men are viewed as breadwinners and women as economically dependent (see also Abramovitz, 1988).[4] Eileen Boris and Peter Bardaglio (1983) view the welfare state as a form of patriarchy in which women have shifted their economic dependence from their husbands to the state but in which women continue to be subordinate in the family and the economic system.

Barbara Ehrenreich and Frances Fox Piven (1984) recognize that the American welfare state is seriously flawed and that the principal program for single mothers, Aid to Families with Dependent Children (AFDC), not only perpetuates poverty with its low benefits but that the welfare bureaucracy systematically degrades and humiliates its clients. Yet, they are pessimistic about the possibility of deriving sufficient income from employment, given the low-wage work that so many women are obliged to do. Social welfare programs have at least offered poor women the choice of staying home with their children, a choice that affluent wives have. According to Ehrenreich and Piven, poor women may want that choice, and they write that, "Even with a vast expansion of child-care services, some women may prefer to remain at home with their small children rather than do double duty as full-time employees and full-time homemakers" (p. 168). In 1988, however, Congress reduced that option by imposing a work requirement in AFDC for mothers of very young children (Bergmann, 1987; Cherry and Goldberg, 1988; Goldberg, 1987). Now poor women no longer have the choice of remaining at home with their children.

The analysis of poverty by gender has been criticized for overlooking or downplaying racial and ethnic inequalities (Brenner, 1987; Lewis, 1983; Malveaux, 1985, 1987). Pearce, though recognizing that "disadvantages suffered by poor women are exacerbated by race and prejudice for minority women," nonetheless has held that "for a woman race is a relatively unimportant consideration in determining economic status" (1978, pp. 30, 34). However, in the United States, black and Hispanic single mothers suffer poverty rates 50 percent greater than their white counterparts, and black women are three times as likely as white women to be in the economically vulnerable position of single motherhood. Three-fifths of poor, single-mother families in the United States, moreover, are women of color and their children (U.S. Bureau of the Census, 1989, pp. 11–14).

Evelyn Nakano Glenn (1985) argues that women of color do not merely face an intensification of the inequalities suffered by white women. As black feminist Sojourner Truth recognized more than a century ago, black women have not been protected against the hardships of either slave or wage labor (Fauset, 1988, pp. 131–132). The reproductive roles of white women have usually been favored over their market roles by devices such as the family wage or protective labor legislation (Kessler-Harris, 1982; Ursel, 1986), but black women's reproductive roles have generally been ignored in favor of their roles as marginal workers (Glenn, 1985). Owing to racism and limited economic opportunities for black men, black women have historically been obliged to assume major economic responsibilities for their families by entering a labor market in which they have faced both racism and sexism.

We believe that in the United States the problem of color cannot be minimized. In fact, we considered the possibility that racial injustice, as reflected in the economic condition of minority women in the United States, may be such a powerful factor as to make the feminization of poverty uniquely American. Existing analyses of inequality do not yet appear to have integrated the impact of gender, race, and class (Glenn, 1985; Bernard, 1987). Particularly in chapter 2, which focuses on the United States, we have tried to make a contribution to the understanding of this complex issue.

Undoubtedly, broad social forces such as patriarchy, industrialism, and the nature of the economic system have an important impact on the feminization of poverty. It is difficult, however, to identify and disentangle the contribution that each makes. Our analysis of the feminization of poverty assumes the context of an industrial society characterized by the increasing centrality of the service sector, theory-based technology, and the widespread absorption of women into the labor force—what some have termed postindustrialism (Bell, 1976, 1989; Block, 1987; Axinn and Stern, 1988).[5] The low wages that women earn, the unpaid work that they do in the home, and the social assignment of child care and domestic work solely to women reflect the continuing influence of patriarchy. Certainly, but not only in the United States, racism must be considered. Different economic systems—capitalism, socialism, and the more regulated market economies of western Europe—may well have a different effect on the emergence of the feminization of poverty.

Building on this analysis we will use the following four-factor framework for our crossnational analysis of the feminization of poverty:

1. *Labor market factors* such as women's participation in the labor force, part-time employment, unemployment, ratios of women's to men's wages, and sex segregation in the labor market for all women and for particular subgroups such as women of color.

2. *Policies to promote the labor market equality of women* such as equal pay legislation or affirmative action. These policies can increase women's economic opportunities or counter their economic inequalities. Often, too, these policies are designed to assist other disadvantaged groups such as minorities. The enactment and implementation of such policies reflect the degree of societal commitment to decreasing women's economic inequities. The extent to which women themselves have organized to effect equalization policies must also be considered.

3. *Social welfare benefits or government income transfers* such as those provided to the general population and specifically to women and their families. The scope and adequacy of these benefits or the social wage can be a significant deterrent to the feminization of poverty.

4. *Demographic factors* such as rates of divorce, remarriage, unmarried motherhood, and teenage pregnancy, which contribute to the prevalence of single motherhood.

Of course, these four factors interact and cannot be considered fully independent of one another. In fact, it is difficult to decide whether certain programs like child care or maternity benefits should be considered as part of labor market policy or social welfare policy. Moreover, it should be kept in mind that these factors operate in a historical-cultural context that changes over time.

CHOICE OF STUDY COUNTRIES

For our crossnational study we have chosen seven industrialized countries: five capitalist and two socialist. The capitalist nations are Canada, France, Japan, Sweden, and the United States. The two socialist countries are Poland and the Soviet Union.

We have grouped the capitalist countries according to the level of resources that they devote to social welfare. Canada, Japan, and the United States spend less than one-fourth of their total resources on social welfare. The term "reluctant welfare state" (Wilensky, 1965), originally applied to the United States, includes all three although there are differences among the lower spenders.[6] Sweden and France are examples of "advanced welfare states," spending approximately one-third of their gross national product (GNP) on social welfare (see table 1.1).[7]

Among advanced welfare states there are differing degrees of private ownership of economic enterprise. In Sweden, for example, ownership is overwhelmingly private. In France, government ownership is more extensive, although this has been fluctuating depending upon the orientation of the ruling political party. Similarly, among the less developed welfare states the degree of economic planning can differ. In Japan, as compared to the United States, the government is considerably more involved in economic planning (Johnson, 1982).

There are some other differences among the capitalist countries. These include the distribution of family income, with Japan being the most egalitarian and the United States among the least (World Bank, 1988, p. 273). There is a range in per capita income, even among these wealthy capitalist nations; in 1987 the GNP per capita of the United States was 45 percent higher than that of France, and in the preceding year the difference was even greater (see table 1.1). The capitalist countries also vary in their commitment to full employment. Japan and Sweden are among a handful of capitalist countries with a long-standing commitment to full employment, whereas the other capitalist countries in this study have from time to time allowed unemployment to climb to relatively high levels (Therborn, 1986). Full employment is potentially a mechanism for improving women's economic position by raising the general level of wages. However, full employment has been defined almost exclusively in terms of male employment (Armstrong and Armstrong, 1988). Women's labor force participation rates and

Table 1.1
The Seven Study Countries, Selected Indicators

	Population 1987 (millions) (a)	Area (sq. kilometers) (a)	GNP per capita (US $)		Social Expenditures %GDP		(d)
			1986 (b)	1987 (c)	1980	1985	
Canada	26	9,976	14,120	15,160	19.5	22.6	
France	56	547	10,720	12,790	30.9	34.2	
Japan	122	378	12,840	15,760	16.1	16.2	
Sweden	8	450	13,160	15,550	33.2	32.0	
U.S.	244	9,373	17,480	18,530	18.0	18.2	
Poland	38	313	2,070	1,930	NA	NA	
U.S.S.R.	283	22,402	4,550	NA	NA	NA	

	Military Expenditures % GNP, 1984 (e)	Distribution of Labor Force by Sector, 1980, % (f)		
		Agriculture	Industry	Services
Canada	2.3	5	29	65
France	4.1	9	35	56
Japan	1.0	11	34	55
Sweden	3.1	6	33	62
U.S.	6.4	4	31	66
Poland	2.5	29	39	33
U.S.S.R.	11.5	20	39	41

Sources:
(a) World Bank 1989, pp. 165, 232
(b) UNICEF, 1989, p. 95
(c) World Bank, 1989, p. 165
(d) OECD, 1988, pp. 16-17
(e) Sivard, 1987, pp. 43-44
(f) World Bank, 1988, p. 283

the extent to which they work full time need to be taken into account, too. In a full employment economy like Japan's, women's participation rate is relatively low; in Sweden, substantial numbers of women—over two-fifths—work part time. In the socialist countries, the constitutional guarantee of full employment appears to have been maintained until now in the developed areas of the economy. High rates of unemployment have recently been reported in underdeveloped areas and republics of the Soviet Union.

In Poland and the Soviet Union, the two socialist countries studied in this book, there are differences in the extent of industrial development. Poland retains a larger proportion of its workforce in agriculture and has had more limited experience with and commitment to a collectivist economy than the Soviet Union. These socialist countries differ from their capitalist counterparts, not only with respect to the obvious differences in ownership and control of the economic system, but in the extent of their economic resources. Although the two socialist countries are among the wealthier nations from a world perspective, the GNP per capita in the Soviet Union and Poland is considerably lower than those of all five capitalist countries (see table 1.1). The two socialist countries are also not as far along the industrialization or postindustrialization continuum as the capitalist countries in our study (see table 1.1).

Among the seven nations there are substantial differences in geographic area, population size, and demographic heterogeneity. Japan, Poland, and Sweden are examples of homogeneous countries, whereas the United States and the Soviet Union are quite heterogeneous. Clearly there are important cultural and historic differences between and among the capitalist and socialist nations.

This book looks at a wider range of countries than has generally been selected for previous crossnational comparison. Readers with an interest in social welfare or labor market policy, and those with an international or feminist perspective, may be familiar with the condition of women in the capitalist countries of North America and western Europe. The inclusion of two socialist nations in this study of the feminization of poverty is an opportunity to hold industrialization constant while examining the condition of women in contrasting economic systems. In effect, we will have data to test some of the differing assumptions that have been held about the economic status of women in socialist countries. Japan has recently emerged as one of the world's leading industrial powers. Its inclusion in this study provides an opportunity to explore the condition of women in a country that has industrialized rapidly while retaining many traditional expectations of the role of women. Because of what appear to be obvious similarities to the United States, the study of Canada and of women in that country has been somewhat overlooked. Chapter 3 on Canada not only provides data on a subject that may have been neglected but can also highlight some of the differences between these two North American neighbors that have been obscured by their apparent likeness.

The chapters on the North American countries, particularly the United States, are relatively lengthy. One reason is that these two countries have a well-developed statistical capacity and thus offer the scholar rather voluminous data. In the United States, demographic heterogeneity and the availability of statistics on people of color make it possible to present data on minorities and to explore the relationship among poverty, gender, and race.

COMPARING THE FEMINIZATION OF POVERTY
CROSSNATIONALLY

This study began with the recognition that the economic, social, and political inequality of women is a global phenomenon and that in the United States a trend toward the feminization of poverty has been discernible since the mid–1970s. In attempting to answer the principal question of this study, whether feminization of poverty exists in other industrialized countries with which the United States can be compared, we found that there is no research that addresses this question directly. Indeed, the recognition of the gender component in poverty is a relatively recent phenomenon in both the developing and industrialized worlds. In the developing world, for example, as was discovered at the International Women's Year Conference in Mexico City in 1975, "many nations had never thought to collect information on women as a distinct category," and "few had much information on the condition and status of women in their own nations" (Leahy, 1986, p. 3).[8] In the industrialized world, crossnational data are only beginning to be collected through such international organizations as the United Nations and its affiliate, the Economic Commission on Europe (ECE), the International Labor Organization (ILO), and the Organization for Economic and Cultural Development (OECD).

In addition to these international organizations, the Luxembourg Income Study (LIS) has facilitated crossnational comparison of family poverty (including single-parent families) through the use of a uniform poverty standard (Smeeding, Torrey, and Rein, 1988). The influential work of Alfred J. Kahn and Sheila B. Kamerman (1983; 1988) has provided much crossnational data on economically vulnerable families, including single mothers, in a number of capitalist countries.

Research in this area is complicated by the fact that some countries have not developed an official poverty standard; others, including the Soviet Union and France, do not gather or publish national income data. In the socialist countries, there has been a reluctance to identify poverty, much less to identify it by gender. There is a dearth of statistics describing the poverty or racial and ethnic minorities, and even Canada, which has a well-developed statistical capacity, lacks data on the poverty of minority women.

There are a number of crossnational studies that deal with one or more of the factors in our framework for analyzing the feminization of poverty. There are comparative studies of the welfare state (Flora and Heideheimer, 1981; Furniss and Tilton, 1977; Wilensky, 1983). Other authors have done crossnational work on labor market policy (Cook, Lorwin, and Daniels, 1984; Farley, 1985; Ginsburg, 1983; Jenson, Hagen, and Reddy, 1988). Still others have addressed policies to promote the economic equality of women (Schmid and Weitzel, 1984; Steinberg, 1980). Leahy's work (1986), which compared the status of women in two socialist and two capitalist countries, not only offered data on women in the Soviet Union and the United States, but also developed indicators for assessing women's equality. As far as we are aware no study before our own has addressed the four factors simultaneously or crossnationally.

DEVELOPMENT AND PLAN OF THE BOOK

This book developed out of the earlier collaboration of a group of women faculty at the Center for Social Policy of the Adelphi University School of Social Work. The Center has sponsored studies dealing with the lives and conditions of women graduate students (Goldberg, 1980) and of elderly women without close kin (Goldberg, Kantrow, Kremen, and Lauter, 1986). It has also done work in the area of labor market and social welfare policy (Goldberg and Viswanathan, 1982; Johnson and Goldberg, 1986; Goldberg, 1987; Goldberg and Kremen, 1987; Cherry and Goldberg, 1988). Several of the faculty members who collaborated on the earlier studies of women contributed to the development of this crossnational study, which combines the Center's interests in women, work, and welfare. Chapter 8's author, Sophie Wojciechowski (1975), contributed a chapter on Poland to an early collection on social services in nine countries (Thursz and Vigilante, 1975). Over the course of the years, Wojciechowski has stimulated her colleagues to adopt an international perspective.

In order to assure the desired diversity of countries for our sample, we invited scholars from other universities to contribute to this volume. All of our authors were asked to address each of the four factors that we have linked to the feminization of poverty. They were also asked to give special attention to the particular circumstances of single mothers and to address the dual role.

Drawing on the work of each of our authors, we conclude the volume with a discussion of our crossnational findings on the feminization of poverty, the common condition of women, single parenthood, and the dual role. Based on our analytic framework we venture to predict where the feminization of poverty is latent, or likely to emerge, unless countermeasures are taken. We propose some policies that we believe can prevent the emergence or increase of poverty among women in industrialized nations. We also consider the political feasibility of achieving such policies and programs in the United States.

Our research has been a challenging journey. It has brought us closer to an understanding of what is common in the lives of women and deepened our appreciation of the problems confronting poor women. Enriched by knowledge of programs and policies that have addressed the economic inequality of women in other nations, we have returned eager to share the knowledge that we believe can benefit women in our own country.

NOTES

1. We prefer not to use the term "female-headed families," which implies that the normal family is male-headed. The term also raises a question about the designation for families in which there is a single male or father with no wife present. We prefer, instead, the U.S. Bureau of the Census term "families with female householder, no husband present," "female-householder families," "families supported by a single woman," or, where there are children in the home, "single-mother, lone-mother, or mother-only families."

2. There is some evidence that women predominated among paupers in earlier centuries (Abramovitz, 1988; Katz, 1986). If that were true among the poor, generally, not only the economically dependent or paupers, then we might refer to the trend since 1960 as the "refeminization of poverty."

3. Russell defines "social wages" as "the system of state expenditures on public goods and income transfer payments for the ongoing maintenance and renewal of capitalist labour supplies," or what has been termed "social reproduction" (1986, pp. 309–310).

We use the term to refer to the income, goods, and services derived from the welfare state.

4. For a critique of the position that public welfare has served this function, see Frances Fox Piven (1988).

5. Some writers, such as Stephen S. Cohen and John Zysman (1987), have criticized the term postindustrialism, holding that the criteria for distinguishing industrial from postindustrial societies are not clear. It is not certain that postindustrialists have specified what is intrinsic to the wide variety of service jobs or what makes them fundamentally different from jobs in the primary and secondary sectors. Yet, we do think it important to call attention to the fact that most jobs in the U.S. economy are in the service sector.

6. Writing in the 1960s, Harold L. Wilensky assumed that there would be progress toward the welfare state, however reluctantly. In the 1980s, retrenchment rather than reluctance has been more characteristic of the U.S. welfare state.

7. The categorization of Canada as a ''reluctant welfare state'' might be questioned since its difference from Japan, the lowest spender, is 6.4 percent and its difference from Sweden, an advanced welfare state, amounts to 9.4 percent. For fuller discussion of social welfare in Canada, see chapter 3.

8. This conference and the conference in Nairobi, Kenya, sponsored by the United Nations, acted as a stimulus for the collection of data on women on a worldwide and on a regional basis. In preparation for the Nairobi conference, Sivard (1985) compiled her important study on the status of women throughout the world. The Economic Commission on Europe (ECE) published a comprehensive study on the economic role of women in Europe and North America (1985). There were regional follow-ups to the Nairobi conference, among which was the Nordisk Forum in 1988 that examined the status of women in the Scandinavian countries. Preliminary findings from our seven-country study were presented in a keynote speech to the Nordisk Forum, held in Oslo, Norway.

REFERENCES

Abramovitz, M. (1988). *Regulating the Lives of Women: Social Welfare Policy from Colonial Times to the Present*. Boston: South End Press.

Armstrong, P., and H. Armstrong (1988). ''Taking women into account: Redefining and intensifying employment in Canada.'' In J. Jenson, E. Hagen, and C. Reddy, eds. *Feminization of the Labor Force: Paradoxes and Promises*. New York: Oxford University Press.

Axinn, J., and M. J. Stern (1988). *Dependency and Poverty: Old Problems in a New World*. Lexington, MA: Lexington Books.

Beauvoir, S. de (1952). *The Second Sex*. H. M. Parshley, trans. and ed. New York: Bantam Books. (Original work published 1949).

Bell, D. (1976). *The Coming of Post-industrial Society*. New York: Basic Books.

————.(1989). ''The third technological revolution: And its possible socioeconomic consequences.'' *Dissent* 36 (Spring): 164–176.

Bergmann, B. (1987). ''A fresh start in welfare reform.'' *Challenge* 30 (6): 44–50.

Bernard, J. (1987). *The Female World from a Global Perspective*. Bloomington: University of Indiana Press.

Block, F. (1987). ''Rethinking the political economy of the welfare state.'' In F. Block, R. A. Cloward, B. Ehrenreich, and F. F. Piven, eds. *The Mean Season: The Attack on the Welfare State*. New York: Pantheon.

Boris, E., and P. Bardaglio (1983). "The transformation of patriarchy: The historical role of the state." In I. Diamond, ed. *Families, Politics and Public Policy*. New York: Longman, Green.

Brenner, J. (1987). "Feminist political discourse: Radical versus liberal approaches to the feminization of poverty and comparable worth." *Gender and Society* 1 (4): 447–465.

Cherry, R., and G. S. Goldberg (1988). "Fresh start or false start?" *Challenge* 31 (3): 48–51.

Cohen, S. S., and J. C. Zysman (1987). *Manufacturing Matters: The Myth of the Post-industrial Economy*. New York: Basic Books.

Cook, A. H., V. R. Lorwin, and A. K. Daniels, eds. (1984). *Women and Trade Unions in Eleven Industrialized Countries*. Philadelphia: Temple University Press.

Economic Commission on Europe (1985). *The Economic Role of Women in the ECE Region: Developments 1975/1985*. New York: United Nations.

Ehrenreich, B., and F. F. Piven (1984). "The feminization of poverty: When the family wage system breaks down." *Dissent* 31 (Summer): 162–168.

Farley, J., ed. (1985). *Women Workers in 15 Countries*. Ithaca, NY: ILR Press.

Fauset, A. H. (1971). *Sojourner Truth: God's Faithful Pilgrim*. New York: Russell & Russell.

Flora, P., and A. Heideheimer, eds. (1981). *The Development of Welfare States in Europe and North America*. New Brunswick, NJ: Transaction Books.

Furniss, N., and T. Tilton (1977). *The Case for the Welfare State*. Bloomington: Indiana University Press.

Ginsburg, H. (1983). *Full Employment and Public Policy: The United States and Sweden*. Lexington, MA: Lexington Books.

Glenn, E. N. (1985). "Racial ethnic women's labor: The intersection of race, gender and class oppression." *Review of Radical Political Economics* 17 (3): 86–108.

Goldberg, G. S. (March 1980). *What Do Women Students Need and Want? Preliminary Findings of the Alumnae Survey, Adelphi University School of Social Work*. Paper presented at the Annual Program Meeting, Council on Social Work Education, Los Angeles.

———.(September 1987). *Welfare Reform: Some American Illusions and Some New Initiatives*. Paper presented at the Fourteenth European Regional Symposium of the International Conference on Social Welfare, Special Meeting of the International Network on Unemployment and Social Work, Rome, Italy.

Goldberg, G. S., R. Kantrow, E. Kremen, and L. Lauter. (1986). "Spouseless, childless, elderly women and their social supports." *Social Work* 31 (March/April): 104–112.

Goldberg, G. S., and E. Kremen (1987). "The feminization of poverty: Only in America?" *Social Policy* 17 (Spring): 3–14.

Goldberg, G. S., and N. J. Viswanathan (April 1982). *Social Policy and the Work/Welfare Choice*. Paper presented at the Annual Meeting of the Eastern Sociological Association, Philadelphia.

Granovetter, M., and C. Tilly (1988). "Inequality and labor processes." In N. J. Smelser, ed. *Handbook of Sociology*. Newbury Park, CA: Sage Publications.

Jenson, J., E. Hagen, and C. Reddy, eds. (1988). *Feminization of the Labor Force: Paradoxes and Promises*. New York: Oxford University Press.

Johnson, C. (1982). *MITI and the Japanese Miracle: The Growth of Industrial Policies 1925–75*. Stanford, CA: Stanford University Press.

Johnson, H. C., and G. S. Goldberg (1986). *Government Money for Everyday People: A Guide to Income Support Programs*. Lexington, MA: Ginn Press.

Jones, E. F., et al. (1986). *Teenage Pregnancy in Industrialized Countries: A Study Sponsored by the Alan Guttmacher Institute*. New Haven, CT: Yale University Press.

Kahn, A. J., and S. B. Kamerman (1983). *Income Transfers for Families with Children: An Eight-country Study*. Philadelphia: Temple University Press.

Kamerman, S. B., and A. J. Kahn (1988). *Mothers Alone: Strategies for a Time of Change*. Dover, MA: Auburn Publishing Company.

Katz, M. B. (1986). *In the Shadow of the Poorhouse: A Social History of Welfare in America*. New York: Basic Books, Inc.

Kessler-Harris, A. (1982). *Out to Work: A History of Wage-earning Women in the United States*. New York: Oxford University Press.

Leahy, M. E. (1986). *Development Strategies and the Status of Women: A Comparative Study of the United States, Mexico, the Soviet Union and Cuba*. Boulder, CO: Lynne Rienner Publisher, Inc.

Lewis, D. K. (1983). "A response to inequality: Black women, racism and sexism." In E. Abel and E. K. Abel, eds. *The Signs Reader: Women, Gender and Scholarship*. Chicago: University of Chicago Press.

Malveaux, J. (1985). "The economic interests of black and white women: Are they similar?" *Review of Black Political Economy* (Summer): 5–27.

———. (1987). "The political economy of black women." In M. Davis et al., eds. *The Year Left 2: Toward a Rainbow Socialism: Essays on Race, Ethnicity, Class and Gender*. London: Verso.

Myles, J. (1988). "Decline or impasse? The current state of the welfare state." *Studies in Political Economy* 26 (Summer): 73–107.

Organization for Economic and Cultural Development (1988). "OECD in figures." *OECD Observer*, no. 152 (Supplement, June/July). Paris: OECD.

Pearce, D. (1978). "The feminization of poverty: Women, work and welfare." *The Urban and Social Change Review* 11 (1 and 2): 28–36.

Piven, F. F. (September 1988). *What Happened to the Promise of Women's Power? The Case of American Social Policy*. Paper presented at the Conference on Public Policies and Gender Politics, Social Science Research Council and the Wagner Institute, City University of New York.

Russell, B. (1986). "The crisis of the state and the state of crisis: The Canadian welfare experience." In J. Dickinson and B. Russell, eds. *Family, Economy and State: The Social Reproductive Process under Capitalism*. New York: St. Martin's Press.

Sarvasy, W., and J. Van Allen (1984). "Fighting the feminization of poverty: Socialist feminist analysis and strategy." *Review of Radical Political Economics* 16 (4): 89–110.

Schmid, G. and R. Weitzel, eds. (1984). *Sex Discrimination and Equal Opportunity: The Labor Market and Employment Policies*. New York: St. Martin's Press.

Scott, H. (1986). *Women and the Future of Work*. Unpublished paper, Cambridge, MA.

Sivard, R. L. (1985). *Women . . . A World Survey*. Washington, DC: World Priorities.

———.(1987). *World Military and Social Expenditures, 1987–88* (12th ed.). Washington, DC: World Priorities.

Smeeding T., B. B. Torrey, and M. Rein (1988). "Patterns of income and poverty: The economic status of children and the elderly in eight countries." In J. L. Palmer, T. Smeeding, and B. B. Torrey, eds. *The Vulnerable*. Washington, DC: Urban Institute Press.

Steinberg, R. S., ed. (1980). *Equal Employment Policy for Women*. Philadelphia: Temple University Press.

Therborn, G. (1986). *Why Some Peoples Are More Unemployed than Others: The Strange Paradox of Growth and Unemployment*. London: Verso.

Thursz, D., and J. L. Vigilante, eds. (1975). *Meeting Human Needs: An Overview of Nine Countries*. Beverly Hills, CA: Sage Publications.

Tocqueville, Alexis de (1945). *Democracy in America*. F. Bowen, trans., P. Bradley, ed. (2 vols.). New York: Vintage Books. (Original work published 1835).

UNICEF (United Nations Children's Fund) (1989). *The State of the World's Children*. New York: Oxford University Press.

U.S. Bureau of the Census (1988). *Money Income and Poverty Status in the United States: 1987*. Current Population Reports, Series P–160, No. 161. Washington, DC: U.S. Government Printing Office.

————.(1989). *Poverty in the United States: 1987*. Current Population Reports, Series P–60, No. 163. Washington, DC: U.S. Government Printing Office.

Ursel, J. (1986). "The state and the maintenance of patriarchy: A case study of family, labour and welfare legislation in Canada." In B. Russell and J. Dickinson, eds. *Family, Economy and State: The Social Reproductive Process under Capitalism*. New York: St. Martin's Press.

Wilensky, H. L. (1965). "Introduction: The problems and prospects of the welfare state." In H. L. Wilensky and C. N. Lebeaux, eds. *Industrial Society and Social Welfare*. New York: The Free Press.

————.(1983). "Political legitimacy and consensus: Missing variables in the assessment of social policy." In S. Spiro and E. Yuchtman-Yaar, eds. *Evaluating the Welfare State*. New York: Academic Press.

World Bank (1988). *World Development Report 1988*. New York: Oxford University Press.

Wojciechowski, S. (1975). "Poland's new priority: Human welfare." In D. Thursz and J. L. Vigilante, eds. *Meeting Human Needs: An Overview of Nine Countries*. Beverly Hills, CA: Sage Publications.

2

The United States: Feminization of Poverty Amidst Plenty

GERTRUDE SCHAFFNER GOLDBERG

The United States is a very wealthy country with a very unequal distribution of income. In 1987, the GNP per capita of the United States was 50 percent higher than the U.S. poverty level for a family of four. Yet, in that same year, there were over 32 million impoverished Americans (U.S. Bureau of the Census, 1989, p. 7).

Along with the persisting American paradox of poverty amidst plenty is a newer paradox. At the very time when women have been emancipating themselves from unpaid domestic work, the families with a female householder and no husband present have become preponderant among the poor. Such families have probably always suffered a high risk of poverty, but they have not always been the majority of poor families. In 1960, when the poverty rate of families with a female householder and no husband present was higher than in the late 1980s, these families constituted less than one-fourth of poor families. They are now the majority (U.S. Bureau of the Census, 1989, p. 11).

Since 1960, millions of American women have entered the labor force, but for many of these women, paid employment has not meant economic independence or true emancipation. As we examine labor market factors and government policies to reduce sex discrimination and inequality in the workplace, we find that while most women work, many do not earn enough to escape poverty.[1]

Disadvantaged in the workforce, American women who support themselves frequently require government income transfers or social welfare to escape poverty or economic deprivation. Yet, at just the time when the number of single mothers and female householders had risen very significantly, the U.S. government cut back the social programs that relieve the poverty of these women and their families (Bawden and Palmer, 1984; Piven and Cloward, 1985).Through a combination of tax reduction and greatly increased defense spending, the federal government during the 1980s created a huge budgetary deficit that contributes to the impression that social expenditures are fiscally irresponsible (Schlesinger,

1986). The effect of these government policies has been to create a poor state in a rich nation, one that cannot afford to pay for social welfare.[2] Thus, despite its abundant resources, the United States denies to women not only a fair market wage, but a decent social wage as well.[3]

In the United States, there is, in addition to gender, another important piece to the poverty puzzle. Nearly three-fifths of all poor families with a female householder and no husband present are either black or Hispanic (U.S. Bureau of the Census, 1989, pp. 11–14). American women of color are "doubly disadvantaged," but they are also said to be "doubly ignored," overlooked in analyses that are concerned with either racial or gender inequality (Malveaux, 1985). Yet, the feminization of poverty in the United States can only be understood by considering both of these forms of inequality, along with that of social class. Thus, in discussing each of the four factors that we have linked to the feminization of poverty—labor force, equalization, social welfare, and demographics—we present data regarding women of color.

AMERICAN WOMEN AND WAGE WORK

The increase in women's labor force participation in the post–World War II period has been striking in its sheer magnitude, proportions, and composition. The number of women in the workforce has increased by over 35 million since 1950, or nearly three-fold (table 2.1). From 1950 to 1975 alone the percentage increase was equal to that of the entire sixty years preceding 1950 (Kessler-Harris, 1982, p. 310). As a result of these increases, the labor force participation rate for women age 16 and over rose from about one-third in 1950 to well over one-half (56.0 percent) in 1987. The proportion rises to about two-thirds if the traditional working years, 16 to 64, are considered (U.S. Department of Labor, Bureau of Labor Statistics, 1989, calculated from pp. 17, 39, 75, and 97). Between 1950 and 1987, women increased their share in the labor force from just under 30 percent to 45 percent.

Employment has always been fairly common for women between leaving school and getting married but far less so after marriage and childbirth (Mott, 1982, p. 6). The revolution in women's employment, then, is not just in its size but in the tendency for married women and mothers, including those with young children, to go out to work.[4] Whereas less than one-third (30.4 percent) of women with children under age 18 were employed outside the home in 1960, almost two-thirds (65.6 percent) were in 1987. The increases were even more dramatic for the mothers of children under age 6 whose rates of participation nearly tripled since 1960. In 1987, over half (54.0 percent) of the women with children under 3 were in the labor force—an increase of over 50 percent in just a dozen years. The participation rate of single mothers with children under 18 was 69.2 percent, somewhat higher than the 63.8 percent figure for married mothers (U.S. Department of Labor, Bureau of Labor Statistics, 1989, pp. 804–806).

Table 2.1
Labor Force Participation of Women, Age 16 and Over, 1950–1987

(numbers in millions)

	Number	Rate	Proportion Labor Force
1950	18.4	33.9	29.6
1960	23.2	37.7	33.4
1965	26.2	39.3	35.2
1970	31.5	43.7	38.1
1975	37.5	46.3	40.0
1980	45.4	51.5	42.5
1985	51.1	54.5	44.2
1987	53.7	56.0	44.8

Source: U.S. Department of Labor, Bureau of Labor Statistics, 1989, pp. 17, 74, 75, 133.

The factors that have increased women's labor force participation are diverse and often interrelated. Labor-saving devices and declining birth rates have freed them to work outside the home. Divorce and changing consumption norms (preference for goods produced in the market rather than "homemade") have increased women's economic need for employment, and feminist thinking has emphasized economic independence and self-fulfillment through employment (Bergmann, 1986, chapter 2; Brown, comments by Carter and Lebergott, 1987; Degler, 1980, chapter 5; Kessler-Harris, 1982, chapter 11; Smith, 1986).

The factors influencing women's decisions to enter the labor force vary in relation to their social and economic circumstances and the eras being considered. In a discussion primarily concerned with poor women, however, it is especially important to bear in mind the estimate made by the Women's Bureau of the Department of Labor that approximately two-thirds of working women are widowed, divorced, separated, never married, or have husbands with annual incomes under $15,000 (Christensen, 1988b). Despite the fact that women are still regarded as secondary workers, their incomes are of primary importance to themselves and their families.

Paralleling the changes that have increased the need for women to become employed is the increased availability of jobs to which women have traditionally had greater access. More open to women's employment than the goods-producing sector, employment in the service sector has grown dramatically in the postwar era (Kornbluh, 1987). In the period from 1970 to 1984, 22 million of 23 million new jobs in the economy were in service industries (Axinn and Stern, 1988).

Women's vastly increased labor force participation has not been associated with commensurate improvement in their position in the labor market. The 30 years following World War II were generally a time of economic expansion and rising real wages, but it was not until the end of this interval that women began to press their claims for equality. Since the mid–1970s, employment conditions generally have deteriorated. The position of women has actually improved somewhat, as discussions of the wage gap and occupational segregation will show, but not nearly enough to achieve parity with men or for many employed single mothers to escape poverty.

Since the early 1970s, American business has attempted to maintain its profitability in the face of increased international economic competition, the creation of natural resource cartels like OPEC in the developing nations, and the accelerated growth of a low-profit service industry. Business responded to these changes, not primarily with capital investment or innovations that would increase productivity, but primarily with a strategy that came to be called "restructuring"—wage freezes; the development of alternative work arrangements that increase the flexibility with which workers can be hired, fired, and scheduled; the reduction of internal labor markets or career paths; and globalization or the shift of capital and business operations to lower-wage areas of the world (Harrison and Bluestone, 1988; Appelbaum, 1987).

Although American industry has tended to eschew changes that would increase productivity, technical innovation is nonetheless affecting the design, distribution, and amount of work. The overall employment effects of technological advance are debatable (Leontieff and Duchin, 1986), but computerization of office work, for example, could reduce the amount of clerical jobs for women (Christensen, 1988b). Computer technology, moreover, is being implemented in such a way as to eliminate both entry-level positions and the jobs that traditionally formed the rungs of career ladders from semiskilled to skilled work (Appelbaum, 1987).

Government policy has abetted restructuring rather than protected rights of workers. The federal minimum wage remained the same between 1981 and 1990 and fell substantially in real value. Cuts in welfare programs for working-age Americans reduced alternatives to low-wage or degrading work (Piven and Cloward, 1985). Deregulation of transportation and communications industries and a laissez-faire stance by the National Labor Relations Board weakened the power of labor to resist these changes (Axinn and Stern, 1988), as did anti-union tactics of the federal government itself in its role as employer. Tight monetary policies that, in the early 1980s, created the highest unemployment rates since the Great Depression also tended to depress wages and weaken workers' positions vis-à-vis management.

One result of these strategies on the part of business and government has been called the "pauperization of work" (Morehouse and Dembo, 1988), or the replacement of higher paid jobs by those at or close to the minimum wage. Between 1972 and 1988, real weekly earnings of nonsupervisory workers declined by 15 percent (calculated from Morehouse and Dembo, 1988, p. 7).

Bennett Harrison and Barry Bluestone have used the metaphor of a "U-turn" to describe the decline in real annual wages after 1973 following a steady rise since the 1950s. Women, though still much more likely to be in the lower-wage workforce than men—defined as less than half of the inflation-adjusted 1973 median—were nonetheless somewhat less likely to be in that disadvantaged position in the mid–1980s than in the early 1970s (Harrison and Bluestone, 1988). Neither the pauperization of work nor the U-turn applies directly to the experience of women. The significance of the general decline in real wages to which these concepts refer is that such a trend has made it difficult for an economically disadvantaged group—women or minorities—to make significant gains in its position concurrently. Trends in the last two decades have resulted in an increasing number of jobs that resemble those traditionally held by women.

Another result of restructuring was an increasing wage gap between the shrinking manufacturing sector and the expanding service sector that so many women were entering. Whereas the average weekly wage of service workers in 1970 was 62 percent that of workers in manufacturing, the ratio was 51 percent ten years later (Kornbluh, 1987). The ratio of retail-trade to manufacturing earnings fell from 64 percent in 1977 to 44 percent in 1988 (calculated from Morehouse and Dembo, 1988, p. 7). The level of service-sector wages relative to manufacturing wages is lower in the United States than in some other major industrial nations (Waldstein, 1989).

Part-time and Other Contingent Work

Contingent work is the term used to describe alternative work arrangements such as part-time employment, temporary work, and homework, which give employers greater flexibility in hiring, firing, and wages and fringe benefits (U.S. Department of Labor, Women's Bureau, 1988). In recent years employers have been selecting a core group of employees, investing in their development, and encouraging their attachment to the firm; at the same time they have been employing a peripheral or contingent group from whom they remain relatively detached, even at the cost of high turnover (Mangum, Mayall, and Nelson, 1985). The notion of a dual or segmented labor force with largely insurmountable barriers between good jobs and bad jobs can thus be extended to internal labor markets or to core and contingent workers within firms.[5] In both cases the less desirable employment track is for women and minorities.

Over one-fourth of women workers (27.0 percent) were employed part time at any one time in 1987, but many more workers are so employed at some time during the year (Kornbluh, 1987, citing Terry, 1981). Moreover, this proportion underestimates part-time employment by omitting substantial numbers of persons on temporary part-time schedules or with two part-time jobs.[6] It also omits persons on full-time schedules who work less than thirty-five hours a week (Appelbaum, 1987).

According to one study, the proportion of women workers employed part time increased by about 18 percent between 1954, the first year for which data on part-time employment were collected, and 1977 (Appelbaum, 1987, citing Deutermann and Brown, 1978). The 1970 figure of 27.5 percent is roughly equivalent to the 1987 proportion. Thus, the proportion of female part-timers has not risen measurably since 1970, although 5 million more women were working part time in 1987 than in 1970 (U.S. Department of Labor, Bureau of Labor Statistics, 1989, p. 711). In the United States, women make up two-thirds of the part-time workforce. Yet, in other capitalist countries, part-time work is even more likely to be women's work (OECD, 1988, p. 149).

Part-time employment can be seen as a way to combine work in the home and in the labor force, but its economic consequences, both current and future, may be negative. In recent years, median hourly wages for part-timers have been 40 percent less than for full-time workers (Levitan and Conway, 1988; Plewes, 1987). Part-timers get lower wages than full-time workers largely because they are overrepresented in low-paid industries and occupations but also because they earn less than full-timers even when they are in the same job categories (Long and Jones, 1981; Owen, 1978).

Part-time employees are much less likely than full-time workers to be covered by health insurance and pension plans (Levitan and Conway, 1988). About 70 percent of part-timers have no employer-paid retirement, and 42 percent have no health insurance coverage (Kornbluh, 1987). Since the United States does not have national health insurance, part-time workers suffer more severe economic consequences than in other industrialized countries. For single women and those not covered by a husband's pension or health benefits, the lack of fringe benefits can be especially disadvantaging (Christensen, 1988b). Part-time employment may permit flexibility for some women, but ''the 'bottom line' has been an expanded pool of low-wage, contingent laborers unprotected by basic benefits'' (Levitan and Conway, 1988, p. 10).

In the capitalist countries, a distinction is made between part-time work that is a matter of choice and part-time work that is involuntary. A distinction such as this is less appropriate for women than for men. A substantial minority of women (24 percent) who work part time would work more hours if suitable child care were available (Presser and Baldwin, 1980). While voluntary part-time employment is much more common than involuntary, the latter has grown three times faster than the former since 1970 (calculated from U.S. Department of Labor, Bureau of Labor Statistics, 1989, p. 711). Involuntary part-time employment is closely associated with poverty, especially among women who maintain families (Appelbaum, 1987; Kornbluh, 1987).

Temporary work, much of it subcontracted from temporary help agencies, is also work done primarily by women, and it has been growing five times faster than the total workforce. Women between the ages of 25 and 54 comprise almost two-thirds of the temporary workforce (Plewes, 1987). By definition, temporary work lacks job stability, and like other forms of contingent work, it tends to be lower in pay and limited in both fringe benefits and opportunities for upward mobility.

Unemployment

Even though unemployment rates had come down from their post-Depression peaks early in the 1980s, more than 3 million women were unemployed at any one time in 1987, a rate of 6.2 percent (U.S. Department of Labor, Bureau of Labor Statistics, 1989, pp. 15, 405). The number unemployed at some time during any year tends to be more than twice that figure (pp. 405, 473). Unemployment rates for female householders consistently exceed the national women's average (U.S. Bureau of the Census, 1986b, pp. 9, 17). In 1985, the Coalition of Women and Employment and the Full Employment Action Council issued a report stating that official unemployment rates for divorced, separated, widowed, or single women were consistently one and a half to two times higher than the national average or the official unemployment rate for married women with a spouse present (p. 4).

Official unemployment statistics omit involuntary part-time workers and those who stop looking for work because they do not expect to find it (discouraged workers). Real joblessness rates that take into account these other types of unemployment are double the official rates (Coalition on Women and Employment and Full Employment Action Council, 1985; Morehouse and Dembo, 1988).

As a result of cutbacks in unemployment insurance in the 1980s, the economic consequences of unemployment have become more severe. This can be especially problematic for female householders since they are more than twice as likely as other families to lack another form of protection against unemployment: more than one worker in a household (U.S. Bureau of the Census, 1988c, pp. 36–37).

Women's Wages

Seemingly stuck for more than a decade at the 60-percent mark or below, the ratio of women's to men's full-time wages began to climb in 1982. At first, pay equity experts were cautiously optimistic, pointing out that one-fourth of the gain was due to a decline in men's earnings and recalling as well that the ratio had gone over 60 percent for several years in the 1950s but had nonetheless sunk to the low level where it remained until 1981 (National Committee on Pay Equity, n.d.). The ratio has proceeded to climb, first to 63 percent in 1982, to 64 percent in the next two years, to 65 percent in 1986 and 1987, and to 66 percent in 1988 (U.S. Bureau of the Census, 1988c, p. 2; 1989a, p. 52). Despite this upturn, the wages of American women who work full time, year round, are still about one-third less than men's.

While the reversal of men's fortunes has contributed to reduction of the wage gap, a more important reason is said to be the maturing of the female workforce. Indeed, this phenomenon was anticipated by Paul Burstein (1985) who maintained that women's salaries were formerly stuck because the large numbers of women who entered the workforce with relatively little experience in the preceding decades temporarily pulled down the averages for women or kept them from improving. Cynthia Goldin (1987), who makes a similar point, argues that the rise in women's wages is likely to be sustained. Those who have proposed this explanation of trends in the wage gap have not dealt with the question crossnationally or asked whether mass labor-force entry of women in other countries has been associated with static female/male wage ratios. Another reason for the wage-gap reduction that began in 1981 may be the decline in labor force segregation in the preceding decade.

The differences in wages between women and men remain even when education is held constant. In 1982, the female/male earnings ratios for full-time, year-round workers with high school diplomas, college degrees, and five or more years of college were 62.6, 62.2, and 66.3 percent, respectively (Cherry, 1989, p. 136; see also U.S. Bureau of the Census, 1986b, p. 31). Men and women with the same amount of education tend to have different earnings potential, partly because higher percentages of women still major in lower paid fields like education, humanities, and health sciences. However, after reviewing a number of studies that attribute the wage gap to differences in human capital—education, skill, experience—Barbara Bergmann (1986, chapter 4) concluded that only half of it was explained by such factors. Citing evidence from court cases pertaining to discrimination in major corporations, Bergmann concluded that discrimination—biased evaluations of women's performance and assignment to jobs—is at the core of women's poor wages and poor position in the labor market.

The wage gap between men and women who are full-time, year-round workers hardly tells the whole tale about earnings differences. The full-time wage gap pertains to just under one-third of the women who received income from any source in 1987 and to a little over half the men. When the earnings of all female and male workers were compared, the ratio in 1987 was 53 percent, considerably lower than the 65 percent ratio of full-time, year-round workers (U.S. Bureau of the Census, 1988c, p. 23).

Contributing to women's low wages was the failure of Congress to raise the minimum wage during most of the 1980s. Nearly two-thirds of the 6.7 million hourly and salaried workers who earned the minimum wage or less in 1986 were women (Shapiro, 1987). Single mothers, whose educational attainments tend to be lower than those of married mothers (U.S. Bureau of the Census, 1986b, p. 9), are more likely to have low-wage jobs and hence especially handicapped by a stagnant minimum wage. Thus, while the median income of full-time women workers rose during the 1980s, millions of women clearly lost ground.

Occupational Segregation

After extensive review of the evidence Alice Ilchman, chair of the Committee on Women's Employment and Related Issues of the National Research Council, concluded, "The segregation of the sexes into different occupations, industries and (within firms) specific jobs is one of the most stable and striking features of the American workplace" (Reskin, 1984, p. vii). Examining both cross-sectional and times-series data on female employment from 1890 to 1980, Goldin (1987, p. 199) found that although there have been shifts in the sex composition of some major occupations, most sectors and most industries have been either male or female intensive during the entire century. While there have been increases in the number of women physicians, lawyers, and judges, these professionals total less than one-half percent of all employed women (Milkman, 1987).

The closer one looks at the labor market the more sex segregation one finds. Of the 503 occupational categories in the detailed classification scheme of the Department of Labor, 187 categories were at least 90 percent male or 90 percent female in 1980, and 275 were at least 80 percent single sex (Reskin and Hartmann, 1986, p. 7). The detailed classification scheme, moreover, understates segregation because it combines in one category several occupations that are predominantly one sex or the other, thereby creating the illusion of integration.[7] Sex segregation at the firm or establishment level is even more marked than within occupational or industrial categories (Bielby and Baron, 1984).

Using the detailed classification scheme of the Department of Labor, two researchers (Beller, 1984; U.S. Bureau of the Census, 1986b, citing unpublished work of Ryscavage) found that occupational segregation declined significantly in the 1970s. Andrea H. Beller found that the proportion of women who would have to change occupations for the workforce to be completely integrated dropped from 68.3 percent to 61.7 percent during the 1970s. Weighing a variety of data, including the expected greater growth in female occupations, Beller and Kee-ok Kim Han (1984) predicted only a modest decline in occupational segregation in the 1980s.

Women and men are not only separate but unequal at work. Female occupations tend to be lower in status, pay, and opportunities for mobility. Donald J. Treiman and Heidi I. Hartmann (1981) estimated that wages drop $42 annually for each additional percent female in an occupation, and that the expected median wage in an occupation filled exclusively by women was less than half the median for an exclusively male occupation. Francine D. Blau (1984) estimated that 35 to 40 percent of the sex differences in average earnings can be accounted for by sex segregation.

One explanation for these wage differences is that society simply devaluates whatever tasks women perform. An example of this is the process of resegregation, whereby women's widescale entry into formerly male-dominated fields like teaching or secretarial work leads to a decline in prestige and pay scales (Reskin, 1988). Another explanation of wage differences is that women are "crowded" into fewer occupations than men, resulting in an oversupply and reduction of wages in women's occupations and the reverse in men's (Bergmann, 1986).

Some factors that may play a part in occupational segregation are socialization regarding the "proper" roles of the two sexes, discrimination, and women's family responsibilities. It has been argued that women prefer predominantly female occupations because they are often extensions of the nurturing role and because they are more easily combined with family responsibilities (Oppenheimer, 1970), but women have nonetheless moved into nontraditional occupations when opportunities have arisen, such as during wartime and in recent decades (Reskin and Hartmann, 1986, p. 77). Women's choices probably play a role in occupational segregation, but the different education, socialization, and family responsibilities associated with these choices are themselves related to sexism.

Minority Women at Work

In the mid–1980s, one-fifth of the female labor force consisted of women of color (Malveaux, 1987). Experts disagree as to whether they are significantly more disadvantaged in the labor force than other women. For example, Burstein (1985) emphasizes the common economic marginality of all women workers, while Phyllis A. Wallace concludes that the labor market experiences of black women are different from both white women and black men. "Employment discrimination against black women," she holds, "is composed of generous doses of sex discrimination (experienced by all women) and a lingering amount of racial discrimination" (1980, pp. 56–57).

Owing to the depressed economic condition of black men, black women have historically had higher labor force participation rates than white women (Goldin, 1987; Wallace, 1980), but the difference in their participation rates had narrowed to less than three percentage points in 1987 (computed from U.S. Department of Labor, Bureau of Labor Statistics, 1989, pp. 155, 174). The similarity in overall participation rates, however, obscures age-group differences. Perhaps as a result of the related factors of their higher unemployment and fertility rates, younger black women are considerably less likely to be in the labor force than their white counterparts, whereas the reverse is true for those age 25 and over, though to a lesser extent. In 1987 white women between the ages of 16 and 19 were 42 percent more likely than black women of the same age to be in the labor force; for those between 20 and 24, the difference was 16 percent (pp. 132–181).[8]

Although black women are less likely than white women to be part-time workers (Nardone, 1986; Plewes, 1987) they are more likely to be employed part-time involuntarily (Levitan and Conway, 1988). Compared to other workers, involuntary part-timers have a higher incidence of poverty, and this is particularly true of the black female householders who are so employed (Kornbluh, 1987).

Black women are at higher risk of unemployment. From 1972 to 1987, they were at least twice as likely as white women to be unemployed (2.5 times in 1987). Among young workers, the discrepancies were even higher. In 1987, for example, black women between ages 20 and 24 were three times as likely to be unemployed as their white counterparts (U.S. Department of Labor, Bureau of Labor Statistics, 1989, pp. 514–537). It has been suggested that the low labor force participation rates of young black women are the result of "the staggering amount of unemployment among them" (Wallace, 1980, p. 77; see also Bowen and Finegan, 1969). While much attention has been paid to the unemployment of young black males—and justifiably—little is paid to young black women whose unemployment rates are as high or higher. The unemployment rates of Hispanic women are higher than those of white women but not as steep as those of blacks (Coalition on Women and Unemployment and Full Employment Action Council, 1985).

Wage differences between white and minority women are less marked than these other labor market indicators. There have been dramatic improvements in the wage levels of black women who, as recently as 1955, had earnings half that of white women (U.S. Bureau of the Census, 1986b, p. 29; U.S. Department of Labor, Bureau of Labor Statistics, 1989, p. 742).

In 1987, the full-time year-round earnings of black women were 91 percent those of white women (U.S. Bureau of the Census, 1988c, p. 20). The relatively narrow gap between the earnings of white and black women may suggest that gender has become a more critical disadvantage in the labor market than race. However, it is important to consider that these wage figures do not include unemployed or discouraged workers, categories in which black women are overerrepresented.

The steep reduction of the wage gap between employed black and white women reflects the narrowing of differences in their occupational profiles. The proportion of black women in private household work has declined very sharply, and the more educated and skilled black women are holding service, sales, clerical, and manufacturing jobs similar to those of other women (Albelda, 1985; Wallace, 1980). Nonetheless, black women appear to have moved into some other segregated jobs such as chambermaid, welfare service aide, nurse's aide, child-care worker, and other low-status occupations in which they are now overrepresented (Malveaux, 1985). Even more concentrated in a few occupations than white women, they are especially vulnerable to changes in the demand for labor in these occupations. Relocation of clerical positions out of urban centers, for example, is expected to have an adverse effect on urban minority women who have only recently entered such occupations (Ginzberg, 1987).

How does the experience of Hispanic women compare with that of other women workers? Hispanic women have lower participation rates than non-

Hispanics (47 percent vs. 55 percent) (U.S. Bureau of the Census, 1986b, p. 4). Like blacks they tend to have higher rates of involuntary part-time employment than whites (Levitan and Conway, 1988). Their unemployment rates are higher than those of white women but not as steep as those of blacks (Coalition on Women and Employment and Full Employment Action Council, 1985). In 1987 their full-time earnings were 16 percent less than those of white women and 8 percent less than black women (U.S. Bureau of the Census, 1988c, p. 20). With respect to wages, they are the most disadvantaged of the three groups of women.

Compared to their white counterparts, minority women are more likely to be unemployed, underemployed, and, in the case of young black women, less likely to be in the labor market. The earnings gap is slim for blacks but wider for Hispanics. The earnings of all three are beneath those of all three groups of men, and within each racial or national origin group women's median yearly, full-time earnings range from 65 percent of men's for whites to 83 to 84 percent for Hispanics and blacks (U.S. Bureau of the Census, 1988c, p. 20). The wage gap is more marked for whites but nonetheless exists between men and women of color.

This overview of women in the workforce shows that as a group, though ever more vital to production outside the home, American women remain secondary in status and income. Among women workers are those who experience not only the disadvantage of gender but of minority race or ethnicity as well.

POLICIES TO REDUCE ECONOMIC INEQUALITY

Policies to reduce the economic inequality of women and minorities have been directed toward decreasing occupational segregation and wage inequalities. Since the 1960s a wide range of public policies has addressed these goals. Nonetheless, these efforts have been wholly insufficient to overcome or to reduce substantially the workplace inequities that have been observed. The policies are relatively recent, the status inequalities they address are deeply entrenched, and the policies themselves, though still standing, have been hobbled by the opposition of the executive branch of government during the 1980s and by the legacy that it has left through conservative appointments to the Supreme Court. Restructuring, too, especially the decline of internal labor markets, has reduced the number of opportunities toward which equal employment policies can be targeted.

Reducing Occupational Segregation

The cornerstone of equal employment opportunity policies is Title VII of the Civil Rights Act of 1964, which forbids discrimination in hiring, training, compensation, and promotion. The Act applies not only to employers but to labor organizations and to joint labor-management committees that control apprenticeship. In 1972, Congress gave the administering agency of Title VII, the Equal Employment Opportunity Commission (EEOC), the right to sue for complainants in court (Reskin and Hartmann, 1986, p. 85). In its early years, the EEOC used the strategy of targeting large, highly visible employers, and it also initiated action that led the courts to overrule state protective legislation for women.

As far-reaching as it is, the Civil Rights Act of 1964 did not include affirmative action, one of the more important and controversial mechanisms for promoting workforce integration. A 1965 Executive Order of President Lyndon B. Johnson, along with subsequent orders, not only extended prohibitions against discrimination to federal contractors but required them to take positive actions to achieve integration—such as advertising job openings to underrepresented groups. A 1971 Executive Order of President Richard Nixon required employers to set goals or timetables for achieving integration. Contractors who failed to comply with the Executive Orders for affirmative action could have their contracts revoked or could be debarred from future government contracts. There has, in reality, been very little debarment, but having to submit a plan is believed to serve as a stimulus to affirmative action (Bergmann, 1986, p. 160).

U.S. laws against sex and race discrimination stipulate serious penalties for offenders, and, unlike laws in some other countries, permit class action suits. The potentially powerful sanctions in U.S. laws have not been automatically applied, and legal suits have not only proved time-consuming and expensive but, in some cases, without consequences for underlying attitudes and policies (Bergmann, 1985).

Evaluations of the effects of antidiscrimination and affirmative action policies suggest that when they have been enforced, significant numbers of positions have been opened to women (Reskin and Hartmann, 1986). Citing increases in their income and changes in their occupations, Burstein (1985) holds that equal opportunity policies have clearly benefited nonwhite women. It is Bergmann's conclusion that affirmative action "has never been seriously tried on a large enough scale and with a severity of enforcement sufficient to make a big dent in the problem of discrimination" (1985, pp. 171–172).

Until 1989, it was not clear that the attempt of the executive branch of government to set its negative seal on the judiciary had succeeded in relation to affirmative action. In 1987, in its first affirmative action case involving a woman (*Johnson v. Santa Clara Transportation Agency*), the Supreme Court decided in favor of a plan giving job preference to a woman road maintenance worker over a marginally better-qualified man (Barbaro, 1988). However, a series of decisions in 1989 led the *New York Times* to conclude that the Court was changing its direction on civil rights (Greenhouse, 1989).[9]

Largely initiated in the 1970s were policies to promote occupational integration through education and training. Title IX of the Educational Amendments of 1972 was the first law to protect students from sex discrimination, but the federal government did little to enforce it (Reskin and Hartmann, 1986); it was halted by Executive Order during the 1980s. The Vocational Education Act of 1976 provided the states with money for sex equity coordinators to meet the needs of groups such as displaced homemakers and single heads of households. Studies of its implementation suggest that legislation of this kind must be accompanied by active monitoring of schools, that affirmative action programs are necessary to attract women to training programs for traditionally male occupations, and that placement provisions following training are also necessary (Reskin and Hartmann, 1986).

Pay Equity

The Equal Pay Act of 1963 was the first law in American history to ban sex discrimination (Degler, 1980). Limited to equal work in the same establishment, the Equal Pay Act did not strike at the heart of inequality in employment—sex-segregated occupations. The drive for comparable worth has been a response to the inadequacies of the Equal Pay Act and to the slow pace of affirmative action. In contrast to the latter, which aims to integrate the labor force, comparable worth or pay equity attempts to increase the rewards of a segregated workplace— that is, to raise pay in female-dominated occupations. Proponents of this approach have attempted to extend the protection of Title VII to pay disputes over comparable worth, to press for pay equity through the collective bargaining process, and to seek passage of pay equity laws at the state level.

A major victory in the pay equity struggle came in 1981, when the Supreme Court determined, in *County of Washington (OR) v. Gunther*, that in wage discrimination cases Title VII is not limited by the equal work standard of the Equal Pay Act. The Gunther case, however, did not rule directly on whether a predominantly female occupation could be considered "comparable" to a predominantly male occupation since the decision hinged on the employer's having ignored its own classification scheme for male and female correctional guards (Kahn and Grune, 1982). The lower courts, in any case, have defeated large numbers of comparable worth cases and regarded the approach as counter to free market principles (Livernash, 1984; Steinberg, 1987).

Political and union pressures have, in a number of cases, led to pay equity settlements in favor of women (Bergmann, 1986). There have been victories at the state level where twenty states have made some pay equity adjustment for state civil service employees (Coleman and Hubbard, n.d.). None of the states, however, has passed legislation covering employees in the private sector (Lisa Hubbard, National Committee on Pay Equity, personal communication, August 1989).

Comparable worth has not been without its critics. Its classification schemes have been seen as reinforcing meritocratic principles and existing class relations (Brenner, 1987). Critics have also charged that it places more emphasis on the inequities of women than those of minorities (Brenner, 1987) and that it does nothing for the unemployed who are disproportionately women of color (Malveaux, 1987). One response to these charges is that affirmative action also accepts existing hierarchies; its approach is to seek access to better positions for those who are excluded from higher echelon jobs. In some pay equity cases, moreover, there have been higher adjustments on the basis of race than on the basis of gender (Steinberg, 1987).

Besides increasing wages for workers in low-paid, segregated occupations, the comparable worth drive has "broadened public thinking on what discrimination is" (Steinberg, 1987, p. 468). Comparable worth, moreover, tends to lend more dignity to the important and undervalued work that women do.

In addition to policies specifically targeted toward expanding employment opportunities and achieving pay equity for women, fuller employment and minimum wage policies have a role to play in reducing the economic inequality of women. Some grou_s of women experience disproportionately high rates of unemployment, and women predominate among minimum wage workers. Although full employment and minimum wage increases would disproportionately benefit women, they have not been the issues receiving high priority from most women's rights organizations.

SOCIAL WELFARE FOR WOMEN AND THEIR FAMILIES

Many women who maintain families by themselves require government income transfers to overcome labor market inequities and to compensate for the lack of a second income. Single mothers benefit from policies designed to meet the needs and risks common to all individuals and families as well as those geared to the economic burdens of both parenthood and single parenthood.

Paying for Essential Goods and Services

Paying for essential goods and services burdens many individuals and families. The United States has a number of programs to pay for these essentials, typically through means-tested, in-kind benefits that either stigmatize recipients, restrict their choices, or both. In 1986, U.S. expenditures for in-kind benefits for the poor exceeded those for cash benefits by 84 percent (U.S. Bureau of the Census, 1987, p. 2). While most countries subsidize housing in this way, health care is offered on a more universal basis, and food is provided either through more adequate cash assistance programs or, in the case of the socialist countries, subsidization of essential goods for everyone rather than for the poor alone.

Perhaps the most glaring omission in U.S. social policy is national health insurance. In this respect the United States is unique among the seven countries in this study. Since the middle 1960s, the United States has had two programs that reimburse health care providers for their services to some of the population: the elderly and disabled in the case of Medicare, and certain categories of the poor in the case of Medicaid. In 1986, however, 35 percent of poor female householder families had neither Medicaid nor Medicare coverage (U.S. Bureau of the Census, 1987, p. 6).

Employer-provided health insurance is the main source of health coverage for people of working age. Women who are unemployed, spouseless and thus not covered by their husbands' insurance, or working for low wages are at risk of not being covered. Forty-eight percent of all unemployed women and 40 percent of those who are divorced or separated have no health insurance from either employer-provided or government programs (Davis, 1988, p. 182, citing National Center for Health Statistics Health Interview Survey). It has been estimated that nearly one-third of the employers who pay the minimum wage to most of their workers offer them no health insurance (Children's Defense Fund, 1988, p. 71). Black women, who have higher rates of unemployment and spouselessness than white women, are more likely to be without both public and private health coverage (Davis, 1988, p. 185).

The poor are beset by problems of affordability and availability of housing. Both problems are addressed by federal public housing and lower-income rental assistance programs, which, however, are not entitlements and thus not available to many who meet income eligibility requirements. Indeed, in 1986, only 19 percent of poor families and less than 30 percent of poor, female householder families received government housing aid (U.S. Bureau of the Census, 1987, p. 6). Moreover, the federal commitment to housing the poor has decreased sharply (Leonard, Dolbeare, and Lazere, 1989, p. 29). By far the largest housing subsidies in the United States are tax deductions on mortgage interest and local property taxes. In the mid–1980s, these tax expenditures were four times public housing outlays and were overwhemingly for the nonpoor (calculated from Bixby, 1988, p. 24; Congressional Budget Office [CBO], 1988b, pp. ix–x).

Homelessness is the most extreme consequence of the failure to treat housing as a basic right. Of the persons deprived of one of the most basic rights in civilized societies, more than one-third are families with children, and of these, about two-thirds are single-parent families (Children's Defense Fund, 1988, pp. 108–109). Another serious result of deficient public support of housing is that in 1985, 69 percent of the 11 million very-low-income renters (below 50 percent of their area median incomes) were paying more than 30 percent of their incomes for rent, and 41 percent were paying more than half (CBO, 1988a, p. 9). Especially burdened by high housing costs are young single parents; under age 25 and nearly all female, they spend, on the average, 80 percent of their incomes on housing (Leonard, Dolbeare, and Lazere, 1989, p. xxii).

The United States has a number of programs to subsidize the cost of food. The largest of these is food stamps, which, along with several other food programs, played a vital role in reducing the nutrition gap between the poor and other Americans in the 1960s and 1970s (Children's Defense Fund, 1987, p. 126, citing a Department of Agriculture survey). Food stamps is an entitlement program and therefore available to all who meet income eligibility criteria. However, food stamp expenditures were cut nearly $7 billion between 1982 and 1985 with resultant tightening of eligibility, reduction of caseloads, and lowering of benefits. Onerous regulations and lack of outreach are important reasons why about one-third of those eligible do not claim or receive benefits. In addition, benefits are based on such a low food budget that it is impossible for most recipients to secure basic nutrients (Children's Defense Fund, 1988, pp. 125–126).

Poor, female householder families are more likely than other poor families to benefit from either food stamps or free school lunches. Yet, in 1986, 20 percent of these women and their dependents got neither (U.S. Bureau of the Census, 1987, p. 6). Two other food and nutrition programs of particular benefit to poor mothers are not entitlements. School breakfast programs are helpful to mothers who work outside the home, especially the sole parent who is employed. In many school districts, including ones in poor neighborhoods, breakfast programs are not available. The Supplemental Feeding Program for Women, Infants, and Children (WIC) serves only about 45 percent of the women and children who are eligible (Shapiro and Greenstein, 1988, pp. 33–34). A symptom of the failure of food programs to prevent hunger are the food pantries and soup kitchens that have arisen during the 1980s and the sharp increase in the numbers of families with children requesting emergency food assistance in American cities (Children's Defense Fund, 1987, p. 24, citing a survey of the U.S. Conference of Mayors).

Risks to Income Security

Unemployment, involuntary part-time employment, and low wages are three risks to income security experienced by people of working age. The first of these market failures is met through unemployment insurance. However, as a result of cutbacks and consequent tightening of both federal and state eligibility requirements, only one-third of the unemployed were covered in 1987, compared to about three-fourths in 1975 (Shapiro and Greenstein, 1988, p. 22). Women are even less likely than men to meet earnings and employment requirements for unemployment insurance (Levitan and Shapiro, 1987).

Inadequate benefits for those who are covered by unemployment insurance are also a problem. Benefits vary by state, with the proportion of wages replaced ranging from 28 percent and 29 percent in Indiana, Alaska, and California to 50 percent in North Dakota (Shapiro and Greenstein, 1988, p. 63, citing unpublished tables of the Department of Labor). Many of the unemployed are impoverished both by lack of coverage and very low benefits. In 1987, 72 percent of unemployed female householders were poor (U.S. Bureau of the Census, 1988c, p. 37).

The minimum wage is intended to guard against pauperization of the employed but has not fulfilled that function in recent years. Instead, persons working at or below the minimum wage, a group in which women are disproportionately represented, have had to turn to social assistance, as have the long-term employed who exhaust their insurance benefits, the unemployed who are not covered, and the underemployed.

The Costs of Parenthood

In a number of industrialized countries a nonmeans-tested family or children's allowance is a cornerstone of family policy. The United States has not laid that foundation to its system. It has no universal allowance to offset the costs of child rearing. In addition to tax deductions for dependents, which benefit higher income families more, the United States has an Earned Income Tax Credit (EITC) for families with low earnings. Parents who are not in the labor force or who are among the long-term unemployed do not benefit. The maximum EITC benefit in 1987 was $851, regardless of the number of children in a family. Congress, however, is seriously considering higher benefits that rise with the birth of the second and third child in a family and a supplemental credit for preschool children (Mark Mazur, U.S. Congress, Joint Committee on Taxation, personal communication, May 1990).

By and large the U.S. government has ignored the needs created by the entry of mothers into the labor force. While women's work is vital to the productive as well as reproductive spheres, neither employers nor government have been willing to pay the price for women's dual labors. Alone among the countries in this study the United States has no national, paid maternity leave. Only a handful of the states offer paid maternity leave under temporary disability insurance programs, and it has been estimated that only 40 percent of women in the labor force have even modest coverage that would allow them partial income replacement for six to ten weeks after childbirth (Kahn and Kamerman, 1987, p. 264). In 1990, Congress passed a bill entitling employees to job-guaranteed, unpaid leave for birth, adoption, or serious illness of a child or parent, but President Bush vetoed it.

Despite the fact that increasing numbers of mothers of preschool children are in the labor force, the federal government has refused to assume major responsibility for meeting the child care needs of employed mothers and their children. Consistent with the lack of centralized concern and planning for child care is the fact that "data are unavailable to develop a comprehensive profile of existing child care programs" (Hofferth and Phillips, 1986, p. 12).

According to a National Academy of Sciences panel, "the United States lags behind almost all industrialized countries in its efforts to address child care needs . . . " (Lewin, 1990, p. A24).

The child care problem seems to be primarily one of affordability, quality, and convenience rather than quantity. Alfred J. Kahn and Sheila B. Kamerman (1987) concluded that for three- to five-year-olds there is sufficient quantity but that it is beyond the reach of the poor. The Children's Defense Fund estimated that decent child care for one youngster costs nearly half the median income of single mothers with one preschool child (1988, p. 180). As for quality, only a small percentage of child care is provided in state-licensed facilities (Cail and Port, 1985). By spring 1990, both houses of Congress had passed child care bills that would, if signed into law, expand the number of child care slots by

800,000 and require some states to establish their own standards of care. An encouraging step, this legislation would nevertheless leave American families a long way from an entitlement to child care. In a time when privatization has been touted, there is no indication that private employers will meet even a fraction of the child care needs that are being ignored by the public sector (Hofferth and Phillips, 1986, p. 16; Kahn and Kamerman, 1987, p. 198).

Single Parenthood

In theory single parents receive private transfers or child support from non-custodial parents. However, in 1986, only 61 percent had ever been awarded child support, and only about one-half of all mothers legally awarded child support got the full amount (Children's Defense Fund, 1989, pp. 19–20). Irwin Garfinkel and Sara S. McLanahan (1986, p. 24) estimate that only 40 percent of white fathers and 19 percent of black fathers pay child support; their average payments, moreover, are much smaller than the contributions of fathers in two-parent homes. Less than one-fourth of mothers with children born out of wedlock have even established paternity, the first step in obtaining child support (Children's Defense Fund, 1989, p. 20). In 1984 and again in 1988, Congress enacted stiffer collection, award, and paternity determination procedures as well as the automatic withholding of the noncustodial parent's paychecks. The effects of these laws will be limited both by understaffing of child support agencies (p. 20) as well as by the incapacity of many poor fathers to pay.

As part of the 1984 Child Support Amendments, Congress, perhaps recognizing the limited incomes of some noncustodial parents, directed the Secretary of Health and Human Services to authorize the state of Wisconsin to use federal money that would otherwise have been spent on public assistance (Aid to Families with Dependent Children or AFDC) to fund a demonstration child support assurance program.[10] The two advanced welfare states in this study have such provisions that, in contrast to social assistance or AFDC, treat child support as a right.

Among single mothers, only widows, who constitute less than 10 percent of single mothers (see table 2.3), have access to social insurance. Average social insurance benefits for a widow (surviving spouse) and her children permit a narrow escape from poverty (Johnson and Goldberg, 1986, p. 6), but the fact that so few single mothers are eligible for these benefits led Alvin L. Schorr (1966) to propose "fatherless child insurance" for the much larger group of children who are "socially orphaned" by the divorce, separation, or nonmarriage of their parents.

The cash assistance program on which the majority of poor single-parent families must rely is AFDC. The benefits of AFDC are below the poverty level in all states, even when the cash value of food stamps is counted. In forty-one states, these combined benefits were less than 75 percent of the poverty level in 1987 (Center on Social Welfare Policy and Law, 1987, pp. 1–6).

In 1974 Congress granted a minimum national benefit to the elderly and disabled poor (Supplemental Security Income or SSI) and indexed those benefits to rises in the cost of living. This it has steadfastly refused to do for poor families with dependent children. Ironically "welfare reform," passed overwhelmingly by Congress in 1988, did not raise a single benefit in a single state. Arguing that most mothers of young children were in the workforce, Congress restricted the right to relief through mandatory work requirements for mothers of very young children and in so doing expanded the labor reserve of the most disadvantaged women workers (Goldberg, 1987). While the rhetoric of reform is education and training for welfare mothers who are required to seek employment, the reality of the state initiatives that preceded the national legislation was very little of either. It is probably unlikely, though not certain at this time, that implementation of the federal reform will include significant educational and training opportunities.

Since public assistance is a last resort for those families whose income from all other sources is insufficient, the low level of AFDC benefits contributes significantly to the poverty of American women. Cash benefits reduced the number of single mothers in poverty by only 11 percent in 1986; the antipoverty effect of these cash income transfers had fallen from 19 percent in 1979 (U.S. Bureau of the Census, 1984, p. 134; 1988b, p. 158).

Crossnational data reinforce the conclusion that one of the world's wealthiest nations is not generous to single mothers and their children. Kahn and Kamerman (1983) compared the incomes of several types of economically vulnerable families with the net wage of an average production worker (APWW) in each of eight capitalist countries. In Pennsylvania in 1979, a single mother not in the labor force and with two children had an income less than half (44.0 percent) of the APWW; if the mother in such a family earned half the average wage, the income was just about 70 percent of the APWW. In both cases these benefits, which were above the fifty-state median, were lower than in any of the other seven countries in this study, all of which have less abundant resources than the United States. The epithet "reluctant welfare state," given to the United States some twenty-five years ago (Wilensky, 1965), has become an understatement.

Political philosophies, such as rugged individualism or antistatism, are sometimes offered to explain why the United States is more reluctant than most other wealthy democratic nations to make fuller use of government income transfers to prevent poverty. Another explanation seems inescapable in view of the fact that so many of the nonelderly who turn to social welfare to compensate for low wages, no wages at all, and insufficient private income transfers are black and Hispanic. Indeed, 55.5 percent of the families receiving AFDC are black and Hispanic (U.S. Department of Health and Human Services, 1990). It seems clear that the racism that has so long infected American social life plays an important role in the inadequacy of the American social welfare system and in the willingness of a society with such abundant resources to neglect so many of its women and children.

Table 2.2
Female Householder Families with Children as Proportion of All Families with Children, 1960–1987

	White	Black (a)	Hispanic	Total
1960	6.0	21.3	NA	7.4
1965	7.3	25.2	NA	9.2
1970	7.8	30.6	NA	10.2
1975	11.4	39.8	NA	14.7
1980	13.4	46.9	22.0	17.5
1985	15.0	49.9	24.7	19.3
1987	15.5	48.4	25.5	19.7

(a) Before 1970, the racial groups were white and nonwhite, which included not only blacks but other racial minorities.

Sources: U.S. Bureau of the Census, 1961, pp. 44–46; 1966, p. 3; 1971, pp. 9–10; 1976, pp. 7–10; 1981, pp. 7–14; 1986a, pp. 13–14; 1988a, pp. 3–6.

DEMOGRAPHIC FACTORS

If the combined income from work and welfare is too low for many women to support their families, then increasing rates of divorce and single motherhood will mean increasing numbers of poor women and children. In 1987, more than 10 million American women were heading households in which there was no husband present, an increase of nearly 6 million since 1960 (U.S. Bureau of the Census, 1989, p. 11).

This discussion concentrates on a particular category of single women: female householders with no husband present and at least one related child under age 18. This population category includes only the single mothers who maintain their own households, not those who live as subfamilies in other households (usually the mothers' parents').[11]

The number of female householder families with children has increased from 1.9 million in 1960 to 5.1 million in 1987 or from 7.4 percent of all families with children to 19.7 percent, about one in five (see table 2.2). The proportion of singe-mother households rose by 37.8 percent in the 1960s, by 72.5 percent in the 1970s, and by 11.9 percent in the first seven years of the 1980s, the latter figure suggesting that the trend has abated but nonetheless continues.

Cross-sectional data underestimate the total number and proportion of women and children who are part of a single parent family at some time during their lives (Bumpass, 1984; Hofferth, 1985). ''A newborn in the United States,'' writes Larry L. Bumpass, "is as likely to spend some time in a single parent family as it is to have an uninterrupted childhood with its natural parents, and the single parent experience is not likely to be brief" (p. 80).

Throughout the period under discussion the rates of single motherhood have been at least three times greater for blacks than for whites. Black women, moreover, remain single mothers much longer than their white counterparts (Bumpass, 1984).

We lack data on Hispanics for the years prior to 1980, but their current rate of 25.5 percent is higher (65 percent) than that of whites but lower (47 percent) than that of blacks. A high proportion of black and Hispanic women, therefore, are in the economically vulnerable position of supporting themselves on a woman's wage or no wage at all; they are, in turn, dependent on a social welfare system that is unresponsive to their needs, perhaps because they are women of color.

In addition to the large increase in the number and proportion of single mothers, there has been a marked change in their marital status (see table 2.3). Since 1960, widows have declined, not only as a proportion of all single-mother householders but, despite population increases, in actual numbers as well. Widows, who are relatively well protected by social policy, fell from nearly one-third of single mothers in 1960 to 7.5 percent in 1987. Since 1960, unmarried motherhood has risen more than five-fold (5.7 times). Currently, one in four (25.1 percent) single mothers has never married, and if subfamilies were included, the figures would be higher.

Among the racial and national origin groups there are striking differences in the marital status of single mothers (see table 2.3). Divorce or separation still predominates among white single mothers. By contrast, black single mothers are almost equally likely to be unmarried as to be divorced or separated. "The difference is that whites marry and increasingly divorce, whereas blacks are increasingly likely never to marry at all" (Garfinkel and McLanahan, 1986, p. 54). Hispanic single mothers are most likely to be divorced or separated, but they are between blacks and whites with respect to both nonmarriage and divorce.

Much has been written about the causes of single parenthood in the United States. The hypotheses run the gamut from increases in the availability and generosity of public assistance for single mothers to unemployment and declining real wages for working-class, particularly black, men.

Charles Murray (1984) has been the chief spokesman for the position that increases in the availability and generosity of public assistance for single mothers have led to increased single parenthood (see also Gilder, 1981). Murray's analysis has been severely criticized and virtually discredited. According to Robert Greenstein (1985), single parenthood continued to increase after the mid–1970s despite a substantial decline in the real value of welfare benefits. David T. Ellwood (1988, p. 61) demonstrates that the highest percentages of children in female-headed families are often in states with the lowest AFDC benefits and that single parenthood is therefore unrelated to the generosity of welfare. Furthermore, the

Table 2.3
Female Householders with Children Under 18 by Marital Status, Race, and Hispanic Origin, 1960–1987
(percentages)

	Never Married						Divorced/Separated						Widowed					
	1960	1970	1975 (a)	1980	1985	1987	1960	1970	1975	1980	1985	1987	1960	1970	1975	1980	1985	1987
All Races/Origins	4.4	8.0	11.7	16.4	22.1	25.1	63.6	69.9	70.5	71.1	68.9	67.4	32.0	22.1	17.8	12.5	9.9	7.5
White	1.9	3.3	5.8	8.4	11.6	14.8	63.3	71.5	74.4	77.7	78.8	77.4	34.8	25.1	19.9	13.9	9.5	7.9
Black (b)	11.5	18.3	24.7	32.7	43.8	46.6	64.4	66.0	61.6	57.9	49.3	46.8	24.1	15.6	13.7	9.3	6.9	6.6
Hispanic	NA	NA	NA	23.1	23.4	27.8	NA	NA	NA	66.8	68.7	65.8	NA	NA	NA	9.9	7.9	6.4

(a) Data not available for 1965.

(b) Before 1970, the racial groups were white and nonwhite, which included not only blacks
     but other racial minorities.

Sources: U.S. Bureau of the Census, 1961, pp. 64–66; 1971, pp. 64–66; 1976, pp.62–64; 1981,
pp. 140–143; 1986a, pp.71–74; 1988a, pp. 79–82.

number of children in single-parent families and, by implication, the number of such families continued to grow between 1972 and 1984, even though the number of AFDC recipients actually declined. For example, during those years, the number of black children in female-headed families grew by more than 25 percent, despite the fact that the number of black children receiving AFDC fell by 15 percent (pp. 59–60).

Increases in the number of single-mother householders are related not only to the propensity of women and men to marry, divorce, or have children but to the tendency of women to establish separate households. The public assistance rolls did expand greatly in the 1960s, and one of the major effects of the increased availability of welfare is said to have been the increased ability of single mothers to live independently (Cutright and Madras, 1974; Ellwood and Bane, 1985; Piven and Cloward, 1987). Garfinkel and McLanahan have shown that changes in the tendency of single women with children to establish independent living arrangements account for part of the growth of female householder families— 30 percent of the growth in the 1950s and 14 percent and 10 percent in the 1960s and 1970s, respectively (1986, p. 53).

William J. Wilson and his associates (1987) attribute the high rates of single and unmarried parenthood among blacks to economic disadvantage: high unemployment and a resultant reduction in the number of "marriageable" males. Their research shows that between 1960 and 1980 the number of marriageable black men—employed males per 100 females of the same age and race—declined significantly in three of four regions of the country, whereas the marriageability of white men changed only slightly. While emphasizing the strength of kinship networks rather than the lack of standard family structures, Carol B. Stack's anthropological study of a low-income black community found that "since many black American males have little or no access to steady and productive employment, they are rarely able to support and maintain their families" (1974, p. 51).

While the marriageability argument may explain why lower-income black men either do not marry or do not stay married, it ignores the unemployment and underemployment among black women. Young women with poor employment outlooks may lack desirable career alternatives to premature motherhood. The finding of Blake and del Pinal (1981), that reproduction is likely to be most valued when alternative means of achieving a more secure and recognized social role are most limited, offers some empirical support for the view that motherhood may be a relatively desirable career for young women with little education and limited employment opportunities. Whatever the effects on unmarried motherhood, unemployment and limited earnings are serious problems for young black women and ones that might well be a source of marital instability in families that are likely to require a second income to avoid poverty. In this regard it is interesting to note the finding of Sheldon Danziger and his associates (1982) that wives' employment reduces both female headship and poverty among nonwhites.

High rates of single parenthood among blacks and, to a lesser extent, Hispanics should not obscure the existence of substantial amounts of single parenthood among white women. Nearly 16 percent of white families with children were single-mother families in 1987. As noted, the great majority of white, single mothers are divorced or separated. Increasing divorce rates have been associated with factors related to advanced industrialization, such as increased independence of women (Cherlin, 1981; Ellwood, 1988; Garfinkel and McLanahan, 1986; Ross and Sawhill, 1975). This argument may seem to conflict with the one previously advanced regarding the positive relationship between wives' employment and marital stability among nonwhites. However, Danziger and his colleagues (1982) found that while wives' employment reduces female headship for nonwhites, it increases it for whites. One explanation of this difference is that the negative consequences of wives' employment are concentrated among couples with traditional attitudes about sex roles in the family (Garfinkel & McLanahan, 1986, p. 68, citing Ross, Mirowsky, and Huber, 1983). Perhaps blacks, whose economic deprivation has long necessitated wives' employment, are less likely to have such traditional values.

Teenage pregnancies and births, both sources of single parenthood, are high in the United States. Pregnancy rates for women ages 15 to 19 are twice those in Sweden, Canada, and France, and rates of birth to women in this age range are higher than in any of the other countries in this study. Overall teenage pregnancy rates in the United States are increased by the high rates among blacks, but the rates for whites nonetheless exceed those of the other capitalist countries in this study by at least 60 percent (Jones et al., 1986). Elise F. Jones and her associates attributed the level of teenage pregnancy in the United States to a high degree of "religiosity" and a consequent unwillingness either to deal openly with sex or to make contraceptive services available to young people. A national survey of adolescent girls revealed the paucity of contraceptive and related services for American teenagers (Weatherley, 1987, pp. 26–27, citing Zelnick, Kanter, and Ford, 1981). Unwanted pregnancies and parenthood are thus related to an inadequate social welfare system, particularly the lack of a universal, national health insurance scheme. Richard A. Weatherley refers to several studies that found that poor teenagers, those most affected by welfare deficiencies, are prone to bear children.

The causes of single parenthood are clearly complex. Ellwood, who has contributed significantly to research on the subject, concludes that "the changes in the structure of the family are probably the result of some sizeable and largely unstoppable changes in social and economic patterns" (1988, p. 46). While increased rates of divorce and single parenthood tend to be characteristic of advanced, industrialized societies, some single parenthood appears to be related to poverty and its antecedents in the labor market and the social welfare system. It is the single motherhood that is born of poverty that is avoidable through more egalitarian social and economic policies. Whatever the causes, the fact remains that at any one time nearly one-fifth of all family households with children are headed by a single woman, and these families are very vulnerable to poverty.

POVERTY: ITS PREVALENCE AND ITS FEMINIZATION

The official U.S. poverty standard is based on an "economy" food plan that is "for temporary use when funds are low" (Orshansky, 1965, p. 6). The economy plan is 75 to 80 percent of a low-cost food plan that was devised by the Department of Agriculture in the 1950s and intended to provide an "acceptable and adequate diet" (p. 5).[12] The U.S. poverty standard has remained the same since 1965, updated only to reflect changes in the cost of living. In 1965, the poverty line for a family of four was about half the median income, but it had fallen to 38 percent of the median in 1987.[13]

Poverty Rates

Poverty continues to descend heavily on women and their families, despite the fact that so many more women have become wage earners since the 1950s. In 1987, nearly half (46 percent) of single-mother families were poor (see table 2.4). More disadvantaged in the labor market, less likely to receive child support, and more frequently dependent upon an inadequate welfare system, black and Hispanic single mothers have shockingly high poverty rates—about three-fifths of their total population (U.S. Bureau of the Census, 1989b, pp. 13–14). The rates for whites are lower, but nonetheless a substantial minority, nearly two-fifths, are poor.

Trend data indicated that for all groups of female householders for whom data are available, the rates of poverty dropped at least 22 percent between 1960 and 1970, the time of the war on poverty. Rates continued to drop in the 1970s— by 9.5 percent for all female householders with children between 1970 and 1979, the low point in the entire period. Thereafter, the rates for these families rose by 20.7 percent between 1979 and 1982, during the years of recession and welfare retrenchment, and they were still 16.4 percent above the 1979 level in 1987. The rise was steepest for white single-mother families, almost one-fourth (23.6 percent) between 1979 and 1987.

The rates of poverty for female householder families exceeded those of other families (largely married couples but some single male householders) in 1960, but differences in rates are considerably higher now (see table 2.4). This is true for all female householder families but particularly for those with children. Whereas the rate for single-mother families was 3.6 times that of other families with children in 1960, it was 5.6 times higher in 1987.

We have reasoned that both low wages and a single wage play a part in the poverty of single-mother families. The two sets of comparisons that follow— one focusing on family composition and gender and the other on family composition, gender, and the employment status of parents—illustrate these effects. Both give 1987 poverty rates, and both pertain to parents with children.

Table 2.4

Poverty Rates by Type of Families and Presence of Children, 1960–1987, Selected Years

With/Without Children	All Families	Married Couple/ Families	Male House-holder, No Wife Present	Married Couple/ Male Householder (a)	Female Householder, No Husband Present
1960	18.1	NA	NA	15.4	42.4
1970	10.1	NA	NA	7.2	32.5
1980	10.3	6.2	11.0	6.3	32.7
1987	10.3	6.0	12.5	6.3	34.3

With Children	All Families	Married Couple/ Families	Male House-holder, No Wife Present	Married Couple/ Male Householder (a)	Female Householder, No Husband Present
1960	19.7	NA	NA	15.7	56.3
1970	11.6	NA	NA	6.9	43.8
1980	14.7	7.7	18.0	8.9	42.9
1987	16.2	7.8	17.6	8.3	46.1

(a) Before 1972 data were only available for all families and for female householder families; the remaining families are assumed to be either married-couple families (largely) or male-householder families, no wife present.

Source: U.S. Bureau of the Census, 1989b, p.11.

Table 2.5

Poverty Rates by Household Type, Race, and Hispanic Origin, 1987

Families With/Without Children

(1) Female Householders				(2) Male Householders				(3) Married Couple			
White	Black	Hisp.	All	White	Black	Hisp.	All	White	Black	Hisp.	All
26.7	51.8	51.8	34.3	10.3	24.3	15.7	12.5	5.2	12.3	18.1	6.0

Families With Children

(1) Single Mother				(2) Single Father				(3) Married Couple			
White	Black	Hisp.	All	White	Black	Hisp.	All	White	Black	Hisp.	All
38.7	59.5	60.7	46.1	15.1	29.6	NA	17.6	7.0	12.3	NA	7.8

Source: U.S. Bureau of the Census, 1989b, pp. 11–14.

	Single mothers	Single fathers	Married- couple families
Poverty rate	46.1	17.6	7.8

Source: U.S. Bureau of the Census, 1989b, p. 11.

	Employed (a) single mothers	One spouse employed	Both spouses employed
Poverty rate	33.1	14.7	3.9

(a) Employed means in the labor force. Only the employment of the spouse or
    spouses is considered.

Source: U.S. Bureau of the Census, 1989b, pp. 88, 90.

Single-mother families have poverty rates more than twice (2.6) those of single
fathers, and nearly as large a difference (2.3) is also found between families
with an employed single mother and families with one employed spouse (typically
the male). Two-parent households have the lowest poverty rates. The family
with an employed single mother suffers a poverty rate 8.5 times that of a family
with two employed parents.

While single mothers have lower educational attainments than married mothers, their poverty rates are high even when they are relatively well educated.
For younger white single mothers the poverty rates in 1980 were 45 percent for
high school graduates and 31 percent for those with one or more years of college.
At both educational levels black and Hispanic young single mothers had poverty
rates of 45 percent or more. In general, increased schooling is associated with
lower poverty rates for single mothers, but educational attainment is clearly no
guarantee against poverty for these women (Zopf, 1989, p. 33).

The high poverty risks of minority women have already been identified. Table
2.5 illustrates the effects on poverty of both race or ethnicity and gender. In all
marital categories, poverty rates are higher for minorities than for whites. At
the same time, single female householders and single mothers have at least twice
the poverty rates of their male counterparts, regardless of race or national origin.
The relationship, moreover, is even more marked when the poverty rates of
female householder and married-couple families are compared. Among blacks,
for example, single-mother families have poverty rates nearly five times those
of two-parent households. These data underscore the need to consider the double
disadvantages of women of color.

Feminization of Poverty

Since 1960, great increases in divorce, separation, and nonmarriage of parents have resulted in a much larger number and proportion of women being exposed to the economic hazards of having to support themselves and their families. A group with high poverty rates to begin with has more than doubled in size. At the same time the poverty rates of married-couple families with and without children are less than half their 1960 rates, and the decline is nearly that great for married couples with children. In contrast, the declines are under 20 percent for both groups of female householders (see table 2.4). Since 1980, the growth of female householder families has slowed, but their rates of poverty have increased.

The results of these changes in family composition and in incidence of poverty is the feminization of poverty. It was first discernible in the mid–1970s (see table 2.6), when female householder families constituted 45 percent of poor families, and single-mother families already predominated among poor families with children. In 1987, the former made up over half the poor and the latter were three-fifths. The trend toward the feminization of poverty has continued, although at a somewhat slower pace after 1975 than in the preceding fifteen years.

Poverty is likely to remain feminized in America in the near future, despite the fact that the trend toward increasing preponderance of women among the poor seems to be abating. The high rates of poverty of American women should come as no surprise after the discussion of adverse labor market conditions, the failure to mount and sustain a vigorous campaign to reduce gender and racial inequality in employment, and the very limited antipoverty effects of social welfare programs.

FEMINIZATION OF POVERTY, FEMINIZATION OF POWER

The feminization of poverty has occurred alongside the increased power and politicization of American women. In the 1960s, a long-dormant women's movement was aroused, and the descendents of suffragists and social feminists began to organize, demonstrate, lobby, seek political office, and influence the political process.[14] The contemporary women's movement is widely credited with making American women more conscious of their status and their rights, and it has been an important force behind gains in the workforce and the political sphere (Harrison, 1988; Palley, 1987). Its promotion of women's entry into politics, its lobbying and mobilization of support for antidiscrimination laws, and its suits in response to violation of these laws have benefited poor women, minority women, and blue-collar women. At the same time, the mainstream of the movement, as represented by the National Organization for Women (NOW), is thought to be middle class in orientation (Degler, 1980; Eisenstein, 1981). While the movement has favored expansion of child care, pay equity, and maternity leave,

Table 2.6
Poor Female Householder Families as Proportion of All Poor Family Households by Presence of Children, 1960–1987 (in thousands)

With/ Without Children	Poor Female Householder Families	All Poor Families	Percent Female Householder Families
1960	1955	8243	23.7
1965	1916	6721	28.5
1970	1952	5260	37.1
1975	2430	5450	44.6
1980	2972	6217	47.8
1985	3474	7223	48.1
1987	3636	7059	51.5
With Children			
1960	1476	5328	27.7
1965	1499	4379	34.2
1970	1680	3491	48.1
1975	2252	4172	54.0
1980	2703	4822	56.1
1985	3131	5586	56.1
1987	3296	5516	60.0

Source: Calculated from U.S. Bureau of the Census, 1989b, p.11.

it has not made these its top priorities (Hewlett, 1986), and even though both middle-class and poor women are, as human service providers and beneficiaries, adversely affected by retrenchment in the human services (Erie, Rein, and Wiget, 1983), the women's movement has not functioned as a major defender of the social welfare system. Nor has the movement, by and large, defined a hike in the minimum wage as a women's issue.

NOW has also been regarded as a white women's organization (Loiacono, 1989). Yet, black women were among the founders of NOW, and currently one-fourth of the seats on the NOW board are reserved for women of color. Nonetheless, minority women often do not feel at home in either civil rights or women's rights organizations. They may well ''need a place where they can be both black and female'' (Loiacono, 1989; see also Lewis, 1983).

The Labor Movement

Women's voice in the labor movement can influence both the outcome of political decisions that bear on work and welfare as well as specific labor-management conflicts (Cook, 1984). In this route to economic and political influence women have gained in numbers. They make up 44 percent of the labor force and 41 percent of union members, up from 25 percent only a decade ago (Nelson, 1987). Traditionally, women have been virtually unrepresented in the leadership of organized labor, even in unions where they have been the majority of the members (Wertheimer, 1984). It was not until 1980 that a woman was elected to the thirty-five-member AFL-CIO Executive Council, and in 1989, there were only three women members.

In the past, organized labor has been unfriendly to women's rights (Raphael, 1974), but there have been some changes. The AFL-CIO, for example, has supported comparable worth since 1979; several pay equity battles have been waged by public sector unions; and some unions have been closely affiliated with organizations promoting pay and job equity, such as the National Committee for Pay Equity and Wider Opportunities for Women. Also a sign of change was the formation in 1974 of the Coalition of Labor Union Women (CLUW), which assembles women unionists across individual union locals and pursues such goals as organizing more women workers, securing passage of legislation to improve the conditions of working women, supporting more women candidates for public office, and increasing women's mobility on the job and in the union (Wertheimer, 1984, citing CLUW News, 1980). Still another promising development in the labor movement has been the growing unionization of clerical workers, an over-whelmingly female group, and the innovative techniques used to recruit them by unions such as 9 to 5: National Association of Working Women, and the Office and Professional Employees Union (Gilpin, Isaac, Letwin, and Mc-Kivigan, 1988; Nelson, 1987; Sidel, 1986).

Union membership is associated with significantly higher wages for women, and it is possible that wide-scale organization could upgrade the postindustrial workforce just as it elevated the once low-paid industrial laborer earlier in the century. As promising as these developments are, a weakened labor movement representing less than one-fifth of the workforce—down from about one-third in the 1950s—and still very male-dominated is a less-than-ideal ally and aegis for women. Yet, the economic future of many women workers as well as that of the American labor movement may well depend on such an alliance.

The Political Arena

Two gender gaps that have emerged in the 1980s could increase women's influence and the forces to fight women's poverty. First, reversing an earlier trend, women have begun to vote in greater proportions than men and to outnumber them at the polls (Kenski, 1988), although it is likely that poorer women and women of color remain underrepresented at the polls.[15]

A gender gap in preference is also discernible—women tend to favor Democrats and candidates who are more opposed to the use of force in foreign policy and more liberal in regard to domestic spending (Kenski, 1988; Klein, 1984; Mueller, 1988). The preference gap, however, has not yet affected the outcome of a presidential election.

While much less of an anomaly in today's American government than in the 1960s, particularly at the state and local levels, women remain a tiny minority of those with formal authority to make and execute national laws. They comprised only 2 percent of the Senate and 6 percent of the House of Representatives in 1989 (Women's Political Caucus of the U.S. Congress, personal communication, July 1989). Indeed, the United States is among the nations with the smallest proportions of women in its national legislature (Mandel, 1988; Sivard, 1985).

There is some evidence that women officeholders tend to represent the interests of women better than their male colleagues. The Center for American Women and Politics (1983, cited by Mandel, 1988) found that women officials had more liberal and feminist views than men of the same party or political orientation. Yet, on economic issues like minimum social security benefits, AFDC levels, or income distribution, women split along traditional liberal and conservative lines (Palley, 1987). Black women in government have been found to be the most liberal group of office holders and to be most identified with feminist issues (Mandel, 1988). It seems important, then, to elect to public office more women of color and more women and men specifically committed to economic justice. Such electoral outcomes would be facilitated by voter registration reforms that would lead to greater participation of the poor and people of color (Piven and Cloward, 1988).

Former member of Congress Bella Abzug, a feminist who has championed the interests of poor women and women of color, believes that "the feminization of poverty leads directly to the feminization of politics" or to women's determination to "have a greater say about the political, economic and social forces that dictate the way they live" (1984, p. 115). While the mechanism for women's mass political mobilization has not yet been created, women's wider recognition of the feminization of poverty and of the factors that contribute to it could give impetus to such mobilization.

There is some evidence to suggest that women respond politically on the basis of both altruism and self-interest (Mueller, 1988). The feminization of poverty is an issue that can evoke both. Most American women are either on their own already or, in view of the high rates of divorce or separation, at risk of becoming single parents or single providers—and poorer, if not actually impoverished, as a result. This is particularly true of women of color but by no means limited to them. Recognition of this common vulnerability could lead large numbers of American women—of all classes and racial or national origin groups—to advocate for the changes in labor market and social welfare policies that underlie the feminization of poverty.

NOTES

1. In 1987, the earnings of 45 percent of women workers were below the poverty level for a three-person family (calculated from U.S. Bureau of the Census, 1988c, p. 23).

2. It was largely in the social sector that government's wherewithal was deficient. The U.S. government bailout of the bankrupt savings and loan industry, approved by Congress in 1989, is estimated at $325 billion to $500 billion over the next three decades.

3. For a discussion of the social wage, see pp.11–12.

4. Barbara Bergmann (1986) takes a long view of the growth of women's labor force participation in the United States, arguing that there has been a steady growth every decade since 1870. However, her view seems to overlook the very dramatic rise in numbers in the post–1950 decades and the fact that large numbers of mothers, even with small children, are now in the labor force. Without this development the "steady march to employment" (p. 19) might have ground to a halt.

5. Dual labor market theory holds that one sector of the labor market, the primary sector, offers jobs that have such attributes as high wages, decent working conditions, and opportunities for advancement. The secondary market has low wages, poor working conditions, and little opportunity to advance (Piore, 1977). Garth Mangum, Donald Mayall, and Kristin Nelson (1985) extend this concept to temporary and core or permanent workers within the same firm. The dual internal labor market concept can also apply to full-time and part-time workers.

6. In 1985, 1.2 million persons held two part-time jobs, and 3.8 million had a part-time as well as a full-time job (Plewes, 1987).

7. For example, women comprised 59 percent of all workers in service occupations in 1980, but they made up 95 percent of all household workers and 12 percent of all workers in protective service occupations, both of which were subcategories of service occupations (Reskin and Hartmann, 1986, p. 8).

8. It should be noted that the labor force activity of young women of both races has increased steadily since 1972 (U.S. Department of Labor, Bureau of Labor Statistics, 1989, pp. 132–181).

9. In 1989, the Supreme Court reversed an eighteen-year precedent that employers, not plaintiffs, have the burden of proving whether a job requirement that is shown statistically to screen out minorities is a "business necessity," and it also ruled that court-approved affirmative action settlements are open to subsequent legal challenges by white workers (Greenhouse, 1989).

10. Under the Wisconsin program, which began in 1987 and is scheduled to run until 1993, there is an administrative formula for child support: 17 percent of the gross income of a noncustodial parent for one child, and 25, 29, 31, and 34 percent for two, three, four, and five children, respectively. Child support in these amounts is withheld from the wages and other income of the noncustodial parent. Children are to receive either the amount paid by their noncustodial parent or an assured benefit, whichever is larger. Unlike social assistance benefits, the assured benefit is not reduced for each dollar of earned income, and it is more a right than a dole. On the other hand, it is likely to be

lower than public assistance—probably $3,000 a year for the first child (Garfinkel and McLanahan, 1986, p. 137).

11. In 1987, the total number of single-mother families exceeded the number of female householder families with children by 1.5 million or 23 percent. The most important reason for using the smaller female householder category here is that data on poverty are collected by family households and are not available for all single-mother families. On the other hand, female householders with children are not only a smaller group than the total lone-mother population, but, since mother-child subfamilies are predominantly never-married women and their children (63 percent in 1967), they differ in marital composition from the total single-mother population (U.S. Bureau of the Census, 1988a, and unpublished tables from the U.S. Bureau of the Census, Marriage and Family Statistics Branch).

12. Mollie Orshansky (1965), the statistician who developed the poverty standard, offered no explanation for the decision to use a temporary food budget. However, 50 million Americans or over one-fourth of the population would have been below the poverty line had the higher cost food plan been used. The lower standard, based on the economy food plan, held the poverty count to 34 million.

13. For a number of years the Bureau of Labor Statistics used a "lower-level" budget for urban families that was initially termed "modest but adequate." When last issued in 1981, this lower-level budget was 67 percent higher than the official poverty standard (Johnson and Goldberg, 1986, pp. 6–7).

14. William L. O'Neill (1971) distinguishes among suffragists, social feminists, and radical feminists. The first were primarily concerned with the vote; social feminists put domestic social reform and the interests of the disadvantaged above those of women; and the radical feminists put women's oppression first. The radical feminists were thus able to confront the inequality of the domestic system. Carrie Chapman Catt epitomizes the suffragist, Jane Addams the social feminist, and Elizabeth Cady Stanton and Susan B. Anthony the radical feminists of the first wave.

15. Kevin Phillips has written:

The American electorate is disproportionately white and prosperous. Blacks constitute 11 percent of the national population, but cast only 7 percent of the total ballots in 1980. Hispanic turnout rates are even lower. One can reasonably suggest that the economic bottom third of the country cast only 20–25 percent of the total vote, while the top third cast perhaps 40–45 percent. This is a much greater imbalance than exists in any other major Western industrial nation (1983, cited by Piven and Cloward, 1988).

REFERENCES

Abzug, B. with M.Kelber (1984). *Gender Gap: Bella Abzug's Guide to Political Power for American Women*. Boston: Houghton Mifflin.

Albelda, R. (1985). "Nice work if you can get it: Segmentation of white and black women workers in the post-war period." *Review of Radical Political Economics* 17 (3): 72–85.

Appelbaum, E. (1987). "Restructuring work: Temporary, part-time and at-home employment." In H. Hartmann, ed. *Computer Chips and Paper Clips: Technology and Women's Employment*, volume 1. Washington, DC: National Academy Press.

Axinn, J., and M. J. Stern (1988). *Dependency and Poverty: Old Problems in a New World*. Lexington, MA: Lexington Books.

Barbaro, F. (1988). "Affirmative action: A review of government actions affecting employment opportunities for minorities and women." In *Issues in Social Welfare 1988–1990 Edition*. Garden City, NY: Adelphi University School of Social Work.

Bawden, D. L., and J. L. Palmer (1984). "Social policy: Challenging the welfare state." In J. L. Palmer and I. V. Sawhill, eds. *The Reagan Record*. Washington, DC: The Urban Institute.

Beller, A. H. (1984). "Trends in occupational segregation by sex, 1960–1981." In B. F. Reskin, ed. *Sex Segregation in the Workplace: Trends, Explanations, Remedies*. Washington, DC: National Academy Press.

Beller, A. H., and K. K. Han (1984). "Occupational sex segregation: Prospects for the 1980's." In B. F. Reskin, ed. *Sex Segregation in the Workplace: Trends, Explanations, Remedies*. Washington, DC: National Academy Press.

Bergmann, B. (1985). "The United States of America." In J. Farley, ed. *Women Workers in Fifteen Countries*. Ithaca, NY: ILR Press.

————.(1986). *The Economic Emergence of Women*. New York: Basic Books.

Bielby, W. T., and J. N. Baron (1984). "Women's place is with other women within organizations." In B. F. Reskin, ed. *Sex Segregation in the Workplace: Trends, Explanations, Remedies*. Washington, DC: National Academy Press.

Bixby, A. K. (1988). "Public social welfare expenditures, fiscal year 1985." *Social Security Bulletin* 51 (4): 21–31.

Blake, J., and J. H. del Pinal (1981). "The childlessness option: Recent American views of nonparenthood." In G. E. Hendershot and P. J. Placek, eds. *Predicting Fertility: Demographic Studies of Birth Expectation*. Lexington, MA: Lexington Books.

Blau, F. D. (1984). "Occupational segregation and labor market discrimination." In B. F. Reskin, ed. *Sex Segregation in the Workplace: Trends, Explanations, Remedies*. Washington, DC: National Academy Press.

Block, F. (1987). "Rethinking the political economy of the welfare state." In F. Block, R. A. Cloward, B. Ehrenreich, and F. F. Piven, eds. *The Mean Season: The Attack on the Welfare State*. New York: Pantheon.

Bowen, W. G., and T. A. Finegan (1969). *The Economics of Labor Force Participation*. Princeton, NJ: Princeton University Press.

Brenner, J. (1987). "Feminist political discourse: Radical versus liberal approaches to the feminization of poverty and comparable worth." *Gender and Society* 1 (4): 447–465.

Brown, C. (1987). "Consumption norms, work roles and economic growth, 1918–80." In C. Brown and J. A. Pechman, eds. *Gender in the Workplace*. Washington, DC: The Brookings Institution.

Bumpass, L. L. (1984). "Children and marital disruption: A replication and update." *Demography* 21 (1): 71–82.

Burstein, P. (1985). *Discrimination, Jobs and Politics: The Struggle for Equal Employment Opportunity in the United States since the New Deal*. Chicago: University of Chicago Press.

Cail, K., and J. Port (1985). "Examining the reality of childcare work." *Changing Work* (Spring): 9–11.

Center on Social Welfare Policy and Law (1987). *Analysis of 1987 Benefit Levels in the Program of Aid to Families with Dependent Children*. Washington, DC: Center on Social Welfare Policy and Law.

Cherlin, A. J. (1981). *Marriage, Divorce and Remarriage*. Cambridge, MA: Harvard University Press.

Cherry, R. (1989). *Discrimination: Its Economic Impact on Blacks, Women and Jews*. Lexington, MA: Lexington Books.

Children's Defense Fund (1987). *A Children's Defense Budget: FY 1988*. Washington, DC: Children's Defense Fund.

———.(1988). *A Children's Defense Budget: FY 1989*. Washington, DC: Children's Defense Fund.

———.(1989). *A Vision for America's Future: An Agenda for the 1990s*. Washington, DC: Children's Defense Fund.

Christensen, K. (1988a). "Independent contracting." In U.S. Department of Labor, Women's Bureau. *Flexible Workstyles: A Look at Contingent Labor: Conference Summary*. Washington, DC: U.S. Department of Labor, Women's Bureau.

———.(1988b). "Women's labor force attachment." In U.S. Department of Labor, Women's Bureau. *Flexible Workstyles: A Look at Contingent Labor: Conference Summary*. Washington, DC: U.S. Department of Labor, Women's Bureau.

Coalition on Women and Employment and Full Employment Action Council (1985). *Joblessness among Women: A Portrait of Female Unemployment*. Washington, DC: National Women's Law Center.

Coleman, C., and L. Hubbard (n.d.). *Survey of State-Government Pay Equity Activity, 1985*. Washington, DC: National Committee on Pay Equity.

Congressional Budget Office (CBO) (1988a). *Current Housing Problems and Possible Federal Responses*. Washington, DC: U.S. Government Printing Office.

———.(1988b). *The Effects of Tax Reform on Tax Expenditures*. Washington, DC: CBO.

Cook, A. H. (1984). "Introduction." In A. H. Cook, V. R. Lorwin, and A. K. Daniels, eds. *Women and Trade Unions in Eleven Industrialized Countries*. Philadelphia: Temple University Press.

Cutright, P., and P. Madras (1974). "AFDC and the marital and family status of ever married women aged 15–44: United States, 1950–1970." *Sociology and Social Research* 60 (3): 314–327.

Danziger, S., G. Jakubson, S. Schwartz, and E. Smolensky (1982). "Work and welfare as determinants of female household headship." *Quarterly Journal of Economics* (August): 521–534.

Davis, K. (1988). "Women and health care." In S. E. Rix, ed. *The American Woman, 1988–89: A Status Report*. New York: W. W. Norton.

Degler, C. (1980). *At Odds: Women and the Family from the Revolution to the Present*. New York: Oxford University Press.

Deutermann, W. V., Jr., and S. C. Brown (1978). "Voluntary part-time workers: A growing part of the labor force." *Monthly Labor Review* 101(6): 3–10.

Eisenstein, Z. (1981). *The Radical Future of Liberal Feminism*. New York: Longman, Green.

Ellwood, D. T. (1988). *Poor Support: Poverty in the American Family*. New York: Basic Books.

Ellwood, D. T., and M. J. Bane (1985). "The impact of AFDC on family structure and living arrangements." *Research in Labor Economics* 7: 137–207.

Erie, S. P., M. Rein, and B. Wiget (1983). "Women and the Reagan revolution: Thermidor for the social welfare economy." In I. Diamond, ed. *Families, Politics and Public Policy*. New York: Longman, Green.

Garfinkel, I., and S. S. McLanahan (1986). *Single Mothers and Their Children: A New American Dilemma*. Washington, DC: The Urban Institute Press.

Gilder, G. (1981). *Wealth and Poverty*. New York: Basic Books.

Gilpin, T., D. Isaac, D. Letwin, and J. McKivigan (1988). *On Strike for Respect: The Yale Strike of 1984–85*. Chicago: Charles H. Kerr.

Ginzberg, E. (1987). "Technology, women and work: Policy perspectives." In H. Hartmann, ed. *Computer Chips and Paper Clips: Technology and Women's Employment*, volume 1. Washington, DC: National Academy Press.

Goldberg, G. S. (September 1987). *Welfare Reform: Some American Illusions and Some New Initiatives*. Paper presented at the Fourteenth European Regional Symposium of the International Conference on Social Welfare, Special Meeting of the International Network on Unemployment and Social Work, Rome, Italy.

Goldin, C. (1987). "Women's employment and technological change. A historical perspective." In H. Hartmann, ed. *Computer Chips and Paper Clips: Technology and Women's Employment*, volume 1. Washington, DC: National Academy Press.

Greenhouse, L. (July 7, 1989). "The year the Court turned to the right." *New York Times*, pp. A1, A10.

Greenstein, R. (March 25, 1985). "Losing faith in *Losing ground*." *The New Republic*, pp. 12–17.

Harrison, B., and B. Bluestone (1988). *The Great U-turn*. New York: Basic Books.

Harrison, C. (1988). "A richer life: A reflection on the women's movement." In S. E. Rix, ed. *The American Woman, 1988–89: A Status Report*. New York: W. W. Norton.

Hewlett, S. A. (1986). *A Lesser Life: The Myth of Women's Liberation in America*. New York: William Morrow.

Hofferth, S. L. (1985). "Updating children's life course." *Journal of Marriage and the Family* 47: 93–115.

Hofferth, S. L., and D. Phillips (1986). *Child Care in the United States, 1970–1995*. Bethesda, MD: National Institute of Mental Health.

Holden, K. C., and W. L. Hansen (1987). "Part-time work, full-time work, and occupational segregation." In C. Brown and J. A. Pechman, eds. *Gender in the Workplace*. Washington, DC: The Brookings Institution.

Johnson, H. C., and G. S. Goldberg (1986). *Government Money for Everyday People: A Guide to Income Support Programs*. Lexington, MA: Ginn Press.

Jones, E. F., et al. (1986). *Teenage Pregnancy in Industrialized Countries*. New Haven, CT: Yale University Press.

Kahn, A. J., and S. B. Kamerman (1983). *Income Transfers for Families with Children: An Eight-country Study*. Philadelphia: Temple University Press.

———. (1987). *Child Care: Facing the Hard Choices*. Dover, MA: Auburn House.

Kahn, W., and Grune, J. A. (1982). "Pay equity: Beyond equal pay for equal work." In E. Boneparth, ed. *Women, Power and Policy*. New York: Pergamon.

Kenski, A. (1988). "The gender factor in a changing electorate." In C. M. Mueller, ed. *The Politics of the Gender Gap: The Social Construct of Political Influence*, volume 12. Sage Yearbooks in Women's Policy Studies. Beverly Hills, CA: Sage Publications.

Kessler-Harris, A. (1982). *Out to Work: A History of Wage-earning Women in the United States*. New York: Oxford University Press.

Klein, E. (1984). *Gender Politics*. Cambridge, MA: Harvard University Press.

Kornbluh, J. L. (January 1987). *The Contingent Workplace: Historical Perspectives on Part-time and Temporary Workers*. Paper presented at the Conference on the Contingent Workplace: New Directions for Work in the Year 2000, Women's Bureau and City University of New York.

Leonard, P. A., C. M. Dolbeare, and E. B. Lazere (1989). *A Place To Call Home: The Crisis in Housing for the Poor*. Washington, DC: Center on Budget and Policy Priorities.

Leontieff, W., and F. Duchin (1986). *The Future Impact of Automation on Workers*. New York: Oxford University Press.

Levitan, S. A., and E. A. Conway (1988). "Part-timers: Living on half rations." *Challenge* 31 (3): 9–26.

Levitan, S. A., and I. Shapiro (1987). *Working but Poor: America's Contradiction*. Baltimore, MD: Johns Hopkins University Press.

Lewin, T. (March 15, 1990). "Panel Asks at Least $5 Billion to Improve Child Care in U.S." *New York Times*, p. A24.

Lewis, D. L. (1983). "A response to inequality: Black Women, racism and sexism." In E. Abel and E. K. Abel, eds. *The Signs Reader: Women, Gender and Scholarship*. Chicago: University of Chicago Press.

Livernash, E. R. (1984). *Comparable Worth: Equal Employment*, 2d ed. Washington, DC: Advisory Council.

Loiacono, S. (1989). "Blacks and the women's movement: Still seeking common ground." *The Crisis* 96 (9): 26–27, 45–46.

Long, J. E., and E. B. Jones (1981). "Married women in part-time employment." *Industrial and Labor Relations Review* 34 (3): 413–425.

Malveaux, J. (1985). "The economic interests of black and white women: Are they similar?" *Review of Black Political Economy* (Summer): 5–27.

————.(1987). "The political economy of black women." In M. Davis et al., eds. *The Year Left 2: Toward a Rainbow Socialism: Essays on Race, Ethnicity, Class and Gender*. London: Verso.

Mandel, R. (1988). "The political woman." In S. E. Rix, ed. *The American Woman, 1988–89: A Status Report*. New York: W. W. Norton.

Mangum, G., D. Mayall, and K. Nelson (1985). "The temporary help industry: A response to the dual internal labor market." *Industrial and Labor Relations Review* 38 (4): 599–611.

Milkman, R. (1987). *Gender at Work: The Dynamics of Job Segregation by Sex during World War II*. Urbana and Chicago: University of Illinois Press.

Morehouse, W., and D. Dembo (August 1988). *Joblessness and the Pauperization of Work in America, Background Paper*. New York: Council on International and Public Affairs.

Mott, F. L. (1979). "Racial differences in female labor force participation." In K. W. Feinstein, ed. *Working Women and Their Families*. Beverly Hills, CA: Sage Publications.

————. (1982). "Women: The employment revolution." In F. Mott, ed. *The Employment Revolution: Young American Women in the 1970s*. Cambridge, MA: MIT Press.

Mueller, C. M. (1988). "Continuity and change in women's political agenda." In C. M. Mueller, ed. *The Politics of the Gender Gap: The Social Construct of Political Influence*, volume 12. Sage Yearbooks in Women's Policy Studies. Beverly Hills, CA: Sage Publications.

Murray, C. (1984). *Losing Ground: American Social Policy, 1950–1980*. New York: Basic Books.

Nardone, T. J. (1986). "Part-time workers: Who are they?" *Monthly Labor Review* 109 (2): 13–19.

National Committee on Pay Equity (n.d.). *Briefing Paper on the Wage Gap*. Washington, DC: National Committee on Pay Equity.

Nelson, A. (1987). "Women in unions." In S. E. Rix, ed. *The American Woman, 1987–1988: A Report in Depth*. New York: W. W. Norton.

O'Neill, W. L. (1971). *Everyone Was Brave: A History of Feminism in America*. New York: Quadrangle/The New York Times Book Company.

Oppenheimer, V. K. (1970). *The Female Labor Force in the United States: Demographic and Economic Factors Governing Its Growth and Changing Composition*. Westport, CT: Greenwood Press.

Organization for Economic and Cultural Development (OECD) (September 1988). *Employment Outlook*. Paris: OECD.

Orshansky, M. (1965). "Counting the poor, another look at the poverty profile." *Social Security Bulletin* 28 (1): 3–29.

Owen, J. D. (1978). "Why part-time workers tend to be in low-wage jobs." *Monthly Labor Review* 99 (6): 11–14.

Palley, M. L. (1987). "The women's movement in recent American politics." In S. E. Rix, ed. *The American Woman 1987–88: A Report in Depth*. New York: W. W. Norton.

Phillips, K. (1983). *Post-Conservative America: People, Politics and Ideology in a Time of Crisis*. New York: Random House.

Piore, M. J. (1977). "The dual labor market: Theory and implications." In D. M. Gordon, ed. *Problems in Political Economy*. New York: John Wiley.

Piven, F. F., and R. A. Cloward (1988). "New prospects for voter registration reform." *Social Policy* 18 (3): 3–15.

———.(1985). *The New Class War: Reagan's Attack on the Welfare State and Its Consequences*, rev. ed. New York: Pantheon Books.

———.(1987). "The contemporary relief debate." In F. Block, R. A. Cloward, B. Ehrenreich, and F. F. Piven, eds. *The Mean Season: The Attack on the Welfare State*. New York: Pantheon.

Plewes, T. (January 1987). *Understanding the Data on Part-time and Temporary Employment*. Paper presented at the Conference on the Contingent Workplace: New Directions for Work in the Year 2000, Women's Bureau and City University of New York.

———.(1988). "Understanding the data on part-time and temporary employment." In U.S. Department of Labor, Women's Bureau. *Flexible Workstyles: A Look at Contingent Labor: Conference Summary*. Washington, DC: U.S. Department of Labor, Women's Bureau.

Presser, H., and W. Baldwin (1980). "Child care as a constraint on employment: Prevalence, correlates, and bearing on the work and fertility nexus." *American Journal of Sociology* 85 (5): 1202–1213.

Raphael, E. (1974). "Working women and their membership in labor unions." *Monthly Labor Review* 97 (5): 27–33.

Reskin, B. F., ed. (1984). *Sex Segregation in the Workplace: Trends, Explanations, Remedies*. Washington, DC: National Academy Press.

————.(1988). "Occupational resegregation." In S. E. Rix, ed. *The American Woman, 1988–89: A Status Report*. New York: W. W. Norton.

Reskin, B. F., and H. Hartmann (1986). *Women's Work, Men's Work: Sex Segregation on the Job*. Washington, DC: National Academy Press.

Roos, P. A. (1985). *Gender and Work: A Comparative Analysis of Industrial Societies*. Albany: State University of New York Press.

Ross, C., J. Mirowsky, and J. Huber (1983). "Marriage patterns and depression." *American Sociological Review* 48: 809–823.

Ross, H. L., and I. V. Sawhill (1975). *Time of Transition: The Growth of Families Headed by Women*. Washington, DC: The Urban Institute.

Ross, S. D. (1970). *Sex Discrimination and "Protective" Labor Legislation*. New York: New York University Law School.

Ryscavage, P. (n.d.). *Changes in Occupational Sex Segregation during the 1970s*. Unpublished. Washington, DC: U.S. Bureau of the Census.

Schlesinger, A. M., Jr. (1986). *The Cycles of American History*. Boston: Houghton Mifflin.

Schorr, A. L. (1966). *Poor Kids*. New York: Basic Books.

Shapiro, I. (1987). *No Escape: The Minimum Wage and Poverty*. Washington, DC: Center on Budget and Policy Priorities.

Shapiro, I., and R. Greenstein (1988). *Holes in the Safety Nets: Poverty Programs and Policies in the States: National Overview*. Washington, DC: Center on Budget and Policy Priorities.

Sidel, R. (1986). *Women and Children Last: The Plight of Poor Women in Affluent America*. New York: Viking.

Sivard, R. L. (1985). *Women . . . A World Survey*. Washington, DC: World Priorities.

Smeeding, T., B. B. Torrey, and M. Rein (1988). "Patterns of income and poverty: The economic status of children and the elderly in eight countries." In J. L. Palmer, T. Smeeding, and B. B. Torrey, eds. *The Vulnerable*. Washington, DC: Urban Institute Press.

Smith, J. (1986). "The paradox of women's poverty: Wage earning women and economic transformation." In B. Gelpi, N.C.M. Hartsock, C. C. Novak, and M. Strober, eds. *Woman and Poverty*. Chicago: University of Chicago Press.

Stack, C. B. (1974). *All Our Kin: Strategies for Survival in a Black Community*. New York: Harper & Row.

Steinberg, R. S. (1987). "Radical challenges in a liberal world: The mixed success of comparable worth." *Gender & Society* 1 (4): 466–475.

Terry, S. L. (1981). "Involuntary part-time work: New information from the current population survey." *Monthly Labor Review* 104 (2): 70–74.

Treiman, D. J., and H. I. Hartmann (1981). *Women, Work and Wages: Equal Pay for Jobs of Equal Value: Report of the Committee on Occupational Classification and Analysis*. Washington, DC: National Academy Press.

U.S. Bureau of the Census (1961). *Household and Family Characteristics: March 1960*. Current Population Reports, Series P–20, No. 106. Washington, DC: U.S. Government Printing Office.

————.(1966). *Household and Family Characteristics: March 1965*. Current Population Reports, Series P–20, No. 153. Washington, DC: U.S. Government Printing Office.

————.(1971). *Household and Family Characteristics: March 1970*. Current Population

Reports, Series P–20, No. 204. Washington, DC: U.S. Government Printing Office.

———.(1976). *Household and Family Characteristics: March 1975*. Current Population Reports, Series P–20, No. 291. Washington, DC: U.S. Government Printing Office.

———.(1981). *Household and Family Characteristics: March 1980*. Current Population Reports, Series P–20, No. 366. Washington, DC: U.S. Government Printing Office.

———.(1984). *Estimates of Poverty Including the Value of Noncash Benefits, 1979 to 1982*. Technical Paper 51. Washington, DC: U.S. Bureau of the Census.

———.(1986a). *Household and Family Characteristics: March 1985*. Current Population Reports, Series P–20, No. 411. Washington, DC: U.S.Government Printing Office.

———.(1986b). *Women in the American Economy*. Current Population Reports, Series P–23, No. 146, by C. M. Taeuber and V. Valdisera. Washington, DC: U.S. Government Printing Office.

———.(1987). *Estimates of Poverty Including the Value of Noncash Benefits, 1986*. Technical Paper 57. Washington, DC: Author.

———.(1988a). *Household and Family Characteristics: March 1987*. Current Population Reports, Series P–20, No. 424. Washington, DC: U.S. Government Printing Office.

———.(1988b). *Measuring the Effects of Benefits and Taxes on Income and Poverty: 1986*. Current Population Reports, Series P–60, No. 164–RD–1. Washington, DC: U.S. Government Printing Office.

———.(1988c). *Money Income and Poverty Status in the United States: 1987*. Current Population Reports, Series P–60, No. 161. Washington, DC: U.S. Government Printing Office.

———.(1989a). *Money Income and Poverty Status in the United States: 1988* Current Population Reports, Series P–60, No. 166. Washington, DC: U.S. Government Printing Office.

———.(1989b). *Poverty in the United States: 1987*. Current Population Reports, Series P–60, No. 163. Washington, DC: U.S. Government Printing Office.

U.S. Department of Labor, Bureau of Labor Statistics (1989). *Labor Force Statistics Derived from the Current Population Survey, 1948–87*. Bulletin 2307. Washington, DC: U.S. Government Printing Office.

U.S. Department of Health and Human Services, Family Support Administration (1990). *Characteristics and Financial Circumstances of AFDC Recipients: FY 1988*. Washington, DC: U.S. Government Printing Office.

U.S. Department of Labor, Women's Bureau (1988). *Flexible Workstyles: A Look at Contingent Labor: Conference Summary*. Washington, DC: U.S.Department of Labor, Women's Bureau.

Waldstein, L. (1989). "Service sector wages: Productivity and job creation in the U.S. and other countries: Background paper." In L. Thurow. *Toward a High-wage, High-productivity Service Sector*. Washington, DC: Economic Policy Institute.

Wallace, P. A., with L. Datcher and J. Malveaux, (1980). *Black Women in the Labor Force*. Cambridge, MA: MIT Press.

Weatherley, R. A. (1987). "Teenage pregnancy, professional agendas and problem definitions." *Journal of Sociology & Social Welfare* 14 (2): 5–35.

Wertheimer, B. M. (1984). "The United States of America." In A. H. Cook, V. R. Lorwin, and A. K. Daniels, eds. *Women and Trade Unions in Eleven Industrialized Countries*. Philadelphia: Temple University Press.

Wilensky, H. L. (1965). "Introduction: The problems and prospects of the welfare state." In H. L. Wilensky and C. N. Lebeaux, eds. *Industrial Society and Social Welfare*. New York: The Free Press.

Wilson, W. J. (1987). *The Truly Disadvantaged: The Inner City, the Underclass and Public Policy*. Chicago: University of Chicago Press.

World Bank (1988). *World Development Report 1988*. New York: Oxford University Press.

Zelnick, M., J. F. Kanter, and K. Ford (1981). *Sex and Pregnancy in Adolescence*. Beverly Hills, CA: Sage Publications.

Zopf, P. E. (1989). *American Women in Poverty*. New York: Greenwood Press.

3

Canada: Bordering on the Feminization of Poverty

GERTRUDE SCHAFFNER GOLDBERG

Canada and the United States have more in common than a border that stretches along one-fifth of the earth's circumference. In addition to advanced industrialism, capitalism, and democracy, both nations have a colonial past, a relatively recent frontier experience, and a federal system of government. English institutions, the individualism of a pioneer community, and a decentralized form of government have all left their mark on these North American neighbors. Yet, there are vast differences in population and power and smaller and subtler distinctions in political and social philosophies. Even apparent similarities, such as the English heritage or federalism, turn out to be somewhat different. This study asked whether there are also differences in the economic status of women.

Canada has been called a "big, small country." It is somewhat larger in area than the United States, but its population of 26 million is only one-ninth the size. Both are federations, one with ten provinces and the other with fifty states. Though its economy is a fraction of the size of the giant U.S. economy, Canada's GNP per capita is nonetheless among the highest in the world (UNICEF, 1989, p. 95; World Bank, 1989, p. 165).

Born in counterrevolution rather than revolution and still maintaining some ties to the mother country, Canada draws on the older British tradition of toryism and not solely on the liberal individualism that has been the prevailing political philosophy in North America (Horowitz, 1966; Lipset, 1985). Influenced by toryism, with its paternalistic concern for the less fortunate, Canadian conservatives are more inclined to support the welfare state than their American counterparts (Horowitz, 1966). On issues of social policy, conservatives like Prime Minister Brian Mulroney have been described as "reluctant but paternalistic collectivists" whose "notions of noblesse oblige . . . entail a rejection of social Darwinism" (Prince, 1987, p. 248).

The reasons why Canadian elites are mildly supportive of the welfare state, however, may be pragmatic as well as philosophical. One respected study (Banting, 1987) suggested that social welfare benefits have created a direct link between citizens and their government that may serve to bolster the government's legitimacy in the highly fragmented Canadian federation. Whatever the reasons, Canada is more comfortable with strong or affirmative government than the United States (Hockin, 1975; Lipset, 1985, 1990). Since government intervention is particularly important to the economic welfare of women and their families, this factor could influence the extent to which poverty is feminized in the two North American nations.

If tempered somewhat on the right by tory paternalism or *noblesse oblige*, liberal individualism is softened on the left by socialist influences. In Canada both socialism and toryism are "admissible and natural if far from commanding" (Hockin, 1975, p. 10). This combination of influences may explain why Canadians are seen as not only more law abiding and elitist than Americans but also more egalitarian (Lipset, 1985).

The phrase "natural if far from commanding" aptly describes the position of Canada's third party, which is social democratic in orientation. While the Progressive Conservatives and Liberals regularly form national governments in Canada, the New Democratic Party (NDP) has garnered nearly 20 percent of the popular vote in most national elections since the mid–1960s (Thorburn, 1985, p. 349) and has formed governments in three of the Canadian provinces in the last decade. The NDP is formally allied with the Canadian Labour Congress (CLC) whose membership, though low by Scandinavian standards, is considerably higher than in the United States—about one-third of the labor force, compared to less than one-fifth (Neill, 1988).[1]

A number of crossnational studies have shown that, other things being equal, countries with decentralized governments like Canada and the United States devote smaller proportions of their resources to welfare than do those with centralized governments (Banting, 1987, pp. 173–174). In 1985, the two North American federations in this study spent between 29 percent and 47 percent less of their gross domestic products (GDP) on welfare than Sweden and France, both of which are centralized polities (OECD,1988b, pp. 16–17).[2] Though its social welfare spending is considerably less than that of these two advanced welfare states, Canada is a less reluctant welfare state than its North American neighbor; its welfare expenditures in 1985 were nearly 25 percent higher than those of the United States.[3]

If Canada has taken a slightly different course from the United States in social welfare, the same cannot be said of the market sphere. The economic relationship between the two North American countries has been described variously as "the closest of any truly independent lands in the world" (Malcolm, 1985, p. 152), asymmetric because of the great differences in size and interdependence (Lipsey, 1985), or "essentially colonial" (Burnham, 1979). The fact that two-thirds of Canada's trade is with the United States is said to have reduced the leeway of Canadian policymakers to respond to the international economic problems that began manifesting themselves in the mid–1970s (Brodie and Jenson, 1988).[4]

The 1988 free trade treaty with the United States, ratified by Canada after a bitter electoral contest, is moving Canada even further into the U.S. economic orbit. One fear of the Canadians who opposed the treaty is that social programs, such as unemployment and health insurance, will be cut back, lest they provide Canadian business with an unfair subsidy or unbalance the "even playing field" on which free trade is predicated. Canadians pride themselves on the quality of their public social services, and it is in this sector that they have maintained an independence from the United States that now seems threatened. Since social welfare benefits are often vital to low-income women, the changes that ensue from the free trade accord could well affect the feminization of poverty.

Already erasing the subtle shading that differentiated the social and economic policies of the two North American neighbors is Canada's move away from the Keynesian economic policies that marked the postwar period. Since the early 1970s, Canada has adopted more restrictive monetary and fiscal policies that give primacy to the needs of business and the requirements of capital accumulation (Myles, 1988; Sharpe, Voyer, and Cameron, 1988; Wolfe, 1984).

One reason for selecting Canada for this study is that it was thought important to include some countries that, like the United States, are racially and ethnically heterogeneous. This apparent similarity, too, turned out to be somewhat superficial. Canada has "visible minorities"—as people of color are designated—and they "undeniably face discrimination both overt and indirect" (Abella, 1984 p. 47).[5] Native or aboriginal peoples, like their counterparts in the United States, are a "depressed and subjugated population" (Bienvenue, 1985, p. 206). Both groups, along with women and the disabled, were targeted for special equalization measures by the Employment Equity Act of 1986. Visible minorities, however, constitute about 6 percent of the Canadian population (Employment and Immigration Canada, 1988, p. B–1); the vast majority of Canadians (over 90 percent) are of European descent, largely British or French, or a combination of these origins. A much smaller group than people of color in the United States, visible minorities have immigrated largely after 1960 and are neither an initially enslaved nor a long-segregated people.

Not included among the four groups targeted for equalization are French Canadians, whose incomes, occupational scales, rates of mobility, and returns on investment from education are, on the average, lower than Canadians of English stock (Breton and Stasiulis, 1980; Clement, 1985). About one-fourth of the Canadian population, French Canadians are geographically concentrated in Quebec. French Canadians are able to wield considerable power in the ethnically and regionally fragmented Canadian federation. From an ultraconservative society fixated at the essentially feudal stage of its founders, Quebec has, since 1960, undergone a *revolution tranquille* in which political and social structures have been catching up with the economic modernization that had been going on throughout the century (Behiels, 1984; Handler, 1988, pp. 83–85).

In a classic study of its social structure, conducted in the mid–1960s, Canada was described as a "vertical mosaic," racially and ethnically stratified but of-

fering some measure of multiculturalism (Porter, 1965). Women were not pic-
tured in the Canadian mosaic. Yet, one study of both gender and race/ethnicity
in Canada found that the level of occupational segregation is much higher for
women than for all but the most highly segregated ethnic groups (Darroch, 1985,
p. 165).

WOMEN'S STRUGGLE FOR SOCIAL EQUALITY

Women had to fight for the right to vote in the Canadian democracy. A
women's movement that began in the 1870s as an effort to open educational
opportunities for women later focused on the suffrage. Women gained the federal
franchise in 1918 but had to wait until 1925 to secure the vote in nine of the
ten provinces. In Quebec, it was not until the eve of World War II that women
achieved that democratic right.

As elsewhere, the right to vote and hold office did not lead to political or
economic power for women. In 1988, seventy years after the federal franchise
was won, only 14 percent of the House of Commons and 15 percent of the
executive cabinet were women (National Action Committee on the Status of
Women, personal communication, July 1989). Though women continue to be
grossly underrepresented, the percentage of women in the House of Commons
did increase five-fold since 1972 (Brodie, 1985, p. 123).

The "second wave" of the Canadian women's movement gained considerable
momentum from the appointment in 1967 of a Royal Commission on the Status
of Women.[6] A response to pressure on the part of a small group of outstanding
women (Marsden,1980), the Commission "awakened women to their collective
subordination" (Brodie, 1985, p. 127) and served as a rallying point for further
protest (Wilson, 1982). A governmental body, the Canadian Advisory Council
on the Status of Women, was established to continue to propose policies to
improve women's condition, and the National Action Committee on the Status
of Women (NAC) was organized to pressure the government to implement the
wide range of equalization measures proposed by the Royal Commission.[7]

Today NAC is the major women's rights organization in Canada, representing nearly 600 organizations with a membership of 3½ million people
(NAC, personal communication, April 1989). The NAC coalition encompas-
ses not only women's organizations but grassroots or community-based
groups as well (Adamson, Briskin, and McPhail, 1988). NAC appears committed to a wide range of social and economic issues facing women of all
social strata. It has been suggested that the existence of the New Democratic
Party and its progressive positions on women's issues may account for the
fact that the women's movement in Canada has been more inclined than its
American counterpart to focus on public policies such as day care, pensions,
and labor legislation (p. 124).

In its vigorous campaign against the free trade treaty NAC argued that the
agreement would threaten the jobs of women, particularly the elderly, immi-

grants, and women of color, and that it could lead to cutbacks in medical and social programs as well as loosening of Canada's stricter regulations regarding pesticides and acid rain (NAC, 1988). Along with the elderly, the women's movement is said to have emerged as a major champion and political bulwark of the welfare state—a role that NAC's U.S. counterpart, NOW, has not played (Banting, 1987, p. 184). In the past, the Canadian women's movement has been regarded as insensitive to racism or to have failed to regard it as a feminist issue (Stasiulus, 1987). More recently NAC (1987) has expressed a commitment to incorporating the goals of women who bear the double disadvantage of gender and racial inequality.[8]

Since the 1960s, when general awareness of the problems of women in industrial society began to increase, the Canadian government has adopted important measures to deal with these problems. Some of these, such as liberalization of the laws pertaining to abortion and contraception (1969), predated the organized pressure of the women's movement, but the movement fought for and contributed to the passage of a number of reforms during the 1970s and 1980s. Among these measures are: paid maternity leave (1971); amendment of the Canada Pension Plan to permit credits earned during a marriage to be equally divided upon its dissolution (1977); the 1988 Supreme Court ruling that the still restrictive federal abortion law was unconstitutional; the Employment Equity Act of 1986; and several important equalization measures at the provincial level (Adamson, Briskin, and McPhail, 1988). The list of governmental reforms is impressive, but "the government's record in guaranteeing the implementation of . . . legal equalities is less impressive" (Burt, 1984 p. 149).

Since most Canadian women are in the labor force, unionization could be an important means of improving women's economic status. Between 1970 and the mid–1980s, women's membership in unions increased at a faster rate than their participation in the labor force. By 1985, 28 percent of women workers were union members (Neill, 1988), but this was still a minority of the female labor force and a lower membership rate than that of men. Perhaps reflecting the increasing number of women unionists, Shirley Carr was elected president of the CLC, the first woman to hold that position in any western country (Nelson, 1987).

For most of its history the labor movement has not been regarded as an ally in the struggle for women's rights. Feminists contend that unionists have ignored women's issues, even actively discriminated against women, and made little effort to organize them (Phillips and Phillips, 1983). Yet, union membership is associated with higher wages for women and a lower female/male earnings gap (Neill, 1988; Phillips and Phillips 1983, p. 131, citing White, 1980). Moreover, the labor movement has been pressured to champion women's issues by women unionists and by the women's movement (Briskin, 1983). Few unions have undertaken campaigns for affirmative action or made it a bargaining priority, but they have adopted policy statements in support of equal opportunity, including affirmative action (Larkin, 1983). Notwithstanding the earlier record of unions and the remaining difficulties in getting the labor movement to take up women's

Table 3.1
Labor Force Participation of Canadian Women, Age 15 and Over, 1950–1988

(Numbers in thousands)

	Number	Rate	Proportion of Labor Force
1950	1,112	23.2	21.5
1960	1,657	27.9	25.8
1965	2,070	31.3	29.0
1970	2,824	38.3	32.2
1975	3,680	44.4	36.9
1980	4,635	50.4	40.1
1985	5,365	54.6	42.8
1988	5,853	57.4	44.1

Source: Statistics Canada, 1989a, pp.22, 36, 252; for the years 1950–1965, unpublished data from the Labour Force Survey Subdivision.

issues, "unions are one of the key avenues to workplace improvements for women" (Briskin, 1983, p. 260).

PERSISTENCE AND CHANGE FOR WOMEN IN THE WORKFORCE

In all western industrialized countries there has been a growth in women's labor force participation since 1950. This is especially true for Canadian women whose rates were comparatively low at the beginning of the period but, by 1980, above the average for the fifteen countries belonging to the Organization for Economic and Cultural Development (OECD, 1986, p. 140). Between 1950 and 1988 the number of Canadian women in the labor force grew more than five-fold, and their participation rates and share of the workforce both doubled (table 3.1). By the mid–1980s, mothers, even of very young children, were typically in the labor force (Statistics Canada, 1987, p. 32). In 1988, 64 percent of single mothers were in the labor force, a figure just under the rate of 68 percent for married mothers (calculated from Statistics Canada, 1989b, p. 134.)

The factors that led Canadian women to enter the labor market are similar to those that influenced women in the United States (see pp. 18–20 in this volume) and elsewhere in the industrialized world. Owing to declining birth rates and mechanization of housework, women were freer to work outside the home. Their economic need to enter the labor force increased as a result of changing consumption norms and, later, declining real wages and divorce. Still another reason for women's entering the labor force is that expansion of the service sector increased the demand for their labor (Armstrong and Armstrong, 1984).

This tremendous increase in the number of employed women is said to have "revolutionized" the labor force (Dumas, 1988). Yet, women's status in the workforce has hardly been revolutionized. Indeed, "the increasing visibility of women outside the home and the emphasis on female attainment of jobs at the top . . . have camouflaged the lack of basic change in women's work" (Armstrong and Armstrong, 1984, p. 16).

Changes have indeed taken place in the Canadian economy since the early 1970s, but these new developments have made it harder for women to advance, even as they were entering the labor force in record numbers and with new aspirations and greater assertiveness. Unfortunately, the women's movement and the postwar economic boom by and large missed each other. As a result of the economic slowdown that began in the early 1970s and the response of business and government to these challenges, women have had to assert their claims for equality amidst higher unemployment and increasing underemployment. Contributing to this situation was the expansion of the low-wage service sector and the contraction of the secondary sector, never fully developed in the Canadian economy but a natural destination for aspiring blue collar women.[9] Still other developments that made it hard for women to advance in the labor market were the failure of government to provide sufficient child care and other social supports that facilitate handling of dual roles. Indeed, cutbacks in some programs such as social assistance meant that social welfare was doing less to bolster the bargaining power of workers. Finally, there was a resurgent antiunion stance in the private sector that was mirrored in public administration where many women were being employed (Armstrong and Armstrong, 1988; Brodie and Jenson, 1988; Riches, 1986; Ternowetsky, 1987; Wolfe, 1984).

The Canadian labor movement has held its proportion of the labor force since 1970 (Neill, 1988). Yet, it was not strong enough or sufficiently allied with a ruling party to achieve the kind of role in economic decision making that has characterized policymaking in countries where economic planning has considered the welfare of workers as well as of capital (Bellemare and Simon, 1988; Brodie and Jenson, 1988; Wilensky, 1983). Nor was the recently rekindled women's movement, with the likely exception of Quebec feminists, sufficiently conscious of women as an oppressed class or sufficiently adept politically to have influenced the response to economic conditions (Burt, 1984). Thus, economic and political elites in Canada were relatively free to respond to the economic crisis with the combination of antilabor strategies and related post-Keynesian fiscal and monetary policies that have created and countenanced mass unemployment and underemployment and at the same time undermined the capacity of the welfare state to mitigate the consequent losses of income.

Part-time Work and Underemployment

At first advocates for women held that part-time work would help women to achieve equality of employment opportunity. This was the position taken by the Royal Commission on the Status of Women in 1970, but thirteen years later, the Canadian Advisory Council on the Status of Women concluded that "part-time work means exploitation" (White, 1983 p. 12). In the meantime large numbers of Canadian women had entered the labor market as part-time workers.

The economic consequences of part-time work are severe. In general, part-timers are subject to greater occupational segregation and lower wages and fringe benefits, and they are also less likely to be unionized than full-time workers (Evans, 1985, p. 204). The average wage for full-timers was $10.41 (Canadian) an hour in 1984 but only $6.85 for part-timers (Burke, 1986, p. 13). Not unexpectedly, the poverty risk for a head of household who is a part-time worker is five times that of a full-time worker (Thornley, 1987, p. 6). Part-timers are less likely to be covered by employer-sponsored pension plans (Burke, 1986), and they are often denied unemployment insurance benefits because they fail to meet minimum hourly employment requirements per week (Abella, 1984, p. 97). However, in Canada, unlike the United States, part-timers do not have to worry about the lack of health fringe benefits because all citizens have health insurance, regardless of employment status.

A change in Canada's definition of part-time employment from less than thirty-five to less than thirty hours a week has, since the mid–1970s, served to underestimate its extent and to distort crossnational comparisons.[10] We can estimate that if the thirty-five-hour cutoff were still used, about one-third of women workers would be part-time workers instead of the official rate of one-fourth (table 3.2). Part-time work is "largely the preserve of women" in Canada (Burke, 1986, p. 10). This was true in 1950 and it was even more the case over three decades later when women made up over 70 percent of all part-timers (table 3.2).

In the decade from 1975 to 1985, part-time employment grew more than twice as fast as full-time opportunities, and was the "single fastest growing component of the employed Canadian labor force" (Burke, 1986, p. 10) Part-time work has increased throughout the Canadian economy (Lévesque, 1987), but it nevertheless remains concentrated in the service industries where women are overrepresented (Akyeampong, 1987).

While all part-time employment has grown rapidly, involuntary part-time work has grown much faster (Akyeampong, 1987). The incidence of this form of unemployment or underemployment is considerably higher among women than men and is highest among young women ages 15 to 24 (p. 28). The designation "voluntary" can itself be misleading because for many women part-time employment is "not so much the free choice or an ideal solution as a necessary compromise between conflicting pressures and responses to working conditions" (White, 1983, p. 12).

Table 3.2
Part-time Employment Rates for Canadian Women, 1953–1988

	Less Than (a) 35 Hours	Less Than 30 Hours	Women as Proportion of Part-time Workers
1953	10.7	NA	63.5
1960	16.7	NA	66.5
1965	22.1	NA	67.9
1970	30.8	(23.3)	67.4
1975	(26.8)	20.3	69.5
1980	(31.5)	23.8	72.6
1985	(34.5)	26.1	72.0
1988	(33.3)	25.2	72.0

(a) In 1975, Statistics Canada changed the definition of part-time work
     from less than 35 hours per week to less than 30. This resulted in
     a reduction of 24.4% in part-time employment in 1975. Assuming that
     the relationship between the two would have remained constant, we
     figured the rate for the former definition of part-time work (less
     than 35 hours) which is the standard used by the OECD.

Source: Statistics Canada, 1984, pp.212, 215, 297, 302; 1989b, pp. 212, 215;
for the years 1953-1970, unpublished data from the Labour Force Survey
Subdivision.

Unemployment

In the early 1980s, Canada was among the countries with "mass unemployment"—rates of 10 percent or more (Therborn, 1986). Although unemployment
rates have dipped below the double-digit line since then, they were still 8.3
percent for men and 7.4 percent for women in 1988 (Statistics Canada, 1989b,
pp. 206–207). Canadian unemployment rates had previously followed the American pattern, but Canada has adhered to tight monetary and deficit reduction
policies that have continued high unemployment throughout the 1980s (Sharpe,
Voyer, and Cameron, 1988).

In Canada, as in the United States, official unemployment rates underestimate
joblessness by excluding those who have ceased to look for work (discouraged
workers) and involuntary part-time workers. Unemployment rates, moreover,
pertain to the average proportion of the labor force unemployed at any time

during the year but do not measure the total number exposed to unemployment at some time during the year. Thus, in 1985, when the unemployment rate for women was 10.7 percent, more than twice that proportion experienced unemployment at some time during the year (Statistics Canada, 1987, pp. 42, 44). Lone mothers are particularly prone to unemployment. In 1988, their rates were 14.7 percent, compared to 8.8 percent for married mothers (calculated from Statistics Canada, 1989b, p. 134).

Pat Armstrong and Hugh Armstrong assert that the high proportion of women in the labor market has permitted the government to downplay the problem of unemployment. If the unemployed worker is a woman, it is assumed that she is a secondary worker with a spouse to support her; if the male is unemployed, he is assumed to have his wife's earnings on which to fall back (1988, p. 75).

Women's Wages

Canadian women who worked full time year round in 1987 had earnings almost two-thirds (65.9 percent) those of men. This is slightly higher than the U.S. figure for that year. Whereas the Canadian ratio has risen slowly but steadily from 58.4 percent in 1967 to 62.1 percent in 1977 to 65.9 percent ten years later, the narrowing of the U.S. wage gap has taken place largely since 1981. Because women are more likely to work part-time than men, full-time ratios underestimate the earnings gap. Thus the ratio for average earnings was 57.6 percent in 1987, 8 percent lower than for full-time earnings (Statistics Canada, 1988, p. 10).

Discrepancies in full-time earnings of men and women tend to fall as education increases but are nonetheless large at all educational levels. In 1982, women with less than a ninth-grade education earned 57.3 percent that of men with comparable schooling, while the ratio for those with postsecondary education was 69.7 percent. Among holders of university degrees, however, the proportion is slightly lower (Statistics Canada, 1985, p. 40).

An inadequate minimum wage plays a part in the inequality and poverty of Canadian women. In 1985, a single parent supporting one child on a full-time, year-round job paying the minimum wage would have earned an income ranging from 56 percent of the poverty line in the province of British Columbia to 73 percent in Saskatchewan (Thornley, 1987, p. 4) There have been increases in the minimum wage in some provinces since the mid–1980s, but nowhere is it truly a safeguard against family poverty. Under half of the workforce, Canadian women are more than three-fifths of those earning the inadequate minimum wage. A more adequate minimum wage would thus be an important strategy for reducing the wage gap.

Occupational Segregation

The "double ghetto" is a phrase that has been coined to describe the combination of segregated domestic work and segregated market work that is the typical pattern for Canadian women (Armstrong and Armstrong, 1978; 1984). Fifteen of twenty-one detailed occupational categories were at least 75 percent male or female in 1988. Women were 80 percent of clerical workers and 79 percent of medical and health workers. Men were 84 percent of professionals in the natural sciences, 98 percent of construction workers, and 94 percent of those in machining. Between 1976 and 1988 the proportion of women in clerical occupations, medicine and health, and teaching increased. The proportion of women in managerial and administrative work has increased *very* substantially since 1975 (Statistics Canada, 1985, p. 51; 1989b, table 14), yet women have remained less than one-fifth of upper-level managers (1985/1986) (Employment and Immigration Canada, 1988, p. B–8). Within such female-dominated occupations as medicine and health women tend to have jobs in nursing, supervising, and related assisting occupations, while men are much more likely to be independent practitioners; similarly, in retailing, women are the great majority of sales clerks, and men are much more likely to be supervisors (Boyd, 1982).

Women and men are not simply separate at work; they are unequal. Women are concentrated in low-wage, low-productivity industries (Armstrong and Armstrong, 1989). Moreover, levels of pay often depend more on the sex of the worker than on what he or she does: "by giving different job descriptions to what men and women do, employers . . . have been able to keep women in the lower-paying categories" (Landsberg, 1982, p. 36). Patricia M. Evans found that the average wages of sole-support mothers in the primary sector were substantially below those earned by men in the secondary sector. She concluded that the labor market distinction among low income individuals "may be more rooted in sex than sector: to be a women is to be a secondary worker" (1985, p. 188).

While it is possible to point to sex differences in human capital—education, skill levels, and job commitment—past and present discrimination also contribute to occupational segregation and consequent inequalities. It is true that women are still underrepresented among those who earn masters degrees (41 percent) and doctorates (27 percent), but they obtain more than half of the bachelor's degrees and have more than doubled their college enrollment since 1970 ("Education in Canada," 1986). Most women have finished high school but are still segregated into the most menial jobs in clerical, sales, service, and factory work (Armstrong and Armstrong, 1983, p. 4). As Armstrong and Armstrong conclude, "gross inequalities cannot be explained away by differences in education, skills, hours of work or occupational distribution" (1978, p. 38).

The concentration of women in relatively few occupations also contributes to inequality. In 1988, nearly three-fifths (58.0 percent) of women were in just three of twenty-one occupations: clerical, service, and sales. Like women, men, too, are highly segregated at work, but they are more dispersed (Statistics Canada, 1989b, table 14). Here, too, women's mass entry into the labor force has not changed much. At the turn of the century those women who worked were concentrated in teaching, domestic service, and dressmaking; nearly ninety years later they remain occupationally concentrated, although the occupations have changed (Marcotte, 1987). Concentration in relatively few occupations not only limits women's career choices but obliges them to compete against one another, thus driving down wages (Armstrong and Armstrong, 1978; Bergmann, 1986). Concentration also leaves large numbers of women vulnerable to changes in a particular industry, such as the computerization of clerical work.

Minority Women at Work

For visible minority women the problem is neither labor force participation, which, for women aged 25 to 64, exceeds overall rates for Canadian women (McLaughlin, 1986); nor is it unemployment, which is lower than average (with the exception of Haitian women in Quebec). The problem, instead, seems to be underemployment. Women of color are "often forced to shuffle between a series of low-paying jobs which offer little security" (Abella, 1984, p. 3). Occupationally, minority women are somewhat less likely than the total population to be managers and professionals and much more likely to be unskilled manual workers (Statistics Canada, 1990, p. 198).

Data on average income early in the 1980s indicate a range of income among women of color, some groups exceeding the average both for women of European descent and for the total women's labor force and others falling below. Japanese and Pacific Island women have incomes well above the average (13 percent and 30 percent), whereas Indo-Chinese and Central/South American women fall below (about 15 percent). Moreover, there is evidence that the incomes and occupations of some groups, such as Filipino, Indo-Pakistani, and black women are highly bifurcated, with professional occupations on one end and lower-paying processing and service occupations on the other (Stasiulis, 1987).

The problems of native women are quite different from those of visible minorities. Their participation rates are lower than average, they have very high rates of unemployment, partly because they live in remote and rural areas, and their earnings are also substantially below those of all other Canadian women (Abella, 1984).

Some minority groups are clearly disadvantaged in the labor market. However, what figures are available suggest that gender is a greater obstacle in the labor market than ethnicity. The average incomes of all groups of men, except native peoples, exceed both the overall average for women and the average for each of the women's groups. Within every ethnic group, moreover, the average incomes of men are substantially higher than those of women (Stasiulis, 1987).

POLICIES TO PROMOTE WOMEN'S ECONOMIC EQUALITY

Labor market segregation and its concomitant, lower wages for women, suggest that far more effective measures are needed to remedy the economic disadvantages of Canadian women. Despite federal and provincial initiatives, "there has been little headway in the struggle for affirmative action or equal pay for work of equal value'' (Nemiroff, 1984, p. 105). Since the mid–1980s there have been some new initiatives, but it is unlikely that they will achieve substantially greater integration of the labor force or more equitable pay in women's occupations.

Affirmative Action

The affirmative action record in the early 1980s was not a promising one. Only 49 of 1,130 firms approached by the Affirmative Action Directorate of the Canadian Employment and Immigration Commission between 1979 and 1983 entered into affirmative action agreements (Knopff, 1985, p. 87).

Canadian affirmative action policies, unlike those in the United States, are not mandatory. Canadian officials have, for some time, recognized that a voluntary approach will not work. In 1982, the Minister Responsible for the Status of Women urged that in view of ''pronounced resistance'' to affirmative action, Canada should follow the mandatory approach of the United States (Erola, 1982).

In 1986, Ottawa passed the Employment Equity Act, which requires federally regulated employers and Crown corporations with 100 or more employees (about 4 percent of the workforce) to identify and eliminate discriminatory employment practices and to institute positive policies to ensure that disadvantaged groups achieve representation proportionate to their numbers in the workforce. Covered by the Act are about 900 companies, some of the biggest in the Canadian economy and ones that might serve as models for other employers (Hatter, 1988). The Act, however, has no power to compel employers to change their pattern of hiring (Daenzer, personal communication, June 1988). Similarly, the Jobs Strategy Program, which provides various types of training and work experience to the long-term unemployed and other disadvantaged workers, does not mandate job equity. The legislation that established this program has only a minor clause encouraging employers to pay attention to the needs of women and visible minorities (Daenzer, 1988).

Encouraging to advocates of an integrated workforce is a 1988 ruling by the Canadian Supreme Court that the Federal Human Rights Act permits a Human Rights Tribunal to order recalcitrant companies to adopt affirmative action programs (Hatter, 1988). However, the tribunal itself used a very minimal standard for integration.

In its role both as contractor and as employer the federal government has taken steps toward occupational integration. The Federal Contractors Program, adopted in 1988, requires that all government contractors with 100 or more employees, which are bidding on contracts worth $200,000 or more, commit themselves to employment equity. All contractors are subject to on-site compliance review, and failure to honor a commitment to employment equity can result in loss of opportunity to bid on future contracts (OECD, 1988a, p. 165). Affirmative action measures undertaken by the federal government on behalf of its women employees resulted in the doubling of the proportion of women managers in the civil service from 6 percent in 1983 to 13 percent in 1986 (Hatter, 1988). Concurrently, however, efforts to reduce public-sector jobs and wages were adversely affecting opportunities for the many women who were either employed as government workers or seeking employment in the public sector (Armstrong and Armstrong, 1988).

Pay Equity

The drive for pay equity has progressed further in Canada than in the United States. With women's groups playing a major role, Ottawa passed a bill in 1977 requiring that work performed by employees in the same unit be assessed by criteria of skill, effort, responsibility, and conditions of work to determine pay scales (Marsden, 1980). However, most employers are under the jurisdiction of the provincial governments. While Quebec preceded the federal government by passing such legislation in 1975 (National Council of Welfare, 1979, pp. 24, 56), the other provinces are just beginning to follow suit.

Ontario passed a bill in 1988 requiring public and private sector employers to pay the same wages to women performing jobs different from but of equal value to those performed by men in the same unit (McKay, 1988). Unlike American states, where pay equity has been confined to the public sector, the Ontario law applies as well to private employers. This difference prompted the director of the National Committee on Pay Equity in Washington to comment that "Ontario has gone the furthest in the world" (Freudenheim, 1989b). Ontario employers are directly required by law to establish pay structures that respect the equal value principle.

The pay equity concept has gathered a large following in Canada. Indeed, Ontario's legislators voted unanimously for the province's 1988 law (Freudenheim, 1989b). Women's groups are very supportive; unions also endorse the approach but believe that collective bargaining is necessary to supplement legislation (Marcotte, 1987, p. 2). Employers, however, are resistant. Reflecting views of business and political elites, the Royal Commission on the Economic Union (Macdonald Commission) held that comparable worth or pay equity policies "can serve to move Canadians too far away from a market-determined to an administered wage system" (1985, p. 34). By the mid–1980s only a handful of over fifty pay equity claims received by the Human Rights Commission since 1978 had been settled in favor of the claimant (Marcotte, 1987, p. 51).

Equal opportunity and pay equity policies have been endorsed at the highest levels of the Canadian government. Affirmative action and comparable worth laws have been passed at federal and some provincial levels, and there has been some judicial support for these policies as well. The need for mandatory approaches and stiffer penalties for noncompliance is manifest and has been acknowledged in official government reports. Yet, the reluctance to impose such controls persists, and so do the resultant labor market inequities.

WOMEN AND THE SOCIAL WELFARE SYSTEM

Paralleling the growth of unemployment and underemployment has been re-trenchment in some of the programs that protect citizens against risks to income security. While some analysts emphasize declining growth rates or impasse rather than cutback (Myles, 1988), it is hard to make that argument in regard to people of working age. Keith Banting, for example, points out that while programs for the elderly have continued their steady, incremental expansion, the "dominant pattern in other areas of income security has been a dreary one of restraint and retrenchment, for the most part incremental but occasionally more severe" (1987, p. 187). Graham Riches (1986), who studied the rise of voluntary food banks, which were particularly numerous in the high unemployment areas of western Canada, attributed their existence to a "collapse" of the public safety net. As the chief beneficiaries of the programs for the nonelderly, women and their children have been most affected by social policies that resulted in a shakier, if not collapsing, safety net.

An attempt is made here not only to identify trends in Canadian social policy but to determine how income transfer programs are addressing the needs of women and their families. In describing policies and programs to meet the needs of lone-mother families it is useful to think of four levels of provision: programs that help all citizens to pay for the costs of basic goods and services such as health care; programs that protect workers and their families against risks to income security such as unemployment; programs that reduce the costs or al-leviate the burdens of parenthood; and programs specifically geared to the eco-nomic problems of single parenthood. Single parents may benefit from programs of each type, and, indeed, programs geared generally to parenthood may be especially vital for those who lack a second adult with whom to share parental responsibilities. If the combination of these efforts is insufficient, there is, as a last resort, social or public assistance to lift incomes to a designated level of adequacy.

Generally Experienced Needs

Canada has been a leader in the area of health care. National health insurance, with its universal coverage, has not completely overcome the inherent tendency of better educated consumers to utilize a public system more effectively than lower-income and less well-educated people (Badgley and Charles, 1978, pp. 71–86) Nor does a universal system of health care insure against the dif-ference in standards of living that contribute to the inequities in the health status between rich and poor Canadians (Terris, 1990). Yet, Canada spends less of its per capital income on personal health services than the United States. Notwith-standing delays in nonemergency surgery or special tests and the lesser avail-ability of some forms of medical technology, Canadian health care is considered comparable in quality to that which is available south of the border but unaffordable for millions of people (Freudenheim, 1989a; Iglehart, 1989; Malloy, 1988; Terris, 1990). Health insurance was not cut back during the 1980s, despite threatened reduction of federal outlays. There is, however, some fear that this program, particularly, will be viewed as an unfair subsidy to Canadian business because, unlike some of their American counterparts, Canadian employers do not provide this fringe benefit.

Canada does not treat housing as a basic human need or an entitlement (Tester, 1987). While homelessness is nowhere near the problem it is in the United States, Canadian social policy, unlike that of the advanced welfare states, does not provide housing subsidies to all who cannot afford decent housing. According to representatives of single-parent organizations across Ontario, single-parent families on social assistance spend 50 to 70 cents of every dollar on shelter and, nonetheless, live in substandard housing (Gorlick, 1989).

Risks to Income Security

Canada has a relatively generous system of unemployment insurance. Despite some retrenchment in the late 1970s, it remained more likely to cover the unemployed and more generous in rates of income replacement than most OECD countries (Therborn, 1986, pp. 66–67). Nonetheless, dramatically increasing unemployment in the 1980s resulted in the exhaustion of employment benefits and consequent pressure on social assistance caseloads (Riches, 1986). Single mothers, whose unemployment rates nearly doubled between 1975 and 1983 (Evans and McIntyre, 1987), were among those less likely to qualify for benefits.

Citing budgetary deficits, the Canadian government announced further restrictions in eligibility and duration of unemployment insurance benefits in spring 1989. Members of the opposition Liberal Party linked cutbacks to the free trade agreements, and the *New York Times* held that they foreshadowed a trend in Canadian social policy ("Ottawa is moving," 1989). This was not the beginning, but perhaps an intensification, of a trend toward narrowing welfare-state provisions that had been going on for a decade.

Supporting Parenthood

The scope of Canada's programs for parents is relatively wide. There is a family allowance, available for each child in a family, regardless of income. Canada also has a refundable child tax credit that is income tested, but, unlike the U.S. Earned Income Tax Credit, it is available to families with incomes nearly as high as the median and is not restricted to those with an employed parent.

In addition to defraying some of the costs of childrearing, Canada also insures women against income loss from childbearing. Since 1971, its unemployment insurance program has included paid maternity leave. At this writing, moreover, Canada is expected to extend its unemployment insurance program to include a paid parental leave for either mothers or fathers.

While programs such as the children's allowance and maternity leave are a recognition of the costs of parenthood, they provide relatively modest benefits. The children's allowance was $31.28 ($25.66 U.S.) monthly per child in 1988, and the more generous child tax credit provided a maximum of $46.58 ($37.84 U.S.) monthly per child. Together these two benefits met 8 percent of the 1986 poverty level for a single parent and child (calculated from National Council of Welfare, 1987, p. 66), but, particularly for families with two or more children, they provide a helpful income supplement. However, subsequent, partial deindexation of both of these benefits—not raising them by the full increase in the cost of living—will contribute to their slow decline in real terms (Banting, 1987, p. 188).[11] Maternity benefits are limited to fifteen weeks or less than four months, and, in 1989, they replaced 60 percent of earnings up to a weekly maximum of $339 ($275 U.S.). The relatively wide scope but limited adequacy of Canadian social policy could be interpreted as a compromise between reluctant collectivism of Canadian conservatives and the recognition that the welfare state can serve to legitimate the federal government.

Subsidized child care not only reduces the costs of parenting but lessens the pressure of women's dual roles. Canada, however, "has not been a leader" in child care (Ledoux, 1988, p. 4). The recommendation of the Royal Commission on the Status of Women, that a national day care program be financed by the federal government, has not been implemented. One government study found that only 9 percent of working parents has access to a licensed child care arrangement (p. 5); another reported the figure at 13 percent in 1987 (National Council of Welfare, 1988a, p. 4). The number of childcare spaces more than doubled between 1980 and 1987, but this growth was not sufficient to keep up with increasing need. A report from Ontario concluded that "the cost and availability of day care stood out as a primary barrier to labor force participation of lone parent females" (Doyle and Mitchell, 1988, p. 7). Nor is the private sector taking up the slack.[12] In 1988, legislation that would double the number of child care slots was introduced in Parliament but not acted on. Thus while the likely adoption of parental leave betokens government encouragement of greater equality in the home and some expansion of social welfare, the paucity of subsidized child care reflects the persisting failure of the Canadian state to lighten the burdens of women's dual role.

Single Parenthood

Since child support is typically either inadequate or nonexistent (Pask and McCall, 1989), a program of major importance to single parents is government-assured child support. Such benefits are provided when an absent parent defaults or makes payments below a specified minimum level. The federal government has not implemented recommendations by women's advocates that it assure a minimum income guarantee to the heads of one-parent families or to the children in such families regardless of whether the absent father provides support (Canadian Advisory Council on the Status of Women, 1979a; Freiler, 1986). However, contributing to the old-age security of divorced women, including those who have been single parents, is the 1977 amendment to the Canada Pension Plan to permit pension credits earned by both spouses during a marriage to be equally divided between them at the dissolution of their marriage (Canadian Advisory Council on the Status of Women, 1979a).

Social Assistance

Unlike its American counterpart, the Canadian Social Assistance program (CAP) is available to all persons with deficient incomes rather than restricted to special and often stigmatized categories of dependents such as single-parent families. It was thus believed to be less vulnerable to backlash (Leman, 1977). However, in the 1980s, Canadian provinces imposed work requirements on the mothers of young children similar to those that have restricted their right to relief in the United States (Evans, 1988; Evans and McIntyre, 1987). Such work requirements, which have failed to address either the need for significant upgrading or for expanded employment opportunities, have had the effect of expanding the low-wage labor pool in an already depressed labor market.

Social assistance benefits are relatively low in Canada. Like American states, the provinces are allowed to set benefit levels for recipients, and although the federal legislation refers to "the provision of adequate assistance," it has not made adequate provincial grants a condition for its financial contribution (Riches, 1986, p. 5). It is in this critical respect—the inadequacy of social assistance benefits—that Canada and the United States are more alike than different.

None of the provinces provides social assistance benefits equal to the Canadian poverty level. In 1986, a single parent (not employed outside the home) and her 2-year-old child would have been entitled to benefits ranging from 59.3 percent of the poverty level in New Brunswick to 84.3 percent in Prince Edward Island, with the median around 70 percent (National Council of Welfare, 1987, pp. 66–69). In the three western provinces hardest hit by recessions, social assistance and unemployment benefits for families were reduced from 8 to 15 percent in real terms between 1982 and 1985, and even more steeply for employable individuals (Banting, 1987, p. 190).

Compared to the United States, Canada began and ended the 1980s with a broader range of programs to meet basic needs and more generous, though declining, aid for the unemployed. Some support for the parental role is also more characteristic of Canadian policy, although it, too, has failed to provide the major service needed by the increasing numbers of mothers who have entered the labor force—licensed, affordable child care. The family allowance and the child tax credit, though indicative of state support for the parental role, were too low to supplement significantly the low incomes of parents, among whom single mothers are especially disadvantaged. The incomes of single parents were supplemented not by special programs that established child support as a right or recognized the heavy burdens of mothers who must perform dual roles without the support of a second parent. Instead, poor single mothers turned, as a last resort, to public assistance programs that were, in some cases, declining in benefit levels and becoming more restrictive in eligibility. Thus, single mothers and their families were not only handicapped by the failure of the Canadian state to meet the needs of parents generally and by the lack of programs geared especially to their income deficiencies but by its failure to require the provinces to provide a minimally adequate standard in social assistance. It has been said that "the ideological difference between the two North American nations, though slight by international standards . . . appears to have a considerable difference in welfare state development" (Kudrle and Marmor, 1981, p. 112). The Canadian welfare state is more developed than the American one, but it is far from a guarantee against the poverty of lone-mother families.

DEMOGRAPHIC FACTORS

Demographic changes in the last quarter century have left increasing numbers of women dependent on insecure incomes and a less protective safety net. Between 1966 and 1986 the number of single-parent families increased by 130 percent, nearly three times the rise in husband-wife families, and of these single parents the overwhelming majority were women—82 percent of all one-parent families and 94 percent of those between ages 15 and 24. In 1986, single-mother families were 13 percent of all families with children (Moore, 1987). In Toronto, the proportion was much higher: 23 percent or nearly one in four (Doyle and Mitchell, 1988, p. 1). Lone parenthood, of course, is more prevalent than these cross-sectional data suggest. About 500,000 women were lone parents in 1984, but another 900,000 had passed through the status (Moore, 1989). Lone parenthood in Canada lasts an average of five and a half years (Moore, 1989).

The sources of single parenthood as well as its magnitude have changed. "Demographically, lone parenthood has shifted from being a bio-social and vital sequence coming late in the family cycle when widow(er)hood was the modal form of terminating a union, to being more frequently either the first (and sometimes only) step of family formation, or a stage between union dissolution and subsequent formation of a new union" (Pool and Moore, 1986, p. 9). Widowhood, as in the other countries in this study, has decreased dramatically as a source of lone motherhood, from about two-thirds (66 percent) in 1951 to just over one-fourth (28 percent) in 1986 (Moore, 1987).

Nearly three-fifths (58 percent) of single mothers are separated or divorced (Moore, 1987). After the passage of the first unified federal divorce legislation in 1968, the divorce rate more than doubled and, during the 1970s, almost doubled again. After falling for several years, it rose to an all-time high following passage of the Divorce Act of 1985, which allows divorce after one year's separation, regardless of the cause (Adams, 1988). Maureen Moore, a sociologist at Statistics Canada, writes that "it is not known what ceiling the divorce rate will reach before it starts to abate" (1989, p. 5). Since divorce is the major precipitant of single parenthood, it is also not possible to predict future trends in that status.

Nonmarriage has increased as a path to single motherhood in Canada. The annual number of "ex-nuptial" births more than quadrupled between 1961 and 1985. In 1986, about 15 percent of all single mothers had never married (Moore, 1987). Births to unmarried teenagers, one source of unmarried motherhood, rose from 12.3 per 1,000 to 17.3 per 1,000 between 1960 and 1982, or about 40 percent (Pool and Moore, 1986, citing Romaniuc, 1984).

A study comparing lone and married mothers (Pool and Moore, 1986) found the former are more likely to become parents at a younger age and to have lower educational attainments. They are also more likely to enter the labor force at a later age. Ian Pool and Maureen Moore conclude that "female lone parents must raise children while facing a double disadvantage: a lack of support from a spouse and less job skills by which to gain an income appropriate to the task" (1986, p. 55).

The demographic factors that place women at risk of poverty are of much smaller magnitude in Canada than in the United States. In 1980, Canadian women were more than three times (3.4) less likely to be divorced than their American counterparts (United Nations, 1989, pp. 91, 94). Whereas 15 percent of Canadian single mothers were unmarried, the comparable rate for their American counterparts was 29 percent (U.S. Bureau of the Census, 1988, p. 79). The discrepancy for unmarried teenage motherhood was also marked: 16.4 versus 28 per 1,000 (Jones et al., 1986, p. 72). As a result of these differences, the Canadian rate of single motherhood, 13 percent, is substantially lower than the comparable U.S. figure of 24 percent (U.S. Bureau of the Census, unpublished data).[13]

We lack studies that would enable us to determine with any degree of certainty why the two North American countries diverge so considerably with respect to these demographic factors. The usual explanation is that Canadian society is more conservative. Another possibility is that Canada does not have racial and ethnic minorities as large and as disadvantaged as those in the United States. The rate of single parenthood among American whites is 18 percent, about midway between the 13 percent rate in Canada and the 24 percent overall proportion for Americans. And the birth rate for unmarried white teenagers is almost the same as that of Canadian teenagers—17 per 1,000 compared to 16.4 per 1,000 (Jones et al.,1986, p. 72). While the factors that contribute to family breakups are present in both societies, Canada lacks the large, economically deprived minorities that, in the United States, have long experienced conditions— such as pervasive unemployment and low wages—that place added strains on marriages or keep them from forming in the first place (see pp. 40–41 in this volume). By contrast, in Canada single motherhood does not appear to be related to minority status, and some groups, such as Asians, may well have lower rates of single parenthood than the general population (Moore, personal communication, August 1989).[14]

POVERTY AND ITS FEMINIZATION IN CANADA

Canada has a semiofficial poverty standard referred to as the low-income cutoffs.[15] Unlike the United States, which continues to use a standard developed in the 1960s, Canada updated its cutoffs in 1978 to reflect current consumption patterns. Again, in contrast to the United States, which uses a single standard for all families, Canada has five cutoffs, ranging from rural to large urban areas with 500,000 inhabitants or more. In 1987, the urban cutoffs for a family of four ranged from $18,691 to $22,616 ($14,095 to $17,055 U.S.). The comparable U.S. standard was 18 percent to 32 percent lower. Although the Canadian low-income cutoffs are high by American standards, the Social Planning Council of Metropolitan Toronto (Doyle and Mitchell, 1988) estimated that in Toronto a lone-parent women with one child required nearly 50 percent more than the low-income cutoff to maintain an adequate standard of living.

Poverty Rates

More than half of Canadian single-mother families (56.0 percent) were poor or below the low-income cutoff in 1986. Their poverty rates were over five times those of couples with children. Rates for male single parents were less than half those of female single parents but nonetheless double those of couples with children. These differences in poverty rates of female single parents, their male counterparts, and two-parent families suggest, as did comparable U.S. data, that both female gender and single parenthood influence the extent of poverty. Another way to document the poverty of lone-mother families is to point out that in 1986 their average incomes were just under two-fifths that of two-parent families (Battle, 1988b, pp. 31, 89).

A Statistics Canada study of family expenditure patterns (Moore, 1987, pp. 34–35) gives further evidence of the economic disadvantages of single-female households. Conducted in seventeen major cities, the survey found that lone mothers spent almost half their before-tax incomes on food, shelter, and household operations, compared to just over one-third for husband-wife families with children. Lone mothers were less likely to live in single, detached dwellings and more than twice as likely as couple families to rent their living accommodations. They were also much less likely to have such time-saving appliances as microwave ovens, freezers, dishwashers, automatic washing machines, and clothes dryers.

Existing data on family poverty do not permit an evaluation of trends in the poverty of single mothers since 1970 nor a comparison of their rates with those of other families over this time span.[16] Data from the 1980s reveal that the poverty rates of single mothers increased by 6.0 percent from 1981 to 1986, compared to rises of 9.5 percent for couples and nearly 50 percent for single fathers. In the recession years, earlier in the decade, all three groups experienced even higher increases in poverty rates. While the poverty rates of families with a father or an adult male were more sensitive to recession than those of single mothers, who have a much more tenuous labor market position to begin with, the rates of single mothers, nonetheless, remain much higher than either (Battle, 1988b, p. 31).[17]

The Luxembourg Income Study (LIS) has applied the U.S. poverty standard to income data in a number of Western, industrialized countries. According to the lower U.S. standard, the poverty rate of one-parent (both female and male) families was 42.9 percent in the United States (1979), compared to 35.3 percent for Canada (1981). The figure for Sweden was far lower, only 7.5 percent (Smeeding, Torrey, and Rein, 1988, p. 113).

One of the important distinctions among these capitalist countries is the antipoverty effect of their income support systems. Whereas the poverty of Swedish single-parent families was reduced 77.3 percent by a combination of taxes and income transfers, primarily the latter, the comparable figures were 26.5 percent for Canada and only 13.0 percent for the United States. The incomes of single-parent families before taxes and transfers were roughly equivalent in the two North American countries, but the Canadian transfer system had twice the antipoverty effect of the U.S. system. With respect to women and their families, the Canadian state does more to modify market outcomes through social policy than does the United States.

The fact that social welfare benefits have substantial antipoverty effects does not signify that market income is unimportant for single parents. To the contrary, earnings amounted to over 60 percent of the income of the average single-mother family in Canada (Moore, 1987, p. 34). Moreover, lone-mother families with one earner had a poverty rate of 44 percent, compared to 93 percent for those with no earners (Doyle and Mitchell, 1988, p. 6).

Data on poverty provide us with little information concerning the effect of minority status on the poverty of women in Canada. Indeed, none of the statistics that were encountered at this writing provides poverty data by both family composition and race and ethnicity. Experts on the economic and social conditions of single mothers, however, do not tend to believe that single-parent poverty is strongly related to minority status (Moore, personal communication, August 1989).[18]

Feminization of Poverty

In 1986, single-mother families constituted 13 percent of families with children and 43 percent of poor families with children—over two-fifths. The feminization of poverty hardly increased between 1981 and 1986, partly because recession in the early years of the decade led to higher rises in poverty rates of the larger married-couple population. The National Council of Welfare thus concluded that "the 'feminization of poverty' is a striking, long-term trend, although it has not increased during the eighties" (Battle, 1988b, p. 2). Carolyne A. Gorlick, who conducted a longitudinal study of female single parents, wrote that "although there is some debate over whether poverty continues to be 'feminized' . . . , there are nevertheless significant numbers of poor women who are not benefiting from upward swings in the economy and who find themselves (with their children) applying for social assistance'' (1989, p. 6). Pool and Moore, in their report for Statistics Canada, clearly discerned a trend: ''it can be argued that along with widowhood . . . lone parenthood and its attendant disadvantages is leading to a feminization of poverty in Canada'' (1986, p. 9). Regardless of their differences, these informed observers agree that feminization of poverty may well be developing in Canada.

Family poverty has not been feminized in Canada to the extent that it has in the United States, where 59 percent of poor families with children were single-mother families (U.S. Bureau of the Census, 1989, p. 11); the comparable Canadian figure is 42 percent (1986) (Battle, 1988b, p. 31). Thus, Canada could be said to be bordering on the feminization of poverty. Although Canadian women are about as disadvantaged in the labor market as their American counterparts, lower rates of single parenthood and somewhat more expansive social policies have kept women's poverty from becoming as widespread in Canada as in the United States.

To reduce women's poverty, Canada needs to assure greater equity in the labor market and to increase the scope and adequacy of its social welfare benefits. Budgetary constraints and closer economic ties with the United States may lead to a reduction in social welfare rather than the needed expansion. If Canada fails to take steps to improve both the economic and social wage for women, it leaves itself prey to the demographic forces that could increase both the prevalence of poverty and its feminization.

NOTES

1. In power, however, the NDP has seldom defended the rights of workers and has tended to be identified with the most traditional industrial unions (Brodie and Jenson, 1988).

2. The much greater commitment to social welfare of an advanced welfare state like Sweden casts doubt on statements like those of Canadian novelist Robertson Davies, who feels much more at home in Scandinavia than the United States because he considers his country a ''socialist monarchy like Sweden, Denmark and Norway'' (cited in Mitgang, 1988; see also Davies, 1988).

3. It should be noted that more than half the difference in Canadian-U.S. expenditures is accounted for by higher Canadian expenditures for unemployment, which is also a greater problem there.

4. For a different view—that Canada can pursue a more independent monetary policy—see M. C. McCracken, 1988.

5. One of the research reports prepared for the Royal Commission on Equality in Employment (Townson, 1985, p. 347) acknowledged that there is no clear definition of the term ''visible minority.'' Visible minorities appear to comprise all people of non-European origin except Native Americans—Asians, Central/South Americans, Middle

Easterners, and so on. The most numerous visible minorities are Asians who comprise 4 percent of the population. Blacks are a much smaller group, less than one-fifth the Asian population (White, 1989).

6. Royal commissions in Canada perform an important role in regard to policy issues. "They research the issue, hold hearings across the country, receive briefs, and make recommendations for legislative and administrative reform" (Marsden, 1980, p. 243).

7. In its 1970 *Report*, the Commission made 167 recommendations, including adoption of the principle of equal pay for work of equal value, establishment of a national day care program, provision of eighteen weeks of paid maternity leave, and establishment of an advisory body to continue to propose policies to improve the condition of women. Of special relevance to this study is the Royal Commission's conclusion that "the women of this country are particularly vulnerable to the hazards of being poor" (National Council of Welfare, 1979, p. 1).

8. NAC considers native, immigrant, visible minority, and disabled women to be "doubly disadvantaged" (1987). Here, too, French Canadian women are not included among the women considered to be most disadvantaged.

9. The Canadian economy has depended considerably on natural resources or extractive industries. The goods-producing sector fell from 37.5 percent of the labor force in 1951 to 29.7 percent in 1981 (Picott, 1987, p. 11). The long-term structural trend toward a service-dominated economy was accelerated by recession in the early 1980s, which caused the goods-producing sector to decline still further (Lindsay, 1989).

10. In 1975, the only year for which figures based on both definitions of part-time work are available, the former definition resulted in a rate 15.4 percent higher than the current one.

11. An exception to the general pattern is the province of Quebec where, in addition to the family allowance, parents receive $500 at the birth of each of their first two children and the much higher sum of $3,000 for each additional offspring. Adopted in 1988 and believed to be a pronatalist effort to increase a dwindling birth rate among the population of French descent, the benefits will be paid out in monthly installments over a child's first two years (Fulfore, 1988).

12. A survey of 500 Toronto employers found that day care was available in only 0.4 percent of the workplaces studied (Johnson, 1986).

13. Canada counts as single-mother families those in which the single mother is a householder and those in which she and her offspring are subfamilies in other households, such as the mothers' parents (Maureen Moore, Statistics Canada, personal communication, August 1989). Thus the comparable U.S. figure is 24 percent rather than the 20 percent figure used in the previous chapter, which confined its discussion to female householders. For statistics on poverty, both countries use the family household concept.

14. There is some evidence that immigrant women, many of whom are visible minorities, may be unable to divorce or separate from their husbands. They enter the country dependent on their spouses or sponsors, and this dependent status deprives them of entitlements to various forms of government assistance (Stasiulis, 1987, citing Estable, 1986).

15. The underlying assumption of the low-income cutoffs is that a consumption unit is poor if it must spend more than 58.5 percent of its income on food, clothing, and shelter or twenty percentage points more than the average Canadian family spends on such essentials (Battle, 1988a).

16. In 1979, the National Council of Welfare reported that 44 percent of single mothers

were poor in 1975 (p. 6). However, in 1975, a lower poverty standard or low-income cutoff was being used. Had the 1978 cutoff been applied, the proportion would have been larger. The rates of 44 percent (1975) and 56 percent (1986) are thus not comparable.

17. In contrast to increases in the poverty of families with children, the poverty of elderly families continued its steep decline, from 41.4 percent in 1959 to 9.5 percent in 1986, a rate below that of nonaged families. However, in 1986, 42.7 percent of the single or unattached elderly were poor, over three-fourths of whom were women (Battle, 1988b, pp. 35, 40).

18. There are large differences in poverty rates among the Canadian provinces, with rates ranging from 21 percent in Newfoundland, one of the poorer maritime provinces, to 9 percent in Ontario (1986). However, 70 percent of all poor families live in Quebec, Ontario, and British Columbia (Battle, 1988b, p. 10). Since the rates of single motherhood are high in large cities like Toronto, one infers that poor lone-mother families would be even more likely than poor families generally to live in the larger provinces.

REFERENCES

Abella, R. S. (1984). *Equality in Employment: A Royal Commission Report*. Ottawa: Minister of Supply and Services Canada.

Adams, O. (1988). "Divorce rates in Canada." *Canadian Social Trends* (Statistics Canada) (Winter): 18–19.

Adamson, N., L. Briskin, and M. McPhail (1988). *Feminist Organizing for Change: The Contemporary Women's Movement in Canada*. Toronto: Oxford University Press.

Akyeampong, E. B. (1987). "Involuntary part-time employment in Canada. 1956–1986." *Canadian Social Trends* (Statistics Canada) (Autumn): 16–29.

Armstrong, P. (1984). *Labour pains: Women's work in Crisis*. Toronto: The Women's Press.

Armstrong, P., and H. Armstrong (1978). *The Double Ghetto: Canadian Women and Their Segregated Work*. Toronto: McClelland & Stewart.

——— (1983). *A Working Majority*. Ottawa: Canadian Advisory Council on the Status of Women.

——— (1984). *The Double Ghetto: Canadian Women and Their Segregated Work*, rev.ed. Toronto: McClelland & Stewart.

——— (1988). "Taking women into account: Redefining and intensifying employment in Canada." In J. Jenson, E. Hagen, and C. Reddy, eds. *Feminization of the Labor Force: Paradoxes and Promises*. New York: Oxford University Press.

Badgley, R. F., and C. A. Charles (1978). "Health and inequality: Unresolved policy issues." In S. A. Yelaja, ed. *Canadian Social Policy*. Waterloo, Ontario: Laurier University Press.

Banting, K. (1987). *The Welfare State and Canadian Federalism*, 2d ed. Kingston, Ontario: McGill-Queen's University Press.

Battle, K. (1988a). *1988 Poverty Lines*. Ottawa: National Council of Welfare.

——— (1988b). *Poverty Profile 1988*. Ottawa: National Council of Welfare.

Behiels, M. D. (1984). "Quebec: Social transformation and ideological renewal, 1940–1976." In M. S. Cross and G. S. Kealey, eds. *Readings in Canadian Social History*, volume 5, *Modern Canada: 1930–1980's*. Toronto: McClelland & Stewart.

Bellemare, D., and L. P. Simon (1988). "Full employment: A strategy and an objective for economic policy." In D. Cameron and A. Sharpe, eds. *Policies for Full Employment*. Ottawa: Canadian Council on Social Development.

Bergmann, B. R. (1986). *The Economic Emergence of Women*. New York: Basic Books.

Bienvenue, R. M. (1985). "Colonial status: The case of Canadian Indians." In R. M. Bienvenue and J. E. Goldstein, eds. *Ethnicity and Ethnic Relations in Canada*, 2d ed. Toronto: Butterworths.

Boyd, M. (1982). "Occupational segregation: A review." In *Sexual Equality in the Workplace: Proceedings of a Conference Sponsored by the Women's Bureau, Labour Canada, March 17–19, 1982*. Ottawa: Minister of Supply and Services Canada.

Breton, R., and D. Stasiulis (1980). "Linguistic boundaries and the cohesion of Canada." In R. Breton, J. G. Reitz, and V. F. Valentine, eds. *Cultural Boundaries and the Cohesion of Canada*. Montreal: The Institute for Research on Public Policy.

Briskin, L. (1983). "Women's challenge to organized labour." In L. Briskin and L. Yanz, eds. *Union Sisters*. Toronto: Women's Press.

Brodie, J. (1985). *Women and Politics in Canada*. Toronto: McGraw-Hill Ryerson.

Brodie, J., and J. Jenson (1988). *Crisis, Challenge and Change: Party and Class in Canada Revisited*, 2d ed. Ottawa: Carleton University Press.

Burke, M. A. (1986). "The growth of part-time work." *Canadian Social Trends* (Statistics Canada) (Autumn): 9–14.

Burnham, W. D. (1979). "Toward a revitalized confederation." In E. J. Feldman and N. Nevitte, eds. *The Future of North America, Canada, the United States and Quebec Nationalism*. Montreal: Center for International Affairs; and Cambridge, MA: Harvard University and Institute for Research on Public Policy.

Burt, S. (1984). "Women's issues and the women's movement in Canada since 1970." In M. S. Cross and G. S. Kealey, eds. *Readings in Canadian Social History* volume 5, *Modern Canada: 1930–1980's*. Toronto: McClelland & Stewart.

Canadian Advisory Council on the Status of Women (1979a). *Ten Years Later: An Assessment of the Federal Government's Implementation of the Recommendations Made by the Royal Commission on the Status of Women*. Ottawa: Canadian Advisory Council on the Status of Women.

——— (1979b). *Towards Equality in Responsibility: Report to the Parliamentary Committee on Equality*. Ottawa: Canadian Advisory Council on the Status of Women.

Clement, W. (1985). "The Canadian corporate elite: Ethnicity and inequality of access." In R. M. Bienvenue and J. E. Goldstein, eds. *Ethnicity and Ethnic Relations in Canada*, 2d ed. Toronto: Butterworths.

Daenzer, P. M. (June 1988). *Minority Immigrants in the Canadian Labour Force: Bridging Policy and Practice*. Paper presented at the North American Conference on Employment and Unemployment, Adelphi University, Garden City, NY.

Darroch, A. G. (1985) "Another look at ethnicity, stratification, and social mobility in Canada." In R. M. Bienvenue and J. E. Goldstein, eds. *Ethnicity and Ethnic Relations in Canada*, 2d ed. Toronto: Butterworths.

Davies, R. (1988). *The Lyre of Orpheus*. New York: Viking.

Doyle, R., and A. Mitchell (1988). "Lone parents in transition." *Social Infopac* 7 (4): 1–12.

Dumas, C. (1988). "Occupational trends among women in Canada." *Employment and Income Forum* (Statistics Canada, prototype): 19–32.

"Education in Canada" (1986). *Canadian Social Trends* (Statistics Canada) (Autumn): 15–28.

Employment and Immigration Canada (1988). *Employment Equity Act: Annual Report to Parliament 1988*. Ottawa: Minister of Supply and Services Canada.

Erola, J. (1982). "Sexual equality in the private and public sectors." In *Sexual Equality in the Workplace: Proceedings of a Conference Sponsored by the Women's Bureau, Labour Canada, March 17–19, 1982*. Ottawa: Minister of Supply and Services Canada.

Estable. A. (1986). *Immigrant Women in Canada—Current Issues*. Background paper prepared for the Canadian Advisory Council on the Status of Women, Ottawa.

Evans, P. M. (1985). "Work, welfare and the single mother: A dual labor market investigation." Ph.D. dissertation, School of Graduate Studies, University of Toronto.

———(1988). "Work incentives and the single mother: Dilemmas of reform." *Canadian Public Policy* 14 (2): 125–136.

Evans, P. M., and E. L. McIntyre (1987). "Welfare, work incentives and the single mother: An inter-provincial comparison." In J. S. Ismael, ed. *The Canadian Welfare State*. Edmonton, Alberta: University of Alberta Press.

Freiler, C. (1986). "Child poverty re-discovered." *Social Infopac* 5 (4): 1–9.

Freudenheim, M. (1989a, June 29). "Debating Canadian health 'model.' " *New York Times*, pp. D1, D6.

———(1989b, July 27). "A new Ontario law matches women's wages with men's." *New York Times*, pp. A1, A16.

Fulfore, K. (May 23, 1988). "A dubious bribe for raising babies." *Financial Times of Canada* (Toronto), p. 50.

Gorlick, C. A. (1989). "Economic stress, social support and health/wellbeing of low income female single parents." *Transition* (Vanier Institute, Ottawa) 19 (I): 6–8.

Handler, R. (1988). *Nationalism and the Politics of Culture in Quebec*. Madison, WI: University of Wisconsin Press.

Hatter, D. (May 9, 1988). "Age of job equity dawns for a million Canadians." *Financial Post* (Toronto), section 2, p. 15.

Hockin, T. A. (1975). *Government in Canada*. New York: W. W. Norton.

Horowitz, G. (1966). "Conservatism, liberalism and socialism: An interpretation." *The Canadian Journal of Economics and Political Science* 32 (2): 143–171.

Iglehart, J. K. (1989). "Health policy report." *The New England Journal of Medicine* 321 (25): 1767–1772.

Johnson, L. D. (1986). *Working families: Workplace Supports for Families*. Toronto: Social Planning Council of Metropolitan Toronto.

Jones, E. F., et al. (1986) *Teenage Pregnancy in Industrialized Countries*. New Haven, CT: Yale University Press.

Knopff, R. (1985). "The statistical protection of minorities: Affirmative action policy in Canada." In N. Nevitte and A. Kornberg, eds. *Minorities and the Canadian State*. Oakville, Ontario: Mosaic Press.

Kudrle, R. T., and T. T. Marmor (1981). "The development of welfare states in North America." In P. Flora and A. J. Heideheimer, eds. *The Development of Welfare States in Europe and America*. New Brunswick, NJ: Transaction Books.

Landsberg, M. (1982). *Women and Children First: A Provocative Look at Modern Canadian Women at Work and at Home*. Toronto: Macmillan of Canada.

Larkin, J. (1983). "Out of the ghettos: Affirmative action and unions." In L. Briskin and L. Yanz, eds. *Union Sisters*. Toronto: Women's Press.

Ledoux, G. (1988). *Child Care in Canada*. Ottawa: Research Branch of the Library of Parliament, Minister of Supply and Services Canada.

Leman, C. (1977). "Patterns of policy development: Social security in the United States and Canada." *Public Policy* 25 (2): 261–291.

Lévesque, J. M. (1987). "The growth of part-time work in a changing industrial environment." *The Labour Force* (May): 87–104.

Levitan, S. A., and E. A. Conway (1988). "Part-timers: Living on half-rations." *Challenge* 31 (3): 9–26.

Lindsay, C. (1989). "The service sector in the l980s." *Canadian Social Trends* (Statistics Canada) (Spring): 20–23.

Lipset, S. M. (1963). *The First New Nation*. New York: W. W. Norton.

——— (1985). "Canada and the United States: The cultural dimension." In C. F. Doran and J. H. Sigler, eds. *Canada and the United States: Enduring Friendship, Persistent Stress*. Englewood Cliffs, NJ, and Scarborough, Ontario: Prentice-Hall.

——— (1990). *Continental Divide*. New York: Routledge, Chapman and Hall, Inc.

Lipsey, R. G. (1985). "Canada and the United States: The economic dimension." In C. F. Doran and J. H. Sigler, eds. *Canada and the United States: Enduring Friendship, Persistent Stress*. Englewood Cliffs, NJ, and Scarborough, Ontario: Prentice-Hall.

Malcolm, A. (1985). *The Canadians*. New York: Times Books.

Malloy, M. T. (April 22, 1988). "Health, Canadian style." *Wall Street Journal*, special supplement on medicine and health, section 3, p. 21R.

Marcotte, M. (1987). *Equal Pay for Work of Equal Value*. Kingston, Ontario: Industrial Relations Centre, Queen's University at Kingston.

Marsden, L. (1980). "The role of the National Action Committee on the Status of Women in facilitating equal pay policy in Canada." In R. S. Ratner, ed. *Equal Employment Policy for Women*. Philadelphia: Temple University Press.

McCracken, M. C. (1988). "Impact of a more independent monetary policy on unemployment." In D. Cameron and A. Sharpe, eds. *Policies for Full Employment*. Ottawa: Canadian Council on Social Development.

McKay, S. (1988). "Getting even." *Canadian Business* (Toronto) 61 (5): 48–54.

McLaughlin, N. (1986). "The labour force participation of immigrant women." *Canadian Social Trends* (Statistics Canada) (Autumn): 28–31.

Mitgang, H. (December 29, 1988). "Robertson Davies, a novelist of the North." *New York Times*, Section III, p. 13.

Moore, M. (1987). "Women parenting alone." *Canadian Social Trends* (Statistics Canada) (Spring): 31–36.

——— (1989). "How long alone? The duration of female lone parenthood in Canada." *Transition* (Vanier Institute, Ottawa) 19 (1): 4–5.

Myles, J. (1988). "Decline or impasse? The current state of the welfare state." *Studies in Political Economy* 26 (Summer): 73–107.

National Action Committee on the Status of Women (NAC) (July 1987). *NAC Issues*. Toronto: NAC.

——— (1988). *Free Trade: A Bad Deal for Women*. Toronto: NAC.

National Council of Welfare (1979). *Women and Poverty*. Ottawa: National Council of Welfare.

———— (1987). *Welfare in Canada: The Tangled Safety Net*. Ottawa: Minister of Supply and Services Canada.

———— (1988a). *Child Care: A Better Alternative*. Ottawa: Minister of Supply and Services Canada.

———— (1988b). *1988 Poverty Lines: Estimates by the National Council of Welfare*. Ottawa: National Council of Welfare.

Neill, S. (1988). "Unionization in Canada." *Canadian Social Trends* (Statistics Canada) (Spring): 13–15.

Nelson, A. (1987). "Women in unions." In S. E. Rix, ed. *The American Women, 1987–1988*. New York: W. W. Norton.

Nemiroff, G. (1984). "Canada: The empowerment of women." In R. Morgan, ed. *Sisterhood Is Global: The First Anthology of Writings from the International Women's Movement*. Garden City, NY: Doubleday.

Organization for Economic and Cultural Development (OECD) (September 1986). *Employment Outlook*. Paris: OECD.

———— (1988a, September). *Employment Outlook*. Paris: OECD.

———— (1989b). "OECD in figures." *OECD Observer* no. 152 (Supplement, June/July). Paris: OECD.

"Ottawa is moving to tighten its budget" (April 13, 1989). *New York Times*, p. 7.

Pask, E. D., and M. D. McCall, eds. (1989). *How Much and Why? Economic Implications of Marriage Breakdown: Spousal and Child Support*. Calgary, Alberta: Canadian Institute for Law and the Family.

Phillips, P., and E. Phillips (1983). *Women and Work: Inequality in the Labour Market*. Toronto: James Lorimer.

Picott, W. G. (1987). "The changing industrial mix, 1951–1981." *Canadian Social Trends* (Statistics Canada) (Spring): 8–11.

Pool, I., and M. Moore (1986). *Lone Parenthood: Characteristics and Determinants: Results from the 1984 Family History Survey*. Ottawa: Minister of Supply and Services Canada.

Porter, J. (1965). *The Vertical Mosaic*. Toronto: University of Toronto Press.

Prince, M. J. (1987). "How Ottawa decides social policy: Recent changes in philosophy, structure and process." In J. Ismael, ed. *The Canadian Welfare State*. Edmonton, Alberta: University of Alberta Press.

Riches, G. (1986). *Food Banks and the Welfare Crisis*. Ottawa: Canadian Council on Social Development.

Romaniuc, A. (1984). *Fertility in Canada: From Baby-boom to Baby-bust*. Ottawa: Minister of Supply and Services Canada.

Ross, D. P., and R. Shillington (1989). "The changing face of poverty, 1973–1986." *Perception* 13 (1): 8–13.

Royal Commission on the Economic Union and Development Prospects for Canada (1985). *Summary of Conclusions and Recommendations*. Ottawa: Minister of Supply and Services Canada.

Royal Commission on the Status of Women in Canada (1970). *Report*. Ottawa: Information Canada.

Sharpe, A., J. P. Voyer, and D. Cameron (1988). "Unemployment: Its nature, costs and causes." In D. Cameron and A. Sharpe, eds. *Policies for Full Employment.* Ottawa: Canadian Council on Social Development.

Smeeding, T., B. B. Torrey, and M. Rein (1988). "Patterns of income and poverty: The economic status of children and the elderly in eight countries." In J. L. Palmer, T. Smeeding, and B. B. Torrey, eds. *The Vulnerable.* Washington, DC: Urban Institute Press.

Stasiulus, D. K. (1987). "Rainbow feminism. Perspectives on minority women in Canada." *Immigrant Women* 16 (1): 5–9.

Statistics Canada (1984). *Labour Force Annual Averages, 1975–1983.* Ottawa: Minister of Supply and Services Canada.

———— (1985). *Women in Canada: A Statistical Report.* Ottawa: Minister of Supply and Services Canada.

———— (1987). *Women in the Workplace: Selected Characteristics.* Ottawa: Minister of Supply and Services Canada.

———— (1988). *Earnings of Men and Women: 1987.* Ottawa: Minister of Supply and Services Canada.

———— (1989a). *Historical Labour Force Statistics in Actual Data, Seasonal Factors, Seasonally Adjusted Data, 1988.* Ottawa: Minister of Supply and Services Canada.

———— (1989b). *Labour Force Annual Averages, 1981–1988.* Ottawa: Minister of Supply and Services Canada.

———— (1990). *Women in Canada: A Statistical Report,* 2d ed. Ottawa: Minister of Supply and Services Canada.

Ternowetsky, G. (1987). "Controlling the deficit and a private sector led recovery." In J. Ismael, ed. *The Canadian Welfare State.* Edmonton, Alberta: University of Alberta Press.

Terris, M. (1990). "Lessons from Canada's health program." *Technology Review* (February/March 1990): 27–33.

Tester, F. (1987). "Homelessness: What's in the basement, who's in the attic." *Canadian Review of Social Policy* 19: 56–61.

Therborn, G. (1986). *Why Some Peoples Are More Unemployed Than Others: The Strange Paradox of Growth and Unemployment.* London: Verso.

Thorburn, H., ed. (1985). *Party Politics in Canada,* 5th rev. ed. Toronto: Prentice-Hall.

Thornley, D. (1986). *Living on the Margin: Welfare Reform in the Next Decade.* Toronto: Social Planning Council of Metropolitan Toronto.

———— (1987). "Minimum wages and adequate income." *Social Infopac* (Social Planning Council of Metropolitan Toronto) 6 (1): 1–10.

Townson, M. (1985). "The socio-economic costs and benefits of affirmative action for Canada." In R. S. Abella, ed. *Equality in Employment: A Royal Commission Report: Research Studies.* Ottawa: Minister of Supply and Services Canada.

UNICEF (United Nations Children's Fund) (1989). *The State of the World's Children.* New York: Oxford University Press.

United Nations (1989). *Compendium of Statistics and Indicators on the Situation of Women in 1986.* New York: United Nations.

U.S. Bureau of the Census (1988). *Household and Family Characteristics: March 1987.* Current Population Reports, Series P–20, No. 424. Washington, DC: U.S. Government Printing Office.

———— (1989). *Poverty in the United States: 1987.* Current Population Reports, Series P–60, No. 163. Washington, DC: U.S. Government Printing Office.

White, J. (1980). *Women and Unions*. Ottawa: National Advisory Council on the Status of Women.
——— (1983). *Women and Part-time Work*. Ottawa: Canadian Advisory Council on the Status of Women.
White, P. M. (1989). "Ethnic origins of the Canadian population." *Canadian Social Trends* (Summer): 13–16.
Wilensky, H. L. (1965). "Introduction: The problems and prospects of the welfare state." In H. L. Wilensky and C. N. Lebeaux, eds. *Industrial Society and Social Welfare*. New York: The Free Press.
——— (1983). "Political legitimacy and consensus. Missing variables in the assessment of social policy." In S. Spiro and E. Yuchtman-Yaar, eds. *Evaluating the Welfare State*. New York: Academic Press.
Wilson, S. J. (1982). *Women in the Family and the Economy*. Toronto: McGraw Hill Ryerson.
Wolfe, D. (1984). "The rise and demise of the Keynesian era in Canada: Economic policy 1930–1982." In M. S. Cross and G. S. Kealey, eds. *Readings in Canadian Social History, volume 5, Modern Canada 1930–1980's*. Toronto: McClelland & Stewart.
World Bank (1989). *World Development Report: 1989*. New York: Oxford University Press.

4

Japan: A Special Case

JUNE AXINN

Feminization of poverty in Japan? A dramatic increase in the percentage of the poor who are female? A swift rise in single-parent, female-headed families with young children? No, it has not happened. Certainly not in the visible way it appears in the United States.

Since 1955, Japan has experienced high rates of economic growth, with real annual growth rates of 10 and 12 percent in the 1960s and early 1970s and slightly more than 4 percent a year since the oil crisis of 1973. This has led to major changes in the economic and social structure of Japan and in the lives of Japanese women. Many of the shifts that occurred in the United States over the course of the past hundred years have taken place in Japan in less than fifty years. In part the different pace of change and the very different cultural heritage and economic organization of the two countries may account for the different picture that emerges.

This chapter will explore some of the economic, demographic, educational, and cultural shifts that have changed family life and work life for women in Japan. It will analyze the economic status of women and open the door for an examination of the *potential* feminization of poverty in Japan as that country becomes more "developed" and more westernized.

As in the United States, industrialization in Japan has been accompanied by an expansion of education and by demographic shifts that have changed the shape of women's economic lives. There are, however, significant differences in the patterns and terms of their employment. In part these differences stem from the special economic history of Japan and its particular occupational structure; they also reflect major social and cultural diversities between Japan and the rest of the developed world in family roles for women. Taken together the differences

I would like to thank the University of Pennsylvania Research Foundation for partial funding of this chapter.

in economic history and in family structure result in: (1) somewhat lower overall labor force participation rates in Japan than in the United States; (2) a different age pattern of participation; and (3) a much heavier emphasis for Japanese women than for U.S. women on part-time rather than full-time employment.

EDUCATION AND DEMOGRAPHIC CHANGES

As recently as the mid–1960s, only 60 percent of women in Japan went to senior high school; 95 percent attend today. And 32.7 percent go on to college compared to only 5.5 percent in 1960 (Japanese Industrial Relations Series, 1986, p. 6). Note however that women's education level is still below that of men. Although almost 35 percent go on to some form of higher education, as compared to 40 percent of men, most of this—two-thirds—is at junior colleges, which almost no men attend. Further, in the four-year colleges women are not enrolled in the same courses as men. They are not to be found in law, economics, or applied sciences ("Japanese Women," 1988, p. 20).

This longer time in school tends to delay their entrance into the labor force. Counterbalancing this somewhat is the recent delayed age of marriage that has increased women's years of labor force participation before marriage and the beginning of family responsibilities. In most industrialized nations, education has generally operated to increase women's employment opportunities. Studies seem to suggest, however, that in Japan, education has had a positive effect on paid labor force participation of younger workers but a negative effect for middle-aged and older women. Perhaps because of the higher earnings of their husbands, more middle-aged educated women withdrew from the labor force for reasons of child care for longer time periods than did their less educated sisters (Tanaka, 1987a, p. 5).

Birth rates in Japan have come down dramatically. They had reached a pre–World War II high of 30 per thousand population, dropped to 28.1 per thousand in 1950, and then to 11.9 per thousand in 1985 (*Japan Statistical Yearbook*, 1986). The legalization of abortion in 1948 played a major role in that drop, and a drop in the death rates the first year of life was clearly also a factor in the falling birth rate.

The death rate for newborn babies fell from 27.4 per thousand live births in 1950 to 3.7 per thousand in 1984, and the infant mortality rate (deaths up to one year of age) dropped from 60.1 to 6.0 per thousand in the same interval ("About Japan," 1986 p. 36).

Thus, the length of the child-rearing period—the time from the birth of the first child until the time the youngest child enters primary school—is only half of that before World War II. It is now about 8.7 years; it was 19.0 years (Japanese Industrial Relations Series, 1986, p. 5).

Not only has the birth rate fallen but the mortality rate is down as well, and life expectancy for women has increased from 61.5 years in 1950 to 80.5 in 1985 (Ministry of Health and Welfare, 1986). Thus there is a dual impact on the number of "empty nest" years and an increased number of years of potential labor force participation. The Japan Institute of Labor estimates that the average Japanese woman has "about 46 years left to live after being released from child care responsibility" and concludes that "coupled with their changed life cycle and reduced housework due to rationalization, reentry into the labor market is increasing, especially among women aged 40 to 44 who are released from child care responsibility" (Japanese Industrial Relations Series, 1986, p. 5).

LABOR FORCE PARTICIPATION OF WOMEN

Labor force participation of women in Japan is up. Women make up 37 percent of Japan's labor force, somewhat less than the level in the United States and with a different industry, age, and work-time structure.

The most dramatic outcome of the compressed time period in which economic growth has taken place in Japan has been the rapid shift out of agriculture and into industry and then subsequently into the service sector. In 1955, more than half of all female workers were in the agricultural sector; by 1980 only 13 percent were there, 28 percent were in industry, and 58 percent were in the service sector.

But the trend is not just from agriculture to services. Many of the women listed as "in the labor force" are family workers—unpaid laborers in family-run enterprises (as distinguished from housewives whose domestic labor is unpaid and who are not counted as being in the labor force at all). The shift from agriculture to service has meant that the proportion of paid employees in the female population has been increasing. Female family workers were the dominant trend in agriculture, and a majority of those were unpaid. The nonagricultural sector has a much lower rate of family workers (about 15 percent) so that overall the trend out of agriculture has meant a trend out of unpaid, family work and into paid employment (Tanaka, 1987b).

Nonetheless, comparing the situation to the United States, in 1980 it was still the case that only 64 percent of female labor force participants in Japan were paid employees; the rest were either self-employed or, more likely, unpaid workers in family firms. In the United States, by contrast, over 93 percent of female labor force participants were paid employees (Edwards, 1988).

The age cohort comparison with the United States of labor force participation in Japan is in some ways even more dramatic. The labor force activity of Japanese women shifts over the course of a woman's life. Kazuko Tanaka points out: "Female labor force participation varies dramatically over the life cycle, since non-market activities, such as schooling, marriage, childbearing and rearing, strongly affect the probability of women's labor force participation." In discussing the 1980 data, she points to the peak paid employment rates from ages 20 to 24 and notes that there is "a lower participation rate between ages 25 and 34 and a higher second peak between ages 40 and 49" (1987b, p. 14). This second peak is for middle-aged and older married women when their child-caring responsibilities are finished. Even much older women, age 55 and over, have higher rates of participation than in the United States. Of these older women, 30 percent are in the labor force, in contrast to 21 percent in the United States (ILO, *Year Book of Labor Statistics*, 1985; *Labor Force Statistics*, 1986). This is a result, no doubt, of the less mature Japanese pension and retirement system. Widowed or divorced women who had not been in the labor force draw very low pensions. In fact, it is only since the 1985 amendments to the Pension Law that married women have had the right to receive their own pensions at all (''About Japan,'' 1986, p. 35). In contrast, there is ''a sharp drop in the participation rates at ages 25 to 29, and a further drop at ages 30 to 34'' (Tanaka, 1987b, p. 17). Indeed, Japanese married women between the ages of 25 and 34 have the lowest labor force participation rates outside the home of any of the developed countries of the world—only 26 percent (Mincer, 1984, p. 279).

While the proportion of paid labor force activity on the part of women has increased, much of this activity is what is called, in Japan, part-time. Technically part-time means less than thirty-five hours of work a week. In actual practice, most observers agree it can often mean that workers are employed at part-time pay rates and with part-time contracts but for as long as forty hours a week or more. In a country where full-time employment may imply sixty hours of work, a forty- or forty-eight-hour ''part-time'' stint is not considered terribly unusual. Regardless of the number of hours it always means marginal employment—low hourly wages, little or no fringe benefits, and no job security.

Over 22 percent of Japanese female workers are in a part-time bind. Increasingly this part-time work is in the growing service sector. In 1982, the most recent year for which data are available, 63 percent of part-time women workers were in wholesale and retail trade and services, and only 24 percent were in manufacturing. Most of these women worked in small firms: 52 percent in firms with less than thirty workers, only 16 percent in firms with 500 or more employees (Japanese Industrial Relations Series, 1986, p. 14).

Who are these part-time workers? Most of them are older women returning to the labor force. In 1984, 28 percent were over the age of 45; almost 80 percent were over age 35. They are women who left the labor force to rear children and are now finding it impossible, or perhaps undesirable, to return to work for a major Japanese company despite all its benefits and protections.

For although most of these part-time workers have worked in the same company for more than a year (70 percent), most companies (60 percent) do not guarantee their employment. Most of these women work at least six hours a day and nearly half between thirty-five and forty-eight hours a week (''About Japan,'' 1986, p. 24). And yet, their average hourly pay was less than three-fourths that of full-time female employees, and their wages increased at a slower rate than those of regular employees.

Table 4.1 shows clearly the relationship of part-time employment to gender. The proportion of part-time employment has risen steadily since 1960, and that rise has been completely female. Outside of agriculture, male part-time em-

Table 4.1
Trends in Number of Part-time Employees (nonagriculture)

Year	Total			Female			Male		
	Employees (10,000 persons)	Part-time Employees (10,000 persons)	Ratio of Part-time Employees to Total	Employees (10,000 persons)	Part-time Employees (10,000 persons)	Ratio of Part-time Employees to Total	Employees (10,000 persons)	Part-time Employees (10,000 persons)	Ratio of Part-time Employees to Total
1960	2,106	133	6.3%	639	57	8.9%	1,467	76	5.2%
1965	2,713	168	6.2	851	82	9.6	1,862	86	4.6
1970	3,222	216	6.7	1,068	130	12.2	2,154	86	4.0
1975	3,556	353	9.9	1,137	198	17.4	2,419	155	6.4
1980	3,886	390	10.0	1,323	256	19.3	2,563	134	5.2
1981	3,951	395	10.0	1,359	266	19.6	2,592	129	5.0
1982	4,013	416	10.4	1,386	284	20.5	2,627	132	5.0
1983	4,119	433	10.5	1,451	306	21.1	2,668	127	4.8
1984	4,181	464	11.1	1,484	328	22.1	2,697	136	5.0

Source: Japanese Industrial Relations Series, <u>Problems of Working Women</u>, 1989, p. 15.

ployment has remained fairly constant, at about 5.0 percent of male employment; female part-time employment has risen in the same interval from 8.9 percent to 22.1 percent of all female employment.

WAGES AND EARNINGS: THE GENDER GAP

The gap between the earnings of men and women in Japan has grown since 1970. It is difficult to compare income received for equal work because of the heavy weight of the semiannual bonuses (for which there are no good data) in total income; but, overall, in 1984 women earned 51.8 yen for every 100 yen earned by men. In addition to the problem of part-time employment, much of this imbalance stems from the following:

1. Women are located in low-paying industries. They are disproportionately in service industries, and even within manufacturing they are in the low-wage end—textiles and food processing.

2. A high percentage work for small or medium-sized companies, but in Japan the best jobs are with large companies. They have the highest average wages, offer substantial fringe benefits (transportation, large annual or semiannual bonuses), and pursue a life-time employment policy. They hire essentially young graduates, train them, move them around in the company, and tie pay scales to seniority as well as position. The pattern of discrimination starts with recruitment. It continues with the "flexibility" that companies have in the selection of employees for training. Perhaps the most damaging of all, the standard employment policies of large companies in Japan mean that women who leave employment for child rearing stand little chance of being rehired by a major company. Consider table 4.2; 74 percent of all men and 64 percent of all women hired by large firms are under the age of 30. Entering or reentering the labor market at age 40 makes it highly unlikely to enter it at the successful (i.e., well-paid) end of the market.

3. Noncontinuous employment and therefore low average length of service.

4. Lower educational levels than men. This is true for the current cohort of graduates. It is even more the case for older workers. Thus the ratio of women workers holding managerial jobs is much smaller than men who have managerial jobs.

5. The practice of supplementing men's, but not women's, base salaries with dependency and housing allowances and other fringes such as sports club memberships.

6. Lower promotion rates for women.

The Foreign Press Center points out:

A less tangible reason for women's lower pay is the effect of discrimination against women. Female employees have few chances to be promoted to managerial posts or become high-ranking specialists in companies, fewer opportunities for education and training, and little hope of finding employment in major corporations or high-paying areas of industry. . . . [M]ost companies set different requirements for men and women when

Table 4.2
Characteristics of New Hires by Firms with Five or More Employees, 1985 (in thousands)

Size of Firm	Men				Women			
	Total New Hires	Number Occupationally Inexperienced	Number Under 25 Years Old	Number Under 30 Years Old	Total New Hires	Number Occupationally Inexperienced	Number Under 25 Years Old	Number Under 30 Years Old
All Firms	2007.9 (100%)	740.6 (36.9%)	935.9 (46.6%)	1187.9 (59.2%)	2168.3 (100%)	1209.3 (55.8%)	978.5 (45.1%)	1195.6 (55.1%)
1,000 Employees and Over	391.6 (100%)	202.5 (51.7%)	244.4. (62.4%)	289.0 (74.0%)	517.2 (100%)	363.0 (70.2%)	283.4 (54.8%)	328.7 (63.6%)
300-999 Employees	221.3 (100%)	115.8 (52.3%)	130.4 (58.9%)	155.1 (70.1%)	285.7 (100%)	169.9 (59.5%)	134.4 (47.0%)	159.2 (55.7%)
100-299 Employees	319.1 (100%)	126.8 (39.7%)	156.0 (48.9%)	197.0 (61.7%)	361.8 (100%)	200.5 (55.4%)	165.4 (45.7%)	200.3 (55.4%)
5- 99 Employees	1029.9 (100)	278.2 (27.0%)	389.7 (37.8%)	520.1 (50.5%)	928.6 (100%)	440.3 (47.3%)	357.0 (38.4%)	453.1 (48.8%)

Source: Edwards, 1988, p. 246.

recruiting new employees . . . [W]omen have fewer opportunities to learn either through experience working in various departments of a company or through on-the-job training.

Women who reenter the work force after devoting several years to child-rearing responsibilities are at a disadvantage in terms of promotion, which in Japan is generally in accordance with the length of continuous service in an organization ("About Japan," 1986, pp. 20–21).

The Japan Institute of Labor estimates that, controlling for education, age, length of service, and work time, there would still be a discrimination factor (i.e., an unexplained earnings differential) of 10 percentage points for young women and thirty points for women in the 40–49 age group (Japanese Industrial Relations Series, 1986, p. 17).

THE ROLE OF GOVERNMENT

For many years Japan has had protective legislation for women on the books—menstrual leave, released time for nursing, a maximum on hours of work, a prohibition on hazardous labor. Since 1947 the Japanese Labor Standard Laws have prohibited wage discrimination against women. Yet, industrial practice has operated so strongly against economic equity for women that new legislation was required in 1985 to enable Japan to ratify the United Nations Convention on the Elimination of All Forms of Discrimination Against Women (Edwards, 1988, p. 240).

The new legislation, the Japanese Equal Employment Opportunity (EEO) Law, went into effect in the spring of 1986. It prohibits gender discrimination in several areas: vocational training, fringe benefits, retirement, and dismissal. But there are no penalties for violations. In addition, companies are urged not to discriminate on the basis of gender in recruitment, hiring, job assignment, and promotion, but again are not penalized if they do. The legislation does offer subsidies to companies that permit women to take child care leave. It abolishes some special protections of earlier legislation that were seen as hindering rather than helping women. For example, it relaxes the special restrictions on overtime for women in managerial positions and in the professions (Japanese Industrial Relations Series, 1986, pp. 18–24). In sum, equal opportunity is seen as a goal toward which industry should strive, not as a law that should be enforced.

How well is the new legislation working? The law has meant that some new jobs have now opened up to women. For example, it is reported that women now operate cranes and hoist steel at construction sites. At least one woman heads a local tax office, and a woman has become the youngest patrol boat captain for Japan's coast guard. Despite the lack of real penalties for violations, the Labor Ministry and the Japan Federation of Employers Association claim that most large companies have ended the most blatantly discriminatory practices (Chira, 1988, p. 26-L).

But employment advertisements in Japan often do designate gender and age, and an official report in March 1989 pointed out that although 5 million Japanese women had entered the workforce in the past thirteen years, more than 63 percent of all working women who responded to a government survey in 1987 complained of unequal treatment. Few women hold responsible positions as managers or as specialists. Perhaps more important, the report from the former prime minister's office reported that although many private companies may have begun providing equal opportunity for women, women still face discrimination in pay, working conditions, and promotions. An official in the prime minister's office acknowledged that ''general position examinations for promotions may discriminate against women. . . . '' This does not violate the law (*Yamaguchi*, 1989, p. 13-G). Further, it has been reported that many companies attempt to circumvent the law by establishing dual entry-level tracks, separating those who are willing to accept out-of-town transfers and those willing to forfeit promotion opportunities to stay in one location (*Japan Times*, 1988, p. 5). There is some occasional protest from a small women's movement, but by American standards this movement is at a very early stage of development.

CHILD CARE LEAVE AND DAY CARE

A subtle barrier to full-time employment for women with children exists in the nature of the child care leave system and the day care that is available.

Maternity leave has been lengthened an additional two weeks so that a woman is now entitled to six weeks leave before the birth of a child and eight weeks afterwards. The employer does not pay her wages during this time; however, health insurance does provide a maternity benefit of 60 percent of earnings and, in addition, a lump-sum grant upon the birth of the child (Japanese Industrial Relations Series, 1987, pp. 8–9). Women are still entitled to take some time off for nursing, two thirty-minute breaks a day. But most find the traveling prohibitive (Condon, 1985, p. 210). When they have infants or young children, working mothers who are school teachers, nurses, or government workers can request child care leave under the 1985 legislation. Other employers are encouraged but not required to introduce such a system. To date very few have. Despite the carrot of a government subsidy, less than 15 percent of all companies have introduced a policy of child care leave.

Day care is available in Japan. As early as 1950, legislation established the first public day care centers to provide care for young children, with payment on a sliding scale. Since then the number of centers has grown. There are now almost 23,000 day care centers available to care for some 2.1 million young children. There are three major problems however, One is the matter of payment. Despite the sliding scale, many women are not able to afford day care fees. Secondly, most day care centers will not accept very young infants. With maternity leaves of only eight weeks, mothers who want to work are forced to use unlicensed nurseries, unsatisfactory "baby hotels." And perhaps most serious of all, day care centers are for the most part only open from nine to five, making it impossible for women with children to hold full-time jobs. Not only are employment hours considerably longer than that, but the usual pattern must allow for a substantial amount of commuting time. Overall, there is day care, but it is set up for a labor supply system where women leave the labor force completely when their children are infants and then return on a part-time basis. It is not designed to meet the needs of women who wish to work full-time or to support themselves throughout their lives. It is clearly inadequate to meet the needs of either a two-earner family or a single parent family.

THE PART-TIME SOLUTION

Clearly discrimination—overt and subtle—plays a part in the low income and dependent status of women. The heavy reliance on marginal work in small companies reinforces women's secondary economic status. Yet many observers argue that part-time work will probably continue and expand since it appears to suit both employer and employee. The interests of major companies are served as long as life-time employment and wages based upon seniority prevail. Companies use marriage and pregnancy bars to force the retirement of more experienced employees and make possible their replacement by lower paid, inexperienced, or part-time help. As long as a ready supply of labor is constantly available they are under no pressure to change that practice (Cook and Hayashi, 1980, p. 12).

How well does part-time work suit the interests of women? In present-day Japan, the typical work day in a large company is ten to twelve hours, with some attendant socializing. Clearly this leaves little time for child rearing and homemaking. While attitudes are slowly changing, nonetheless most companies still expect employees to demonstrate their "loyalty" by not using all the "sick days" to which they are entitled or not claiming all their vacation time. These conditions seem quite incompatible with the large household responsibilities placed on women. Women have several major jobs in the family.

In the first place, they are expected to take almost complete responsibility for homemaking—shopping, cooking, childrearing, and so on (Condon, 1985, pp. 1–7). They work long hours *away* from home and fewer *in* the home than in other developed countries (Morgan, Rindfuss, and Parnell, 1984). Nor do teenage children, girls or boys, help with household chores to any noticeable extent. Their job is to study, and the mother's job is to further that pursuit. Furthermore, homes are small and thus refrigerators and cabinets are small, necessitating almost daily shopping. Some, but not most, stores are open in the evenings. The food procurement technology is geared to women at home, not women who work full time.

There are extraordinary expectations of mothers regarding their children's education. There is a highly competitive elementary and secondary school system (which operates five and a half days a week), and mothers supervise homework, extra lessons, and frequently, *Jukos* or cram schools. Mother-teacher school conferences are routinely held during the day. The popular phrase "education mama" caricatures a situation that is all too true for many Japanese women. They take their relationship with their children and their children's education to be primary in their lives (Condon, 1985, pp. 120–124; Hendry, 1987, pp. 94–96; Preston and Kono, 1988, pp. 279–280; Shand, 1985, pp. 52–58).

Women, in addition to their responsibilities for their nuclear families, are the caretakers of the aging. It is considered the responsibility of the wife of the eldest son to take care of his parents should they require assistance. Two-thirds of Japanese elderly still live with their children, and while some of these grandparents may serve as babysitters enabling younger women to leave the home for jobs, many of them require and exact the reverse. Women are expected to leave the labor market to become the caretakers of the elderly—usually their husbands' parent or parents (Palmore and Maeda, 1985, pp. 32–42).

Thus, on the "family side" there are serious pulls to keep women out of the labor force on a full-time basis while their children are still in the primary and secondary schools. They are freer to work after that, but often part-time work is the only work available at this point, and frequently this work time is interrupted by a need to care for older parents.

Part-time labor for women would be consistent with household roles as they have been defined and structured in postwar Japan. It also keeps them in dependent marital relationships. *The Economist* put the matter very bluntly: "Japanese women are cramped by a culture that conditions them from an early age to accept the role of obedient wife and doting mother" ("Japanese Women," 1988, p. 20). Once that role is agreed to with all of the ramifications it has assumed in Japanese life, full-time employment becomes very difficult. And without full-time employment and economic independence women will never achieve social independence.

FAMILY STRUCTURE AND DIVORCE PATTERNS

One of the most striking differences between Japan and other developed countries is the apparent stability of Japanese marriages and the intergenerational unity of Japanese families. The divorce rate, which stood at 1.02 per thousand in 1947, rose to a peak of 1.51 per thousand in 1983. In 1986 it dropped back again to 1.37—the lowest of any of the developed nations (Ministry of Health and Welfare, 1986). Seventy percent of older parents live with their children; almost all minor children live with both parents. Over 90 percent of households with children are two-parent households in Japan; only 77 percent of U.S. households are in this category (Statistical Bureau, 1986; U.S. Bureau of the Census, 1989). Further, of the one-parent homes that are female headed in Japan, about 64 percent are the result of divorce. While this represents an increase in the past ten years, it is still only about 2 percent of all families in Japan (Nakano, n.d.).

Certainly the culture supports and enforces traditional family values. Divorce is considered shameful for both men and women. Divorced men are looked upon by their companies as poor managers and therefore poor promotion prospects. For women, "divorce is still regarded as a shameful matter, more so for women than men. . . . Although the wife is more often the aggrieved party, the initiative rarely comes from the women. Many accept that their husband should have extramarital affairs or even keep a mistress as long as it is done relatively discreetly" (Woronoff, 1985, pp. 105–106).

If the culture is not sufficient support for marriage, the economics of divorce make the point even clearer. Most divorces (91 percent) are arrived at by mutual consent, another 8 percent through arbitration, and only 1 percent by family court or judicial decision. About 70 percent of divorced women have custody of their children; fathers retain parental control slightly more than 23 percent of the time (Nakano, n.d., p. 12; Preston and Kono, 1988, p. 293). This is a marked increase in maternal custody since the end of World War II. But only a small proportion of mothers retain a share of mutual property at divorce. Almost half receive no monetary or property settlement at all. Those who do get very low settlements. Overall, 55 percent of divorced mothers must support their children completely on their own, 22 percent of exhusbands support their children, and 7 percent offer partial support ("About Japan," 1986, pp. 29–32; "Japanese Women," 1988, p. 20; Woronoff, 1985, p. 106).

How do these women support their children? About 84 percent work, and, of these, 65 percent are paid workers, while the remainder are in family businesses or are self-employed. Most of the paid wage earners are in small companies and most work part time in the temporary labor market. In fact only 10 percent are regularly employed in companies that employ 1,000 or more workers ("About Japan," 1986, p. 32). As a result, the average income of female headed homes (2.00 million yen) was less than half that of the average household (4.44 million yen) in 1986. The Japanese government admits that "Many single mothers suffer from ill health, and a good number of them, especially those who are divorced, cite problems related to the education of their children and housing" ("About Japan," 1986, p. 32).

Overall, the Japanese government does not have a highly developed system of social welfare supports. In fact it ranks only seventeenth out of nineteen OECD countries in the percentage of GNP it devotes to social programs and services (Preston and Kono, 1988, p. 284).

Perhaps the largest contribution the Japanese government makes to the well-being of women raising children alone in Japan is its contribution to and its oversight of the provision of health care. Through an elaborate complex of systems most of the population is covered by a combination of medical benefits that provides health care with varying contribution rates and co-pay arrangements. The health insurance system is almost universal, financed by individual contributions, employee payments, and government subsidies. The government ensures that prices are controlled and that hospitals, clinics, and other health services are regulated. The system, although far from perfect, does appear to insure some universal level of care for the entire population (Japanese Industrial Relations Series, 1987, pp. 7–11).

There is a small public assistance program, and about one percent of Japan's population gets some aid. In 1984, of the households that received public assistance, 14 percent were female-headed homes, 33 percent were aged, and 44 percent were ill or disabled. The proportion of public assistance going to women struggling to raise children has been increasing in recent years. Thus, for example, a survey by the prime minister's office showed that of 800 fatherless families in the Tokyo metropolitan district who were getting assistance, 70 percent were divorced women of whom only 5 percent were receiving any support from their former husbands. Unfortunately, these assistance grants are very small, and there is no evidence that they lifted these families out of poverty (Preston and Kono, 1988, p. 294).

In addition to the public assistance grants, there is a system of children's allowances, which is a general program for the population at large. Although this is means-tested, the eligibility point is set high enough to include a majority of the population with two or more young children. While the grants are minimal and would hardly be considered an effective means of support for a single parent, they do offer a nod of encouragement in the direction of independence (Japanese Industrial Relations Series, 1987, pp. 30–31).

A second children's allowance system is provided especially for one-parent families. Called a Child Rearing Allowance, the program started with a very low benefit level in 1962 but has risen rapidly to reach a level of about $247 a month for one child, $278 for two children and an additional $14 a month for the third child and each child after that (Nakano, n.d., p. 9). (Apparently, one child is more worthy of support than two or three.) Not only has the size of the benefit increased since the introduction of the program, but the number of beneficiaries has quadrupled, with 90 percent of this increase being an increase in the number of beneficiaries due to divorce.

An alternative to divorce for many unhappily married couples is what is known as "home divorce." The standard picture of a Japanese marriage features a rarely present father, absorbed in long hours of work with long commuting time, few vacations, and little time for family life. Three-fourths of the wives of union members report that they do not eat dinner with their husbands on weekdays. Many have less than ten minutes of conversation a day with them. The father's social life is built around his job, not around his home. Mothers meanwhile build their lives around the education of their children, their own friends, their homes, and their hobbies.

It is a short step from this psychological separation to a physical separation within the boundaries of the same home. *Kateinai rikon* (home divorce) means that no legal divorce occurs, but couples agree to have separate bank accounts and separate beds. They are practically, if not legally, divorced. This quasi-divorce arises in part because of social pressures. Children of legally divorced parents may be discriminated against both in employment and in marriage. Divorce is also a problem for men in business. Many people, especially older people, consider it a social dishonor. For women, there is also an economic risk that is very severe. And most women find it hard to locate another Japanese man who is any different. Thus, the remarriage rate of divorced women is very low. As Kimiko Tanaka, chief editor of *Wife* magazine, was quoted as saying: "The reason most wives don't divorce is very simple. It's hard to find another man. All Japanese men are the same" (Kuriki, 1988, pp. 1, 6).

CONCLUSION

Much has been made of the differences in culture between Japan and the United States—especially regarding family roles and family expectations. Women for many years have been in subordinate positions, and since the end of World War II the importance of parenting, or rather mothering, has held tight sway. Nonetheless one must be struck by some historic similarities with the United States. In the United States there was growing importance given to the role of parenting earlier in the twentieth century, the glorification of middle-class American women as homemakers and mothers, and then the following dramatic changes since the 1960s. Will the homemaker role continue its popularity with women in Japan as education becomes more of a general expectation and less of a novelty? Will the infant feminist movement find new strength as Japan becomes more international?

It has been argued that women work for "pin money," that it is rising prices and rising consumer expectations—the need for a second income in the family—that pushes them into the labor market. Therefore, the story goes, women want to work part-time "just to help out" but not to interfere with their main task of homemaking. What is the evidence of this? Are women becoming dissatisfied with their dependent status? What is the prospect for more freedom for Japanese women? And will that freedom mean more poverty? Ironically Japanese women at this moment are not independent enough to achieve feminization of poverty; they can not afford divorce and economic independence.

Should women achieve more marital independence, they will still face a highly discriminatory labor market that employs women as tea pourers, receptionists, and waitresses. Perhaps the slowing of population growth, the end of the steady flow of young women entering the labor market, will mean that there will be an increase in the demand for women to remain full time in the labor force. The Japanese are a pragmatic people. If the economy can not afford to waste its potential labor supply, we may see a full integration of women into the economy. Whether or not this will carry with it more independence for women—and more poverty for women—is yet to be seen.

REFERENCES

About Japan Series (1986). *Japanese Women Yesterday and Today*. Tokyo: Foreign Press Center.

Chira, Susan (December 4, 1988). "For Japan's working women, a slow recognition." *New York Times*, p. 26-L.

Condon, Jane (1985). *Japanese Women of the '80s: A Half Step Behind*. New York: Dodd, Mead and Company.

Cook, Alice H., and Hiroko Hayashi (1980). *Working Women in Japan*. Ithaca, NY: Cornell University.

Edwards, Linda N. (1988). "Equal employment opportunity in Japan: A view from the west." *Industrial and Labor Relations Review* 41 (2): 240–250.

Hendry, Joy (1987). *Understanding Japanese Society*. London: Croom Helm.

International Labor Organization (ILO) (1985). *Year Book of Labor Statistics*. Geneva: ILO.

Japanese Industrial Relations Series (1986). *Problems of Working Women*. Tokyo: Japan Institute of Labor.

——— (1987). *Social Security*. Tokyo: Japan Institute of Labor.

"Japanese women: A world apart." (May 14, 1988). *The Economist*, pp. 19–22.

Japan Statistical Yearbook (1986). Tokyo: Management and Coordination Agency.

Japan Times (February 29, 1988). P. 5.

Kuriki, Chieko (April 3, 1988). "A separate place." *Chicago Tribune*, pp. 1, 6.

Labor Force Statistics (1986). Tokyo: Management and Coordination Agency.

Mincer, Jacob (1984). *Inter-Country Comparisons of Labor Force Trends and of Related*

Developments. NBER Working Paper Series, No. 1438. Cambridge, MA: National Bureau of Economic Research.

Ministry of Health (1986). *Vital Statistics*. Tokyo: Ministry of Health and Welfare.

Morgan, S. Philip, Ronald R. Rindfuss, and Allan Parnell (1984). "Modern fertility patterns: Contrasts between the U.S. and Japan." *Population and Development Review* 10 (1): 19–40.

Nakano, Hiroshi (n.d.). *OECD Ad-Hoc Conference of National Experts on Lone Parents: National Report of Japan*. Tokyo, Japan: Children and Families Bureau, Ministry of Health and Welfare.

Palmore, Erdman, and Daisaku Maeda (1985). *The Honorable Elders Revisited*. Durham, NC: Duke University Press.

Preston, Samuel H., and Shigemi Kono (1988). "Trends in well-being of children and the elderly in Japan." In John L. Palmer, Timothy Smeeding, and Barbara Boyle Torrey, eds. *The Vulnerable*. Washington, DC: The Urban Institute Press.

Shand, Nancy (1985). "Culture's influence in Japanese and American maternal role perception and confidence." *Psychiatry* 48 (February 1985): 52–66.

Statistical Bureau (1986). *Population Census*. Tokyo: Management and Coordination Agency.

Tanaka, Kazuko (1987a). *Changing Life Cycle Employment of Japanese Women: Education, Home/Paid Work, and Cohort*. Unpublished paper presented at the Annual Meeting of the Association for Asian Studies, April 1987, Boston.

—————— (1987b). "Women, work, and family in Japan: A life cycle perspective." Ph.D dissertation, University of Iowa.

U.S. Bureau of the Census (1989). *Household and Family Characteristics*. Current Population Reports, Series P–20. Washington, DC: U.S. Government Printing Office.

"Working women still lack rights" (February 29, 1988). *Japan Times*, p. 5.

Woronoff, Jon (1985). *Japan: The Coming Social Crisis*. Tokyo: Lotus Press.

Yamaguchi, Mari (March 26, 1989). "Japan admits bias on women in workforce." *Philadelphia Inquirer*, p. 13-G.

5

Labor Market and Family Policy in France: An Intersecting Complex for Dealing with Poverty

JANE JENSON AND RUTH KANTROW

The last decade has brought a number of social, economic, and political changes in France that have affected the situation of women in profound ways. These changes have created a situation that is simultaneously one of risk and of possibility. The risk is that restructuring of production processes, mounting unemployment, and climbing rates of female-headed families would result in greater peril for women's economic well-being. On the other hand women's climbing rate of labor force participation and state policy adjustments to the new conditions has offered them some possibility of economic independence. Therefore the situation of French women facing the 1990s is a complex one in which a variety of social actors pursuing differing strategies have all had and will continue to have an important role in determining whether greater gender biases in the distribution of poverty will develop.

In the 1970s and 1980s crucial decisions were taken by businesses to restructure production in ways that had major impacts on women's employment. At the same time the state made policy adjustments to cope with and react to the economic climate by responding in part to the pressures it was under from not only business but social movements as well. In this context, labor market and family policy were, as they had been at least since World War II, the two major instruments used by French governments for preventing and controlling poverty. As such they became the frontline for prevention of the feminization of poverty.

As France faced the economic crisis of the early 1970s, neither business nor government quite knew how to respond, and both continued the practices on which they had relied throughout the postwar period. This meant that factories hired more semiskilled and unskilled workers and that the service portion of the

Support for this project came from an American Council of Learned Societies (ACLS) fellowship and from Social Sciences and Humanities Research Council of Canada (SSHRCC) research grant #410–88–0912.

economy continued to expand, bringing many new jobs for women in both
industry and commerce. The government, trying to turn aside the worst effects
of economic crisis, extended social services and job protections to the victims
of restructuring.[1]

By the late 1970s, however, both business and the right-wing government
decided that new labor-management relations and less state spending were desirable. Business preferences turned to what has been termed "flexibility," in
which governmental restrictions on labor-management relations are weakened,
if not eliminated, so that managers can employ workers with flexible hours, part-
time, and/or in short-term contracts. Such "flexible" practices then allow businesses to adjust production, to reduce the wage bill, and also to make lower
contributions to the social security programs, which in France are funded by
employers' contributions. Obviously, then, there was also pressure on the government to loosen its regulations so as to permit such flexibility to take hold.
While the Socialists were elected in 1981 on a program of maintaining workplace
protections and increasing state spending for social programs and to reduce
unemployment, by 1983 they too had turned toward "austerity" programs (Ross
and Jenson, 1988, pp. 6–9). The pressure for new labor-management relations
and social and economic policies occurred, moreover, in a situation in which
both the trade union movement and the women's movement were seriously
weakened and did not have the strength to reweight government policy in more
equitable directions.

The result of government and business efforts has been that, despite a massive
increase in the labor force participation rate of women and despite the continued
legal assertion that all citizens have a "right to work," access to a job in France
remains more contingent for women than for men, for whom it is an assumed
social fact.

An irony of the current situation of French women is that while women workers
as a group are more than ever a central pillar of the national economy, many
individual women find themselves in an increasingly precarious position in the
labor force, at risk of unemployment and with fewer and fewer full-time, well-
paid jobs available to them. As a result they are also disproportionately concentrated among those vulnerable to poverty.

WOMEN'S LABOR FORCE PARTICIPATION AFTER 1945

The existence of a large female labor force is not simply a function of business
needs but also the result of long-standing, deep patterns of social change in the
postwar years. The rate of female participation in the labor force before World
War II was higher in France than in most other European countries. The explanation for this lies in the structure of an economy grounded in agricultural
production, luxury goods, and textiles as well as in the demographic effects of
population control and a highly destructive World War I. No matter what the
cause, however, the effect has been that state social programs and economic

Table 5.1
Labor Force Participation Rates by Age, 1988

	Women	Men
15-24	36.1%	37.6%
25-39	74.0%	96.2%
.40-49	70.7%	96.8%
50-59	52.7%	78.7%
60 +	5.8%	10.9%
Overall	45.6%	64.6%

Source: INSEE, 1988, p. 34.

policies have never defined women's work as ''unnatural'' and most of them were designed to reconcile women's dual roles as workers and mothers (Jenson, 1986).

By the late 1960s the percentage of the labor force that was female had begun to rise steadily. In 1969 it was 35.3 percent, in 1979 38.8 percent, in 1984 40.9 percent, and in 1988 43.5 percent (INSEE, 1987, p. 127; INSEE, 1988, p. 34). By 1988, 45.6 percent of all women over age 15 were employed (while 64.6 percent of men were).

Despite such changes in the aggregate statistics, it is even more striking to examine the experience of particular subgroups. As table 5.1 shows, in 1988 almost three-fourths of all women of prime childbearing age worked outside the home, while young women and men (15–24) had nearly the same rates of participation. There has been a rapid increase in the participation rate of women with children. This change is based on the rapidly increasing participation rate of women with children. To illustrate, in all two-parent families having at least one child, 33 percent of the women were in the labor force in 1968, 43 percent in 1975, 54 percent in 1982, and 63 percent in 1987 (Lefaucher, 1988).[2]

Of course, this rising participation rate has not eliminated the wage gap. Among those with full-time jobs, men's incomes are 25 percent higher than women's (INSEE, 1987, pp. 169–171). The location of employment makes a difference, however; public sector jobs display less of a wage gap than do those in the private sector (ECE, 1985, p. 6). The gap is greatest among senior managers and professionals, while it is approximately equal across the other occupations. Another indicator of women's lower economic status is that, while men's incomes range widely, women's are concentrated and lower (INSEE, 1987, pp. 159–161). This means that there is a career ladder for men, which they may ascend with age and seniority; while women are more likely to remain stuck in dead-end jobs and poorly paid throughout their working lives.

A further aspect of the differences in female and male labor force participation is the presence of gender-related differences in the effects of education and

Table 5.2
Variations in the Working Population by Sex and Age, 1975–1985

	1975-1980	1980-1985
Men		
younger than 25	-18,000	-39,000
25-54	- 4,000	-20,000
55 +	-46,000	-82,000
Women		
younger than 25	- 9,000	-29,000
25-54	125,000	136,000
55 +	-12,000	-44,000

Source: INSEE, 1987, p.87.

training. While women are overrepresented in the higher levels of the school system, they tend to gain less from their education. A man with a degree from one of France's *grandes écoles* (the most prestigious institutions) will earn 3.5 times more than a man with no recognized training credentials, whereas the difference for women is only 2.7, again suggesting the narrower range in women's incomes. And, women with a university degree are less likely than men with such credentials to enter management positions (58 percent as compared to 83 percent) (INSEE, 1987, pp. 160–167, 555).

Behind these general characteristics of labor force participation by age, family, and educational categories lies a very important alteration in the gender composition of the French economy in the years of economic crisis. As table 5.2 shows, the only category of the labor force that has increased in absolute size is that of women between the ages of 25 and 54. This means several things. First, it reflects a number of important adjustments in the ways French women now organize their lives, both at work and in the family. Second, it indicates the effects of restructuring of the French economy toward more service-sector employment, as well as the reflection of employers' strategy of increasing the "flexibility" with which they manage their labor forces, including, in particular, hiring more part-time workers (Huet, 1986, pp. 15–17). Both of these aspects of the rising rate of female employment merit further attention.

Table 5.3
Labor Force Participation Rate of Women by Age and Number of Children

	Age of the Woman in 1986			
	25–29	30–34	35–39	40–44
Number of Children (a)				
0	89.0	84.6	81.6	74.9
1	80.6	85.1	81.4	72.3
2	62.4	70.3	73.1	64.1
3	30.2	42.7	50.5	49.8
4	20.9	27.3	37.0	39.0
5 +	11.9	10.8	13.2	14.3
Total	72.5	68.1	68.5	67.3

(a) Children under 18

Source: INSEE, 1987, p. 496, figure 1.

REASONS FOR SHIFTING FEMALE LABOR FORCE PARTICIPATION

The Contribution of Social Change

One important factor lying behind the willingness of women not only to seek employment but also to remain in the labor force throughout their lifetime is the decline in the fertility rate. In 1964 the average rate was 2.90 births per woman and by 1985 it had fallen to 1.82, which is below the rate necessary to reproduce the population. While this second statistic is relatively high for an advanced industrial society, it nevertheless does reflect the fact that French women have begun to reduce their own fertility (INSEE, 1987, pp. 20–21). No doubt legalization of contraception (in 1967 and 1974) and abortion (in 1974) aided this decline in fertility (Jenson, 1987a).

The reduction in fertility is of fundamental importance for women's labor force participation rates. Since the 1960s it has been observed that most women leave the labor force only after the birth of a third child. As table 5.3 shows, women with more than two children behave substantially differently from those with less, no matter what their age (or, by implication, the age of their children). Moreover, the table also shows that the labor force participation of women with one child is virtually indistinguishable from that of those women who have no children. Interesting too are the changes over time. Between 1960 and 1979 it became much less likely that a woman with one child would leave the labor force, whereas the inverse was the case for women with more than three children who, as the following discussion of family policy details, were encouraged to do so (INSEE, 1987, p. 497, figure 3).

Despite these overall patterns, however, there are differences in the ways that particular categories of working women behave after their children are born. The women most likely to depart the workforce are industrial workers or white-collar employees, no matter how many children they have. Women working in a family workplace, for example as artisans or in shops, or employed in agri-culture are much less likely to leave the labor force, and the same is true of women in teaching or management positions. This means, of course, that in-dustrial and service-sector workers continue to provide a pool of employees whose attachment to the labor force is less strong than men's and whose career patterns demonstrate discontinuity (INSEE, 1987, pp. 498–499). Therefore, French employers have available a potential part-time and low-wage industrial and service -sector labor force, and they have been able to base their restructuring strategies on the continued availability of such a labor pool.

A second major change contributing to the rising rates of female labor force participation is the increase in divorce, an increase which has been steady since 1885 but which accelerated in the 1960s even before the 1975 reform of the divorce law. In well over four-fifths of the divorces of couples with children, the women were given custody. Yet, while women get custody they also tend to receive little child support from their former spouses. As a 1985 study showed, only 35 percent of all child support payments were paid regularly and completely, while 13 percent were never paid and a further 36 percent were only partial payments (INSEE, 1987, pp. 523, 527). When a parent is in arrears for support payments, the *Caisse d'Allocations Familiales* (CAF)—the institution that pays family benefits—will make up the missing payments and collect from the delin-quent spouse. Nevertheless, even when the support payments are met, either by a parent or by the state, on average they form less than one-tenth of the family income. The effect of the relatively low level of payments set by the courts means, of course, that women with children to care for are more at risk of being poor. One response is to seek work.

By 1987, 12.5 percent of French families with children were single-parent ones, and the vast majority of these were female-headed. While most single-parent families have been created by divorce or death of a spouse, increasingly they also result from the declining marriage rate (marriages per 1,000 of the population were 7.8 in 1970 and 4.8 in 1986) and the later age of first marriages. Thus, the number of single-parent families consisting of a never-married parent and child almost doubled between 1962 and 1987, when 19 percent of single-parent families fell into that category. Therefore, there is an expanding group of young single women with children who are likely to be employed (Lefaucher, 1987, pp. 1–22). Women who head single-parent families have a labor force participation rate of 76 percent, considerably higher than the female population as a whole (Lefaucher, 1988, p. 2; see table 5.1). For such women between the ages of 30 and 39, the rate is 86 percent (table 5.1).

Despite their high rate of labor force participation, the women heading single-parent families often earn too little to support the family without some kind of transfer payment (CERC, 1988, p. 51). This is the case even though they are more likely than married mothers to work full time (Lefaucher, 1988, p. 44). Overall, then, while there has been a dramatic increase in the labor force participation rates of women, especially those with young children and/or heads of families, there has been a concomitant creation of a group of poor single-parent families dependent on state family benefits. The existence of this "at-risk" group is related not only to patterns of female employment and unemployment but also to rising divorce and declining marriage rates.

The Contribution of Economic Restructuring

As table 5.2 shows, the only category in which the number of women working increased between 1975 and 1985 was that of women between the ages of 25 and 54. Much of this increase was due to the creation of new jobs in the service sector. Therefore, what job creation France experienced in these years disproportionately benefited women because they are concentrated in service-sector work (INSEE, 1987, pp. 127–132).

Women's employment in industry also increased, although more modestly, rising from 19 percent of the industrial workforce in 1969 to 21 percent in 1988. While this rise is not steep, it does indicate that women continued to retain their place in industry that had developed in the postwar years as an important source of jobs, particularly for unskilled workers (Jenson, 1988, pp. 156–157; Thibault, 1986, pp. 155–156). In 1988, 14 percent of all women in the labor force were industrial workers (INSEE, 1988).

There were two major problems with the ways in which women's labor force participation in both the industrial and service sectors shifted. The first was that many of these new jobs were either part-time or temporary ones. The second was that women suffered disproportionately from unemployment.

There has been a significant rise in part-time employment in recent years. Between 1975 and 1986 the percentage of the French population working part time went from 7.5 percent to 12 percent, and women were particularly affected by this change. Between 1982 and 1986, 130,000 women lost a full-time job, while at the same time 450,000 part-time positions were created (Maruani and Nicole, 1987, p. 1). Indeed, 70 percent of the new jobs filled by women were part-time ones, while women were also overrepresented among workers with temporary jobs or contracts that were not permanent (INSEE, 1987, p. 131). Manufacturers, encouraged by the government, often transformed full-time jobs into part-time ones rather than lay off workers; (Bouillaguet-Bernard et al., 1986, pp. 31–32; Jenson, 1988, p. 166). The result was that by 1986, 24 percent of women working in the service sector and 11 percent of women working in industry had part-time contracts; 23 percent of all French women in the labor force were part-time workers (INSEE, 1987, p. 116; OECD, 1988, p. 149, table 5.5).

Despite an initial effort after 1981 to discourage temporary, short-term employment, the Socialist government came to accept that this form of employment was a major element of companies' restructuring strategies, and it moved to liberalize the conditions under which such contracts could be used.[3] Legislation in 1986, recognizing rather than discouraging this kind of employment contract, was designed to prevent employers from using temporary workers for jobs that were normally filled by employees with regular contracts, as well as to regulate the wage rates and social benefits in the direction of equality. At the same time, the unions signed a series of agreements with the association of companies which provided temporary employees to guarantee that the same individual and collective rights available to permanent employees would also be available to people working under temporary contracts.

Despite winning such protections for working conditions and benefits, many French women face new working conditions because of this management of "flexibility." Most such contracts were created as a result of employers' efforts to restructure the labor force in ways that gave them greater discretion in organizing their production processes as well as permitting the deregulation of working conditions. Such changes did not follow from any "demand" on the part of the workers, either women or men. Many had part-time, flex-time, or temporary jobs imposed upon them, and in response they continued to seek full-time and stable work (Kergoat, 1984; Maruani and Nicole, 1987, pp. 1–3).

The creation of part-time or temporary jobs has become a means of redefining the status of employees in many workplaces, creating new divisions across categories by separating women and men, young and old, skilled and unskilled, and married and single workers. Temporary and part-time employees are excluded from the routes upon which career and salary advancement depend—for example, seniority. The role of seniority is extremely important for increasing one's income. While women's salaries rise more slowly than men's in the younger age groups, this difference in the rate of increase disappears with age, an observation attributed to seniority (INSEE, 1987, p. 155). Therefore, if new kinds of hiring practices result in women not accumulating seniority, the effects will continue to haunt them throughout their working lives. Such blockages occur both because part-time and temporary workers are more likely to change employers (as they seek full-time and/or permanent work) and because they are perceived by employers and by unions to be a "different" kind of worker.[4] Incomes are also affected, because many employers differentiate among employees in their employment classification schemas or in the ways that they pay commissions. In many stores, for example, full-time employees receive a substantial commission in addition to their salaries, while regular part-time employees receive only a small bonus. Seasonal part-time employees are the worst off, receiving only their salaries (Maruani and Nicole, 1987, p. 7). Studies of employers' motivations in using part-time workers reveal companies' recognition that such workers are more likely to be transitory employees (because they cannot live on the salary they earn for ten to twenty-two hours a week) and are therefore likely to pay less attention to collective organizing in order to gain improved working conditions, salaries, or other benefits (Maruani and Nicole, 1987, pp. 9–10).

For all of these reasons, analysts have concluded that a new employment status is being created and not simply a new employment time schedule (Maruani and Nicole, 1987). Employers' enthusiasm for part-time and temporary workers in both the industrial and service sectors has meant an increase in the number of women without job security; a decline in professional credentials, which does not depend on any skill differentials but simply on the terms of employment; and a continued wage differential because part-time and temporary workers often both earn lower wages and receive less in other forms of remuneration.

With regard to unemployment, the situation of women has also deteriorated. As more women have entered the paid labor force, in part because of the job creation described above, they have also entered the ranks of the unemployed more than men. Since 1974 women's unemployment rates have always been higher than men's. This pattern holds for all categories of the labor force, for all levels of education and training, for all age groups, and among immigrant workers. In other words, women are more likely to be unemployed and to stay unemployed for longer periods of time than are men (INSEE, 1987, p. 132). Female unemployment rates ranged from 11.1 percent to 13.7 percent between 1983 and 1987, being at least 50 percent higher than those of men each year (OECD, 1988, p. 143, table 5.2).

The following conclusions can be drawn from this discussion of women's labor force participation in France since World War II. First, women have clearly entered the labor force in large numbers, and they seem to be there to stay. Moreover, if job creation has favored women, it is because of their massive concentration in the tertiary sector, which has ballooned at the same time that areas of traditional male employment—industry and construction—have contracted. Yet, this shift in the French economy, by sector and also by type of employment, has not meant that women and men face the same conditions when they work. Service-sector employment is very often part-time or temporary employment. Even the newly created industrial jobs frequently result from conversion of full-time to part-time positions. Therefore, labor force segmentation and low wages remain the lot of French women; their situation can be said to have become even more difficult since the 1960s.

STATE POLICIES DIRECTED TOWARD WOMEN

The changing social and economic situation of women has raised a number of policy issues for the French state. There are two major policy arenas that have had profound effects on women: labor market policy and family policy. Although they are very clearly interconnected, each of these arenas will be considered in turn in order to assess the ways that they have had an impact on the lives of women, especially women at risk of being poor.

For the most part the goal of French labor market policies directed explicitly toward women has been constant in the postwar years; they have been designed to equalize the situation of women and men in the labor force. At the same time, however, macroeconomic policies and labor market policy more generally—not simply those aspects explicitly directed toward women—have operated so as to increase the marginalization of many women in the workforce. Family policies have had different goals over the postwar years, ranging from efforts to increase the average number of children born to each family (pronatalism), to income redistribution, to promotion of more equal gender relations. Nevertheless, by the 1970s and 1980s the expressed goals of both family policy and labor market policy directed toward women were to encourage women's economic independence as well as to facilitate the better performance of their dual roles as workers and mothers.

Labor Market Policies: Forward Toward Equalization, Backward in Restructuring

The place to begin discussing the policies of the French state is in its efforts to reduce the systematic discrimination that women workers have faced historically. Conscious of the discriminatory effects of a laissez-faire labor market, unions and parties of the Left, which held the balance of power during the Resistance and Liberation, inserted their long-standing demand for equal pay for equal work into the program of the first postwar governments. Thus, the Constitution of the Fourth Republic in 1946 affirmed the "right to work" for all French citizens, as did that of the Fifth Republic in 1958. Based on the more general left-wing principle that a proper social order respects everyone's right to earn his or her own living and in that way to become economically independent, this right was intended in part to prevent employers from discriminating against women in their hiring and firing decisions.

The first postwar government also moved to equalize the situation of women and men working in civil service. Women were given access to many categories of employment that had previously been open only to men, and pay scales were integrated (Jenson, 1987b). In subsequent years the civil service moved toward equality more rapidly than the private sector did, with one result being a smaller wage gap. During the 1960s and 1970s the government instituted a series of reforms intended to guarantee professional training, promotion, reentry of women who had dropped out of the labor force to raise children, and improved seniority rights and pensions. Many of the reforms instituted in the 1970s by the government of President Giscard d'Estaing—under some pressure from feminists promoting equal rights—were intended to improve the situation of women with children, especially if they had taken time out of the labor force. Thus, age limits were rescinded in a number of categories, and in others a formula was developed to give credit to women with children, allowing them to exceed the age and time limits for job categories and entrance examinations (Lorée, 1980, pp. 96–99). Finally, in 1982 the Left government removed virtually all sex-based restriction on job categories in the civil service so that women had the same access as men to state employment. Such reforms were important because the civil service has long had a concentration of women in its ranks; many women seeking work in teaching, research, health care, the communications sector, and so on were potentially affected by such new regulations.

There were also efforts to introduce equal pay for equal work across the entire labor force. France ratified Convention 100 of the International Labor Organization in 1952 and the Treaty of Rome of the European Community in 1957, both of which banned pay discrimination on the basis of sex. A 1972 ordinance called for equal pay for work of equal value. Enforcement procedures followed a year later. In 1975 sex discrimination in hiring and firing was prohibited. Then in 1976 France supported the Council of Europe's affirmation of the need to eliminate both direct and indirect discrimination based on sex or family status.

It was, however, the failure of this type of statute to overcome the systemic discriminatory effects of sex-segregated labor markets that led after the election of the Left government in 1981 to the *loi Roudy*. Yvette Roudy, Minister of the Rights of Women in the first Mitterrand government (1981–1986), initiated a series of steps to overcome discrimination in the workplace and in the labor market. The law passed in July 1983 was designed explicitly to fill the gaps in rights and procedures left by the relatively ineffectual decrees of the 1970s. The law was an innovative one because it provided a procedure for drawing existing institutions of workplace representation—primarily trade unions and work councils—into greater responsibility for gender equality. It also made use of new institutions of labor-management relations, established by the Auroux Laws reforming collective bargaining rights, to promote gender equality.

The basic principle of the law is that women may not be (with rare exceptions) excluded from a job solely on the basis of their sex or the supposed characteristics of that sex. All workers must be treated equally, although special provisions for pregnancy and maternity leave and facilities for breast feeding are permitted. For example, France has had paid maternity leaves as part of its labor policy since 1911. Initially, prenatal leaves were available according to need, and postnatal leaves were compulsory and paid at the minimum wage (Jenson, 1986). By the 1980s, the leave period had expanded to six weeks before the birth of the child and ten weeks after, with a 90 percent income replacement. The exception to equal treatment came from the medical and physical aspects of childbirth, and was therefore a different principle than that of parental leave, which is a one-year unpaid leave with job protection available for either parent. Given the wage gap, of course, most often it is the mother who takes parental leave.

With the *loi Roudy*, unions as well as women could make complaints about company practices, and both companies and unions were responsible for designing procedures for change, after consulting with female employees and the state.[5] Thus women no longer had the burden of bringing sex discrimination charges themselves but could be supported by their unions.

Given the continued importance of small business and family business in the French economy, a 1982 law guaranteeing a more equitable status to spouses working together was a further important step toward equality in work. This law as well as the *loi Roudy* and other steps taken by the Ministry of the Rights of Women in the first half of the 1980s all reflected an analysis of the situation of women that located blockages to full workplace equality not simply in hiring and pay practices but also in differences in schooling and training and in longstanding attitudes about women's work. Therefore, the Ministry spent as much effort on encouraging schoolgirls to study science and take up careers in new technology fields as it did in passing legislation banning sex discrimination (Jenson, 1988, pp. 162–164).

In fact this emphasis on training and education was a continuation of the strategy of the 1970s. Even before 1981 analysts blamed the failure of the 1972 law to overcome the wage gap on the fact that jobs done primarily by women were popularly considered less worthy or less important or requiring little more than "natural" skills as compared to jobs done by men, and so they were paid less. In other words, as long as the labor market was sex-segregated so that women and men's work was not directly comparable, women would continue to earn less than men. Therefore, the governments of Giscard d'Estaing in the 1970s and of Mitterrand in the 1980s defined more open and wider access to education and training as a crucial step in overturning the wage gap.

Since the 1970s official government policy has been that every woman must have a real "choice" between working and staying at home.[6] In concrete terms this governmental strategy has meant not only efforts to abolish discrimination via legislation but also changes in fiscal regulations and extension of child care facilities. Tax-law reforms and changes in the family allowance system mean that two-income families are no longer penalized by the tax system. Child care programs have been expanded. Since the middle of the nineteenth century the school system has been the favored route for state-sponsored child care. In 1982, 37 percent of two-year-olds, 83 percent of three-year-olds, and 97 percent of five-year-olds were in the public school system, although compulsory education does not begin until age 6 (Lefaucher, 1988, p. 9). Moreover, the schools extended their child care responsibilities by providing afterschool care and a full lunch, with priority going to children of working mothers. Using the public education system to provide child care, while not perfect—especially with respect to timetables—means that the cost of child care falls on the state, not on parents themselves. The state also finances a system of summer programs for children, although the five weeks of paid vacation that are now the right of all French workers means that much summer child care as well as during other periods of school holidays can be provided by the families themselves.

For children under age 2, who cannot enter the school system, a system of creches has been developed. These are used more by single mothers than by two-parent families, although the most likely solution for a single mother remains a caregiver who is a member of her own family (Lefaucher, 1988, p. 48). These creches too are heavily subsidized by the French government, usually the municipality.

The policy goal of giving women a "choice" about paid work has not applied to single mothers, however, where a principle aim is clearly to foster their economic independence. Therefore, governmental strategy has focused on giving single mothers the means to earn a living to support themselves and their families (Lefaucher, 1988, p. 49). Encouragement of financial independence has taken the form of programs designed by both right- and left-wing governments to get single mothers into the labor force.[7] In 1975, for example, female heads of families were given priority in access to professional training. In 1983–1984 the Ministry of the Rights of Women cooperated with the Ministry of Social Affairs and National Solidarity to design individualized training programs to retrain long-term unemployed single mothers. This program was followed in 1985 and 1986 by a series of other initiatives, undertaken as part of the general governmental efforts against unemployment and poverty, to retrain—or more likely to train—the categories most at risk of falling back on the state for support (INSEE, 1987, pp. 82–83; Lefaucher, 1988, pp. 49–51). The focus on training follows, in part, from the observation that unmarried single mothers are likely to have a lower level of education than divorced or separated single mothers. Therefore, when they do work, their income is also likely to be lower (CERC, 1984, pp. 23, 27). Because of these characteristics of their income-earning potential, unmarried and young mothers have become an important target of poverty programs that intersect both labor market and family policy.

All of these strategies for dealing with the inequality of women in the labor force and the poverty of single mothers were predicated on the notion that the labor market was an entity that responded to training and skills. In other words, analysts believed that women's problems in the labor market were due primarily to their lack of credentials. From the government of Giscard d'Estaing in the 1970s to that of Mitterrand in the 1980s, a whole policy branch of the state—whether in the Ministries of Labor, Rights of Women, or Social Affairs—directed its efforts to training women so that they could enter the labor force and to providing infrastructure to overcome the burdens of child care. Indeed, over one-third of children 2 to 3 years old and 90 percent of those 3 to 4 years old are in child care provided by the school system (Fragonard, 1986, p. 4).

Yet, appearing simultaneously with these initiatives to foster equality were other labor market policies implemented by some of the same branches of the state that undermined the moves toward equality. By the late 1970s notions of a "dual society" in which there would be a well-paid core of skilled workers and a periphery of temporary, part-time, and/or low-paid workers began to appear in the debates among neoliberal ideologues and policy makers (Boyer, 1984, pp. 41–42). In these analyses, which were intended to understand the rapidly rising rate of unemployment after 1974, "women" appeared as one of the categories of the periphery. The notion underpinning all these arguments was that there was not a single labor market but several, and that social groups were differentially located within these markets. After the failure of the first initiatives of the Left government to implement a traditional Keynesian-style economic recovery, there was a retrenchment in the direction of governmental acceptance of business pleadings for greater "flexibility" in the labor market (Ross and Jenson, 1985). Driven by an overwhelming concern for the high rate of unemployment and the fragile competitive position of French firms in the international economy, the Socialist government instituted a series of initiatives to "liberalize" the labor market. This meant that, among other things, a variety of employment contracts was seen as a "solution" to the problems of unemployment. Therefore, in 1982, when the Left government extended employment and welfare protection to part-time workers and moved in 1986 to regulate temporary work, it was clearly stating that it accepted the reconciliation of its social agenda with the continued existence of a segmented labor market, with women located at its periphery.

The political acquiesence in labor market segmentation in the 1980s had two effects on women. The first came as an important unintended effect of the wage-setting strategy pursued by the union movement in the postwar period began to diminish. After 1945 French unions were very weak in the workplace and most of their successes depended on national-level negotiations, especially ones to set the minimum wage. Because they were unable to gain victories in wage-setting from employers directly, they tended to rely on their political clout to ensure that the state-set minimum wage (the SMIG, later the SMIC) rose steadily. Therefore, because so many women in the postwar period were being hired to fill the lowest paid jobs, their minimum wage jobs were better protected against inflation and downward wage pressures than were the jobs of many skilled male workers. And, an unintended effect of this union strategy was to hold down the wage gap between women and men because the best-protected wages were often the minimum ones.

In the 1970s and 1980s, however, the unions lost political influence as the percentage of the labor force unionized plummeted and as their links to the Left parties frayed (Ross and Jenson, 1988, pp. 7–9). Therefore, they were not in a position to organize successful resistance when the Left government backed off its commitments to use the standard French postwar macroeconomic instruments after 1983. Nor could they prevent the emergence of movements among some workers to protect the wage differentials they felt they deserved (Ross and Jenson, 1989, pp. 7ff). Therefore, the wage gap between women and men in France has not closed, in large part because in the 1980s the minimum wage became a less important influence for wage-setting in the labor market as a whole.

A second effect of governmental acceptance of labor-market segmentation in the 1980s was that a profoundly nonegalitarian discourse emerged about the "difference" of women workers: their lower training, their supposed fondness for part-time work, their child care responsibilities. This nonegalitarian discourse about difference coexisted with the discourse of equality which had motivated the *loi Roudy* and certain antipoverty initiatives. The wide-ranging impact of this discourse of "difference" is clearly revealed even in the implementation of equality policies of the French state. In October 1988 the Court of Justice of the European Community issued a finding against the French government for its continued support of policies that promoted or maintained inequalities between female and male workers. Singled out by the Court were a series of special "protections" for women workers—including days off for caring for sick children and the opening of the school year and rest periods—that were not available to men but were not related to pregnancy and childbirth. The French government's justification of such single-sex benefits was that they reflected the "realities" of the family division of labor, in which mothers bore the burden of child care.

While there is always a tension between the reality of women's double burden and the utopian hope that parental responsibilities will be more widely shared, the acceptance by the French government, and by the firms and unions that negotiated such benefits in collective agreements, of the existence of the sexual division of labor reflected a lack of desire on the part of much of that apparatus to challenge tradition. Of course, the decision of the European Court is also important for the political forces seeking greater equality because it provides a weapon in the ongoing policy battles. With the continuation of the discourse of "difference" and with business agitating for greater "flexibility," however, it has become very difficult for those parts of the French state or social movements promoting equality to row against the tide (Jenson, 1989, p. 134).

Family Policy: Adjustments in the Face of New Conditions

Analyses of poverty by French policymakers have focused not only on the resources available to a family at a single point in time but also on a larger conception of resources, including health, education, and work history. Possession of such resources is seen as limiting a family or individual's vulnerability to or risk of poverty over an extended period of time (INSEE, 1987, pp. 234ff.). Antipoverty strategies are designed to overcome such vulnerability, in particular by focusing on groups that are particularly likely to live in poverty, especially the long-term unemployed, single mothers, and young people of both sexes who have difficulty finding permanent employment. Increasingly, pension programs, including special provisions for women whose labor force participation was disrupted due to child care or a broken marriage, have made the elderly a much less vulnerable group than previously (CERC, 1988, p. 17).[8]

As part of this strategy, policymakers have come to realize that the economic well-being of all types of families depends upon women being in the labor force. Family programs are now designed to encourage women to reenter the labor force when their youngest child reaches the age of 3. As long as there is a child under 3 in the family many benefits will make some compensation for the absence (or "loss") of the mother's wage; with no young child in the home, eligibility for several programs terminates. For example, the *allocation au jeune enfant* (AJE, the benefit to a young child)—available to all families from the fourth month of pregnancy until the child is three months old—becomes a means-tested benefit available until the child reaches age 3. The AJE can serve as an important source of supplementary income for mothers of young children who work part time or irregularly. However, the expectation is clear that by the time the child reaches 3, the family's income will be sufficient (albeit perhaps supplemented by other benefits). The *allocation parentale d'education* (benefit to a parent involved in educating a child) is a payment to families with three or more children in which one of the parents gives up work in order to raise the children. This benefit, too, is available only as long as there is a child under age 3 in the family and one parent is not employed full time. It may, however, be combined with part-time work or training programs (in the year before the child turns 3) to allow the parent to reenter the labor force with stronger qualifications.

With programs such as these, the long-standing pronatalist goals of French family policy are reconciled with the goals, on the one hand, of income redistribution and, on the other, of giving married women a choice whether to work or not and of encouraging single mothers to be self-supporting, even if their incomes must be supplemented by social benefits. The coincidence of goals is revealed first by the fact that efforts to insert single mothers into the labor force came simultaneously with the creation of a new benefit for single parents—*allocation de parent isolé* (API)—in 1976. This means-tested benefit is available to pregnant women and to single parents supporting children under 17, or under 20 if the children are in school or an apprenticeship program.[9] Intended to offset the financial strain of becoming a single parent, the API lasts for one year or until the youngest child reaches the age of 3. Therefore, it can be combined with income from low-wage work. Similarly, a major new program was the *complément familial* (family supplement), which in 1977 replaced three earlier programs and clearly marked a move toward a philosophy of redistribution and acceptance of working mothers. It is a means-tested payment, similar in amount to that of the AJE, for families with more than three children whose resources are limited. Access to this benefit no longer depends on families having a single income, as did one of the programs it replaced (Laroque, 1985, pp. 271–272).

But to relate these responses to prevention of family poverty it is important to understand more generally the family policy of the French government. Since the interwar years, the state has assumed responsibility for encouraging childbearing in order to overcome the country's traditionally low birth rate. The system that was selected in the 1930s and enacted in various pieces of legislation was tightly tied to a strategy for the redistribution of income from those with no or few children to those with more. From the beginning the pronatalist design was clear; benefit rates for family allowances rose for each subsequent child. After World War II the redesigned system was even more pronatalist in that it only paid benefits for two or more children.

Overall the primary pillar of family policy remains the *allocation familiale* (family allowance), which goes to all families with at least two children. This basic benefit is indexed to the minimum wage (SMIC) and paid to all families, whether one or both parents are income earners. The definition of "family" is a broad one, meaning any adult(s), whether citizens or not, supporting children under age 17 (or 20 if they are in school). These are substantial payments, especially for more than three children. They amount to about 12 percent of the minimum wage for two children but 27 percent for three children, with an additional 15 percent paid for each additional child. Thus, a family with five children would receive 2,635 francs in 1987, which was 150 percent of the minimum wage or SMIC (Lefaucher, 1988, p. 52). Therefore, families have come to count on the allowances as a crucial source of income. In a 1986 survey study, only 27 percent of the recipients of family allowances thought they would be able to balance the family budget if they did not receive the allowances, and 38 percent thought it would be very difficult or impossible to do so (Grignon, 1986, p. 15).

Around this pillar of family policy intense debates were conducted about the form and specifics of other benefits. Whereas in the politics of the Liberation the Christian Democrats had a great deal of influence and could impose their vision of the ideal family in policy, by the early 1950s the rebalancing of political forces transformed this policy arena into one based less on traditional Catholic notions of the family and more on income redistribution from rich to poor (Laroque, 1985, chaps. 1, 4; Thibault, 1986, pp. 155ff.). The shift is observable in a number of changes. First, the use of family benefits as a mechanism for redistribution occurred as the universality of programs was gradually replaced by a series of income-related benefits such as the AJE and *complément familial*. In the late 1970s and early 1980s in particular the universalistic family allowances lost favor among policymakers—and therefore their budgets did not rise proportionally—while income-related programs that could have redistributive and labor market effects became more popular (CERC, 1984, p. 242).

One striking example, which represents the new trend, was the fate of the *salaire unique* (single salary) benefit. After the war the Christian Democrats had hoped to use this payment as a wage for housewives in order to encourage them to stay home with their children. The payment rate steadily declined. Moreover eligibility declined, too, as access was withdrawn from nonworking wives without children and from mothers with no children under the age of 6. These two shifts reflected, even in the 1950s, the pressure on the French government from

Left parties and unions that opposed policies encouraging women to stay out of the paid labor force (INSEE, 1987, pp. 468–476; Laroque, 1985). By the 1970s this benefit was being used as a way to finance training for women so that they could enter or reenter the labor force, and it finally disappeared with the creation of the *complément familial* as a means-tested benefit for families with at least three children.

Another major shift in family policy in the 1970s came with the clear acceptance that healthy families could indeed have two employed parents. Therefore, programs were developed to subsidize child care expenses and to meet the needs of particular categories of families, especially single-parent families. In the same way, various housing allowances and housing programs were developed to allow *any* family whose resources fell below a means-tested level to raise children in circumstances considered healthy and sound. In addition, fiscal reforms were instituted to remove any tax penalties for families with two earners. Also, as was indicated above, single parents or two-parent poor families often received additional benefits. For example, there is the *allocation de soutien familial* (family support benefit) that goes to all children who are orphans or supported by only one parent (who is not living conjugally with someone). It lasts until the child is 17 years of age and is not means-tested. This is also the benefit paid when a nonresident parent fails to meet child support payments and the state is mandated to collect such payments.

By way of concluding this discussion of family policy, it can be said that there is no evidence in the detailed evaluations of these programs that they serve as a disincentive to work for single parents, who have as a whole a higher rate of labor force participation than do women living with a spouse. There does, however, seem to be some encouragement to women living with a partner to leave the labor force after the birth of a third child; the substantial increase in the benefits for families with more than three children is a legacy of pronatalism in French family policy.

There are two major characteristics of French family policy that need to be stressed. The first is that family policy has been, from the beginning, a terrain of conflict between Right and Left. Whereas the Right has tended to try to use family programs to advance not only pronatalism but also traditional family forms, the Left has moved to use it as a mechanism of income redistribution and to demonstrate acceptance of all kinds of families, including unmarried couples and single parents. Nevertheless, this long-standing dispute has resulted over time in quite consistent policies, demonstrating the effects of compromise. After 1945 both pronatalist and equality goals resulted in a program focused on the needs of children, irrespective of the "morality" or other life situations of their parents. Therefore, nontraditional families have always been recognized in French programs and, indeed, as we have seen, single-parent families have become an increasingly important focus. Secondly, the needs of the labor market as well as the ideology of the Left have dictated that families with two working parents are less penalized in programs and that working single mothers are considered the norm. Child care programs, benefits to supplement inadequate income, and maternity and parental leaves have also been developed. Various benefits are designed to facilitate the combination of paid work and family responsibilities. These compromises have shown that French family policy is a flexible instrument for responding to social changes and for mediating the transition of women from one life situation to another.

FEMINIZATION OF POVERTY

It remains difficult to estimate the extent of the feminization of poverty in France. With a rising concern about poverty in recent years, related primarily to the effects of long-term unemployment for the whole population and especially joblessness among young people, the French state has begun to study the issue more extensively. It has developed a concept of being "at risk" of poverty, which takes into account all the resources, including income, education, training, and health of the family members. Such studies have found that people most at risk are single-parent families, large families, and families with only one wage earner. Moreover, family breakup and/or unemployment, once unemployment benefits have run out, are the best predictors that any particular family will find itself in poverty (Dupré et al., 1986; INSEE, 1987, p. 235). This analysis has sustained French governments' continued attention to using labor market and family policy as tools to fight poverty. And, not surprisingly, young single mothers who have never been in the labor force, and therefore have not accumulated unemployment benefits, are a prime focus of antipoverty thinking, and rightly so. Fully 83 percent of single women, with or without children, who made use of social services in 1985 lacked unemployment benefits either because they had run out or because the woman had never worked (Dupré et al., 1986, pp. 24ff.).

The effects of family benefits are to reduce poverty substantially. For example, one study based on the entire population of 4.4 million families that received one of the benefits administered by the *Caisse National des Allocations Familiales* (CNAF) measured the income of all the families before family benefits were paid. At that point 18 percent fell below the poverty line established by the study.[10] After the payment of all benefits poverty was substantially reduced, leaving 3.5 percent of all families and 13.5 percent of single mothers' incomes still below the poverty line. Overall the CNAF study found that family benefits reduced the numbers of poor, two-parent families by 75 percent. The figure for single-parent families, 63 percent, is smaller but nonetheless considerable. Single-parent families were 16 percent of all families in the sample and 42 percent of the families who remained poor after family benefits were paid (CERC, 1987, p. 54).

Thus there is evidence that family policy does combat poverty. Nevertheless, the legacies of pronatalism in it make it less useful than it might be as an antipoverty device. Except for the year after she becomes a single parent, a lone mother with only one child who is older than 3 is outside the purview of family policy as a redistributive mechanism. For such women the effects of labor market policy and family programs that give them access to training and retraining while their children are young are particularly important. A 1981 study found that in France the income of single-parent families was 76 percent that of two-parent families (CERC, 1987, p. 30. table 19). This statistic can be compared to a U.S. figure of 35 percent (U.S. Bureau of the Census, 1983, p. 93). And, as the paragraphs above have indicated, this outcome cannot by any means be attributed to transfer payments alone. It is an effect of women's paid work combined with family benefits. Indeed the negative effects of women's nonparticipation in the labor force are revealed by the fact that two-parent families with only the man in the labor force had incomes 17 percent lower than single-parent families in which the mother was in the labor force (CERC, 1987). Transfer payments are essential for *all* women because, as study after study shows, women who live in a family with only one wage earner are at risk of poverty.

The combined effects, then, of this complex of labor market and family policies have been to prevent poverty from becoming feminized in France. Nevertheless, the unequal gender distribution of unemployment, part-time work, and low-wage work associated with economic restructuring mean that while poverty may not be severely gender-biased in that country, the goal of gender equality remains to be achieved, and without it women may fall even further behind.

NOTES

1. For an analysis of the politics behind these changes, see George Ross and Jane Jenson (1988).

2. The French state recognizes both married and unmarried couples as two-parent "families" in its statistics.

3. Between 1981 and 1985 the number of temporary contracts went from 985,000 to 1,420,000 and increased another 18 percent in 1986.

4. For example, in everyday language as well as in terms of remuneration, part-time and full-time employees doing the same job are differentially recognized. In stores the full-time employees are considered the skilled workers with professional qualifications (a salesperson, for example), whereas a part-time worker is considered less professional and necessary only as a "stop gap" (Maruani and Nicole, 1987, pp. 8–9).

5. For details of several of these programs see Jacqueline Laufer (1986).

6. On the important distinction between a "choice" and a "right," see J. Laufer (1986, p. 75).

7. The concern about the costs of supporting an unemployed single mother through social welfare as well as the long-standing policy of discouraging mothers from giving up their children for adoption results in the everyday practice of social workers encouraging young, single, and untrained pregnant women to consider abortion (Lefaucher, 1988, p. 37).

8. A number of mechanisms have been devised to improve the retirement benefits of women with discontinuous employment records due to childbearing. See Betrand Fragonard (1986, p. 5).

9. This relatively long extension to children in school reflects the French state's concern to break the poverty cycle by allowing children of poor single parents the time to gain some professional training that will permit them to earn their own living (Lefaucher, 1988, pp. 11ff.).

10. The poverty line in this study was 40 percent of the SMIC per unit of consumption, counting 1.0 unit for the first adult, 1.7 for a spouse, and 0.5 for each child. This scheme was based on the Oxford scale (CERC, 1988, pp. 42–44).

REFERENCES

Bouillaguet-Bernard, P., P. Boisard, and M-T. Letablier (1986). "Le partage du travail: une politique asexuée?" *Nouvelles Questions Féministes* (14–15): 31–52.

Boyer, R. (1984). "Wage labor, capital accumulation, and the crisis, 1968–72." In M. Kesselman and G. Groux, eds. *The French Workers' Movement*. London: Allen & Unwin.

Centre d'Etude des Revenus et des Couts (CERC) (1984). *La Croissance et la crise: Les revenus des français 1960–1983*. Paris: Documentation Française (#77).

——— (1987). *Familles nombreuses, mères isolées, situation économique et vulnerabilité*. Paris: Documentation Française (#85).

——— (1988). *Protection sociale et pauvreté: Protection légale et experiences locales de revenu minimum garanti*. Paris: Documentation Française (#88).

Dupré, J-P. et al. (1986). *La pauvreté-précarité en 1985: Diversité des recours à l'action sociale*. Paris: Centre de Recherche Documentaire (CREDOC) (#4939).

Economic Commission for Europe (ECE) (1985). *The Economic Role of Women in the EEC Region: Developments 1975/85*. New York: United Nations.

Fragonard, B. (1986). "Les fondements du système français." *Dossier CAF* 4: 3–10.

Grignon, M. (1986). *La Famille et la politique familiale*. Paris: CREDOC.

Huet, M. (1986). "Déchiffrer le droit à l'emploi." *Nouvelles Questions Féministes* (14–15): 13–30.

Institut National de la Statistique et des Etudes Economiques (INSEE) (1987). *Données Sociales 1987*. Paris: INSEE.

——— (1988). *Enquête sur l'emploi de 1988: Resultats détaillés*. Paris: INSEE.

Jenson, J. (1986). "Gender and reproduction: Or, babies and the state." *Studies in Political Economy* 26: 9–46.

——— (1987a). "Changing discourse, changing agendas: Political rights and reproductive policies in France." In M. F. Katzenstein and C. M. Mueller, eds. *The Women's Movements of the United States and Western Europe: Consciousness, Political Opportunity and Public Policy*. Philadelphia: Temple University Press.

——— (1987b). "Liberation and new rights for French women." In M. Higonnet, J. Jenson, S. Michel, and M. Weitz, eds. *Behind the Lines: Gender and the Two World Wars*. New Haven, CT: Yale University Press.

——— (1988). "The limits of 'and the' discourse: French women as marginal workers." In J. Jenson, E. Hagen, and C. Reddy, eds. *The Feminization of the Labour Force: Paradoxes and Promises*. New York: Oxford University Press.

——— (1989). "*Ce n'est pas un hasard*: The varieties of French feminism." In J. Howorth and G. Ross, eds. *Contemporary France: An Interdisciplinary Review*. London: Frances Pinter.

Kergoat, D. (1984). *Les Femmes et le travail partiel*. Paris: Ministère due Travail.

Laroque, Pierre, ed. (1985). *La Politique familiale en France depuis 1945*. Paris: Ministère des Affaires Sociales et de la Solidarité Nationale.

Laufer, J. (1986). "Egalité professionelle: Les politiques d'entreprise." *Nouvelles Questions Féministes* (14–15): 73–92.

Lefaucher, N. (1988). *Rapport sur la situation des familles monoparentales en France*. Paris: GRASS/IRESCO.

Lorée, M. J. (1980). "Equal pay and equal opportunity law in France." In R. S. Steinberg, ed. *Equal Employment Policy for Women: Strategies for Implementation in the United States and Western Europe*. Philadelphia: Temple University Press.

Maruani, M., and C. Nicole (1987). *La Flexibilité dans le commerce: Temps de travail ou mode d'emploi?* Working Papers of the Laboratoire de Sociologie du Travail et des Relations Professionelles. Paris: Conservatoire Nationale des Arts et Métiers (CNAM).

Organization for Economic and Cultural Development (OECD) (September 1988). *Employment Outlook*. Paris: OECD.

Ross, G., and J. Jenson (1985). "Pluralism and the decline of left hegemony: The French left in power." *Politics and Society* 14 (2): 147–183.

―――― (1988). "The tragedy of the French left." *New Left Review* (171): 5–44.

―――― (1989). "*Quel joli consensus!* Strikes and politics in autumn 1988." *French Politics and Society* 7 (1): 15–24.

Thibault, M-N. (1986). "Politiques familiales, politiques d'emploi." *Nouvelles Questions Féministes* (14–15): 147–162.

U.S. Bureau of the Census (1983). *Money Income of Households, Families and Persons in the United States: 1981*. Current Population Reports, Series P–60, No. 137, p. 93. Washington, DC: U.S. Government Printing Office.

6

Sweden: Promise and Paradox

MARGUERITE G. ROSENTHAL

Sweden provides an example of an advanced welfare state; indeed, it is probably the most advanced welfare state in the world. Sweden has a high standard of living, liberal social welfare benefits, centralized social and economic planning, full employment policies, and many social policies designed specifically to enhance women's social and economic position in society and to create equality between the sexes.

The country's accomplishments are remarkable. Over the past two decades, women have entered the paid labor force in such large numbers that now nearly all women, including mothers of young children, work. Because of consciously devised wage policies that reduce the salary differences between high- and low-wage earners, the full-time earnings of Swedish women come close to those of men. Generous parental leave policies allow mothers and fathers to stay home with newborns and sick children while maintaining their incomes and preserving their jobs. Publicly supported child care programs, while not universal, are generously supported and have been made a priority for future provision in order to facilitate labor force participation by mothers of preschool children. Full employment policies provide retraining and public works positions for redundant workers when the private market cannot absorb them. These employment policies have included efforts to direct women and men toward "nontraditional" jobs. Other social benefits, such as housing grants and child allowances, relieve the financial burdens of families with children, particularly those with relatively low earnings.

Yet Sweden is not nirvana. The occupational structure is remarkably sex segregated, and women hold very few managerial or other high-status positions. Nearly half of the female workforce works part-time. Household roles, too, remain gender-specific, with women performing most of the caretaking tasks. Women's issues, while on the political agenda, have a difficult time being heard, especially when they directly confront men's interests. Single parents, almost all women, are much better off economically than their American counterparts, but they have a distinctly more arduous life than Swedish women in two-parent families. Some critics claim that the administration of the various social welfare programs and the lack of meaningful enforcement of laws to promote equality keep women from achieving true social and economic equality. Of equal concern, some fear that current economic difficulties may augur retrenchment from the commitment to equality between the sexes and retreat from welfare state programs generally. Thus, to borrow (and somewhat alter) a phrase from Jennifer C. Schirmer (1982), the "limits of reform" may have already been reached.

This chapter will provide a history of the more significant social and economic reforms, examine relevant information about the status of Swedish women today and the social and economic programs and policies that affect their daily lives, and look at some of the problems that are yet to be resolved. A particular look will be taken at those that affect the single parent.

HISTORICAL OVERVIEW

Sweden is composed of a relatively stable and homogeneous population of about 8.4 million who are acknowledged as having one of the highest standards of living in the world. In the late 1800s, it was a poor country whose economy was still agriculturally based. During the early part of the nineteenth century, an upsurge in population had resulted in such destitution and unemployment that emigration to America became a favored means of coping with poverty, and one-fifth of the population left the country (Heckscher, 1984, p. 35; Liljeström, Mellstrom, and Svensson, 1978, chapter 1).

Sweden remained predominantly an agricultural society until well into the twentieth century when its industrial base, predominantly mining and metallurgy heavily tied to export, became increasingly important. By World War II (Sweden was comparatively untouched by that war), slightly more than 30 percent of the economically active population were involved in manufacturing, mining, and construction. Following the war, the industrial sector expanded, and full employment was achieved with 45 percent of the paid workforce engaged in industrial occupations. Industrialization was associated with urbanization, and by 1970, only 20 percent of the population lived in sparsely populated areas (Korpi, 1978). By 1986, less than 5 percent of the working population were employed in agriculture and forestry (Swedish Institute, 1986b).

The 1960s were especially prosperous with full employment, a rising standard of living, and increased leisure time (Swedish Institute, 1986c). Responding to the worldwide economic slump since the 1970s, industrial employment has been declining as a percentage of the total labor force. Nonetheless, the Swedish unemployment rate has remained around 2 percent, largely because of the growth of the public sector and because of consciously devised full-employment policies.

UNIONIZATION, THE SOCIAL DEMOCRATIC PARTY, AND SOCIAL POLICY

Capital in Sweden is highly concentrated, and 90 percent of economically active citizens are wage earners (Korpi, 1978, p. 58). The Swedish workforce is highly unionized, with 90 percent of blue- and white-collar workers belonging to unions. Twenty-three white collar unions, representing secretarial, medical, and public sector workers, have largely female memberships. These unions are consolidated into one of three powerful labor confederations (Heclo and Madsen, 1987, chapter 1). Led by the important Metalworkers' Union, labor has had close ties to the Social Democratic Party, which has controlled the government for all but six years since 1932. The labor movement and the Social Democratic Party have, from the beginning, adopted a pragmatic, reformist approach to economic and social policy.

Beginning in the 1930s, the Swedish government adopted Keynesian economic policies to stimulate the economy and reduce unemployment. Concern about population declines was stimulated by Alva and Gunnar Myrdal's 1934 book, *Crisis and Population*. The result was a broad discussion about the role of government in reducing the economic burdens for families with children. A Population Commission was appointed, and it made many recommendations for governmental intervention. In the 1940s, maternity benefits, housing assistance for large families, tax exemptions for families with children, and subsidized school meals and children's clothing were enacted. Building on voluntary pension and disability insurance schemes, Sweden adopted a basic pension provision to assure an income to all citizens regardless of their employment history. In the late 1940s, a children's allowance scheme was legislated (Scott, 1982). Thus, an elaborate complex of universal and targeted benefits has been created to promote the well-being of the population and to equalize consumption. The Swedish social welfare programs include health insurance, pensions, children's allowances, paid parental leaves, housing assistance, child care, and home care for the elderly.

Sweden is unique among the capitalist countries in its commitment to redistribution of income in order to assure the well-being of its members. As Britta Hoem and Jon M. Hoem stress:

Sweden is firmly committed to the extensive responsibility of its public authorities for the welfare of its citizens within the framework of a democratic society. To this end, public policies influence working life and people's private economic situation more strongly than in many other Western countries. Perhaps more than elsewhere, priority is given to ensuring a decent level of living for everyone rather than to letting market forces provide a wide range of choices to those who can afford it (1987c, p. 4).

Redistribution is accomplished through a steeply graduated income tax, which taxes the highest earners at over 40 percent of their incomes and reduces the ratio of the highest decile of earners to lowest from 8:1 to 5:1 (Åberg, Selen, and Tham, 1987). After transfer payments, the ratio is reduced even further. One study shows that when disposable income is adjusted for family size and the number of earners per household, the ratio drops to about 3:1 (p. 140).

SIGNIFICANT DEVELOPMENTS IN WOMEN'S HISTORY IN SWEDEN

The role of women in Swedish society has undergone a rather remarkable transformation since the 1950s. During the late 1800s, population excesses led to low rates of marriage (about one-fifth of the population never married), emigration, and a surplus of unmarried women. Unmarried mothers and widows were supported by the traditional poor relief system in the rural areas, while in the cities, women's labor was exploited on the rationale that such employment was temporary (Liljeström, Mellstrom, and Svensson, 1978). These attitudes persisted well into the twentieth century. For instance, married women needed their husbands' permission to work outside of the home until 1921 when universal suffrage was achieved. It was not until 1927 that state grammar schools were opened to girls, and separate schools for adolescent girls and boys with separate vocational preparation were maintained until the early 1960s. Until 1939, an employer had the right to dismiss a female employee on the grounds of marriage, pregnancy, or confinement, and not until 1947 did the civil service abolish separate and lower wage rates for women (Statistics Sweden, 1985). The worlds of work and home were traditional and patriarchal until the mid-twentieth century.

Modern feminism in Sweden dates from the late 1950s, following a decade of rapid increases in the percentages of women working. Discussions about sex role expectations were held both in intellectual circles and in the popular press. In 1960, Social Democratic women's organizations were successful in forcing the Party to form a prestigious study group on "women's questions"; Prime Minister Tage Erlander served as honorary chair, and many prominent women were members. The group issued a report in 1964 that supported sex role equality, and in 1969 its recommendations—to use governmental policy in ways to eliminate sex discrimination and to promote opportunities for women to participate fully in all aspects of life—were approved as part of the Social Democratic Party platform (Scott, 1982, chapter 1). The recommendations, nearly all of which have subsequently been legislated, focused on provisions to facilitate women's participation in the workforce, such as day care, as well as measures to promote women's employment and to increase equality in the workplace. Following the recommendations of a parliament-appointed committee, the Swedish Act on Equality between Women and Men at Work was passed in 1980.

Since the late 1960s, Swedish society has continued to be actively engaged in debating issues concerned with women's equality and in creating affirmative measures to deal with some of the more compelling issues that have curtailed women's full participation in economic, social, and political life. This debate and the development of policy have taken place within the context of achieving a high standard of living, a structure of relative wage equality, and a broad system of universal and specific benefits for the whole population.

WOMEN'S LABOR FORCE PARTICIPATION AND PUBLIC POLICY

Entry into the Labor Market

The trend for increased labor force participation by women began in the late 1940s when Sweden, like other industrialized countries, experienced an increased demand for industrial workers. In Sweden, a declining birth rate, the extension of compulsory schooling, the shorter workday and a drop in the numbers of unmarried women available for work all contributed to a reduction in the labor reserve (Liljeström, Mellstrom, and Svensson, 1978, chapter 1; Scott, 1982, chapter 1). Initially, labor shortages were made up by encouraging immigration, largely from Finland but from southern Europe as well. The Swedish trade unions, however, opposed these policies because they threatened wage rates. In the 1960s, government responded by curtailing immigration from countries outside of Scandinavia, and labor shortages began to be filled by married women, including those with young children. Consciously devised economic policies contributed to the massive entry of women into the paid labor force. Principal among these were the introduction in 1971 of separate taxation of spouses. This development had the effect of reducing the marginal tax rate of working wives. Previously, the income of a couple was combined and taxed together, with the wife's income added to her husband's, usually at a point where the tax rate was high. In addition, a solidaristic wage policy, designed to reduce wage disparities between high and low earners, and various employment strategies to encourage full employment contributed to increased numbers of women wage earners (Scott, 1982, chapter 1).

After 1965, there was a dramatic increase in the number of women in the paid labor force. In 1968, about one-half of married women ages 15 to 74 were in the paid workforce, although only one-third of mothers of small children were so involved; by 1981, these figures had grown to over three-fourths of both (Åberg, 1987). By 1985, approximately 80 percent of all Swedish women worked outside of the home; those not working were, for the most part, over 50 years old (S. Gustafsson, 1987).

Full Employment Policy

A hallmark of the Social Democratic government in Sweden has been a commitment to full employment for all workers. While some feared that the massive entrance of women into the workforce might displace male workers or reduce the wage scale, these events did not occur. Instead, the organs of government responsible for labor market policies have had to adjust to include actual and potential women workers in their programs.

The Swedish economy is highly planned and regulated by the government in concert with both employer and labor confederations (Bosworth and Rivlin, 1987; Ginsburg, 1983; Korpi, 1978; Ruggie, 1984). Specific labor market policies are used to stimulate the economy and to promote job creation and a productive workforce (Ginsburg, 1983, chapter 5).

Key to the implementation of this full employment policy is the *Arbetsmar-knadsstyrelsen* (AMS), the Swedish Labor Market Board, a body funded by the Parliament and composed primarily of representatives from the central government, labor, and business. The AMS keeps close watch on the economy and directly intervenes to counteract increasing rates of unemployment through such measures as releasing investment-reserve funds to stimulate investment during periods of economic downturn. It operates a comprehensive and efficient job referral service and provides sophisticated training for workers whose skills are obsolete or insufficient. Trainees are paid stipends while they participate. When the economy is particularly bad, the AMS provides relief work, paid at regular wages, to combat cyclical and seasonal unemployment. Relief jobs are, typically, forestry and road work for men and social services or health-related positions for women, although there have been some attempts to mitigate sex segregation in these positions (Ginsburg, 1983, chapter 7).

The employment service has a very high staff-to-client ratio (about 1:15) and is considered very effective in assisting job seekers in finding appropriate work. Continual labor market analysis is an important component of the AMS's work, and job training and retraining are closely linked to projections for future labor force needs (Ginsburg, 1983, chapter 6; Ruggie, 1984, chapter 4).

These measures have proved to be fairly successful, and unemployment rates in Sweden have remained low. In the 1970s, the unemployment figures averaged around 2 percent (Ginsburg, 1983, p. 119); in the mid–1980s it rose somewhat but remained under 4 percent (Swedish Institute, 1986c). It has since fallen, and in the summer of 1988 the economy was again in an expansive state, and unemployment was not considered a problem. Unemployment statistics do not include workers involved in various labor market programs; students; workers on temporary, state-supported leaves such as parental leave; or pensioners. Nevertheless, a relatively high percentage of Swedes are in the labor force (83 percent of those between the ages of 15 and 65 versus 76 percent of Americans in 1984) (Rivlin, 1987, p. 41).

Part-time Work and Occupational Segregation

Although Swedish women have a very high rate of labor force participation and a low rate of unemployment, the prevalence of part-time work and occupational segregation indicate persisting economic inequality. Nevertheless, wage policies and especially supplementary social welfare benefits have helped women, particularly single mothers, avoid economic deprivation.

Nearly 90 percent of part-time workers are women (Sundström, 1987, pp. 15–16). Between 1970 and 1980, three times as many women entered the work force as part-time workers than as full-time workers. In 1986, 43 percent of working women were employed part time, and, on the average, women in the labor market worked 26.1 hours per week (pp. 15–21). The current trend, however, is for women to increase their working hours. Women with preschool children are most likely to work fewer hours; they are likely to return to longer part-time or full-time work when their children enter school (Persson-Tanimura, 1988; Sundström, 1987).

There are several explanations for the extent of part-time work. Selective recruitment of women to fill part-time jobs during the 1960s and 1970s is one explanation (Ericsson and Jacobsson, 1985). Another is that the newly entering women workers preferred part-time work, and employers accommodated themselves to this preference (Sundström, 1987). Marianne Sundström, who has studied this question extensively, has provided two additional interpretations: (1) marginal tax rates increase as salaries increase, and thus part-time workers take home a greater percentage of their incomes than do full-time workers (when tax rates were cut in 1982, the proportion of full-time female workers increased for the first time in twenty years); and (2) part-time workers are not penalized substantially in their receipt of benefits—including child care, vacation, sick pay, pensions, and especially parental insurance—because the disparity in benefits earned by full- and part-time workers has narrowed. Therefore, women can act on their preferences for part-time work (1987, chapter 8).

Whether women actually prefer reduced hours of paid work, however, is still open to question. Inga Persson-Tanimura (1988) reported on a recent study that shows that women prefer market work to household chores and, indeed, like paid employment as much as men do. Sven Nelander (personal communication, August 16, 1988), who is principal researcher for the *Landsorganisationen* (LO, the industrial labor confederation), described a study that found that one-quarter of women in that labor confederation want more work but in some cases are forced to accept part-time work because work schedules have been geared to a six-hour day. For example, hospitals, which are highly dependent on a female workforce, are organized around six-hour shifts despite the fact that they are short-handed and would benefit from added work hours. Another recent report states that 12 percent of Swedish women who work part-time would prefer to work full-time (OECD, 1988). Thus, many women are being forced to accept part-time work.

The occupational categories that women have filled, both in the private and especially in the public sector, have tended to mirror their traditional caretaking roles. Fully 57 percent of Swedish women work in the public sector. They are mostly in service jobs, particularly child care, nursing, and care of the elderly, in addition to office work (Ericsson and Jacobsson, 1985). These public sector jobs have both provided women with income and have relieved them of providing unpaid services to these same populations.

Swedish women work in a sex-segregated labor market that is characterized by little occupational diversity. In 1985, nearly half of working women were in ten occupations in which they comprised 78 to 98 percent of the workforce: secretaries/typists, nursing assistants, shop assistants, cleaners, childminders, homehelpers, accountants/office cashiers, nurses, junior school teachers, and kitchen staff (National Labor Market Board, 1987, p. 21). Women predominate, that is they comprise more than 60 percent of the labor force, in 44 occupations, while men predominate in 138 occupations (Ericsson and Jacobsson, 1985). Indeed, the sex segregation is so great that one writer concluded that 70 percent of all women would have had to change occupations in order to achieve the same occupational distributions as men (Åberg, 1987, p. 85, citing C. Jonung).

Åberg (1987, p. 86) found that between 1968 and 1981 there were increases in the percentages of women in many occupations dominated by men; however, these gains were more than offset by the growth of occupations with sex-segregated workforces. Perhaps most illuminating is the fact that, in the late 1970s, managerial positions were held by only 0.2 percent of all women as compared to 7 percent of men, and women occupied only 3 percent of senior executive positions (Ericsson and Jacobsson, 1985, p. 20). Although it is difficult to make crossnational comparisons regarding sex segregation in the labor market, this is clearly one area in which Sweden is not a leader.

Immigrant women are a particularly disadvantaged group. Sweden experienced two large waves of immigration in the 1960s during a period of widespread labor shortages. While the largest number came from other Nordic countries, particularly Finland, considerable numbers came from Yugoslavia, Greece, and Turkey. Today, approximately 1 million people, or about one-eighth of the Swedish population, are either foreign born or have at least one immigrant parent (Swedish Institute, 1986a). Current immigration regulations restrict settlement in Sweden to all except citizens of other Nordic countries and political refugees. These restrictive immigration policies are clearly related to the tightening of the labor market.

While efforts are made by the Swedish government to integrate immigrants and to preserve their culture, the shrinking of employment opportunities has had discriminatory effects on immigrant workers. Immigrants are overrepresented in work situations that offer poor working environments, and they frequently do shift work with irregular working hours (Swedish Institute, 1986a). Immigrant women suffer double discrimination: not only are they occupationally segregated because of their sex, but they are quite overrepresented in the least attractive of the "women's work" jobs, such as cleaning and charwork (Leiniö, 1988). Furthermore, immigrant women are typically found in the jobs with the lowest skills and ones that frequently cause physical pain and damage. Even immigrant women who arrived in Sweden with marketable skills have been relegated to very low-level positions (Knocke, n.d.; personal communication, August 9, 1988).

Economic Consequences of Part-time Work and Occupational Segregation

Despite the differences in occupational roles and hours worked, women workers in Sweden fare relatively well in terms of wages. Women's wages rose faster than men's from the late 1960s through the early 1980s (Gustafsson and Jacobsson, 1985; Sundström, 1987), and women have, until recently, profited from the solidaristic wage policy. This policy dates from the 1950s when the LO, the industrial labor confederation, demanded a greater balance in earnings between skilled and unskilled workers and between those in high- and low-productivity jobs. The effort to collapse wage differentials has spilled beyond the blue-collar industries to include white-collar workers as well (Flanagan, 1987). This wage policy has been effectuated through centrally bargained contracts. However, at least one recent investigation (Acker, 1988) indicates that there is a growing trend for individual unions to break away from centralized bargaining, with the result that the age gap between men's and women's full-time wages is now increasing after a twenty-year movement toward greater equality.

By international standards, women's earnings as a percentage of men's are relatively high, but total earnings are clearly affected by part-time work. Women who worked full time earned 78 percent of the wages of full-time men workers in 1985, down from 82 percent in 1983 (Acker, 1988). However, because so many women work part time, only 37 percent of the country's total wages are paid to women (Ericsson and Jacobsson, 1985, p. 18), and the average Swedish woman earns only two-thirds of what the average man earns (S. Gustafsson, 1981). Using data sets from the mid–1970s, Siv Gustafsson (1981) found that when women's and men's education and work history were equal, Swedish women's lifetime earnings were 80 to 84 percent of men's. For American women, the figure was 76 percent.

While social welfare policies help to narrow wage differences between women and men in the short run, women's patterns of labor force participation have significant negative long-term effects. For example, interruptions in work careers can have especially difficult consequences for women who divorce after having established a pattern of part-time work, since their incomes and their opportunities for job mobility are less than those of full-time workers. These problems are particularly acute for those who divorce after children are grown since they are no longer eligible for many of the social welfare benefits available to those with children at home (Wistrand, 1981, p. 35). In addition, since pensions are based on former income, women who are or will be dependent on their own pensions exclusively are economically disadvantaged (Baude, 1979; 1986).

Policies to Promote Equality

Sweden has tried several different approaches to reducing sex segregation in the labor force. The Swedish Labor Market Board, or AMS, has been particularly active in efforts to counteract the job segregation and lower pay that women workers experience. Specifically, it has sponsored programs to upgrade women's participation in higher skilled and higher paying industrial positions. One technique has been to assist industrial expansion into new endeavors and into new geographical locations through loans, grants, and wage subsidies. Since 1974, these funding schemes have used an innovative quota system to promote affirmative action by requiring that newly created positions be filled by at least 40 percent of each sex. Another scheme has provided "equality grants" to subsidize employers for training of employees hired for positions usually filled by workers of the opposite sex.

The AMS has made other efforts to encourage women to take nontraditional jobs. In one well-known experiment, the Kristianstad project, women job seekers were actively recruited for industrial positions normally held by men. The project resulted in the successful employment of many women in nontraditional blue-collar jobs. Subsequently, these techniques were replicated in other districts. However, several observers have concluded that the efforts to increase the numbers of women in such positions were related to labor shortages rather than to a true commitment to desegregating the workforce. In fact, under a less expansive economy, the push to employ women in traditionally male jobs has subsided (Eduards, Halsaa, and Skjeie, 1985; Scott, 1982, chapter 2). In addition, the number of equality grants has declined substantially since the late 1970s (National Labor Market Board, 1987, p. 20), and there has been a reversion to the clear segregation in the blue-collar sector (S. Gustafsson, 1984; Liljeström, Mellstrom and Svensson, 1978; Ruggie, 1984).

The AMS continues to hold to goals of greater job diversity for women. On the national level there is concern that young women leaving secondary school continue to have relatively high unemployment rates because many have studied office skills, for which there is a declining demand. Indeed, higher echelon employees are increasingly expected to do their own word processing, and secretarial jobs are being eliminated. However, women have been reluctant to seek or retrain for industrial jobs, according to one official in the AMS (Yvonne Leimar, personal communication, August 17, 1988). In fact, in August 1988, on a study visit to Sweden, this writer observed total sex segregation in a model training institute in Karlstad: women were only studying word processing and other office skills while only men were receiving training in a variety of highly technical industrial techniques.

Sweden has also used legislation to try to improve the work opportunities for women. In 1980, the Act on Equality between Men and Women at Work was passed. This act bans discrimination at the workplace and applies to both private and public settings. It also seeks to promote greater equality between women and men by establishing goals of more equal distribution of the sexes in job categories through recruitment, training, and promotions. There is an enforcement mechanism through the office of the equality ombudsman (Ministry of Labor, 1985).

It has been generally concluded that the Act on Equality has not been particularly effective, and several explanations have been offered. The law relies primarily upon voluntary compliance, and there has been considerable resistance to affirmative action, particularly among groups of organized male workers. For example, by law, union contracts may state that goals to hire women in order to comply with affirmative action requirements will not be adhered to. In these cases, employers are exempt from compliance with the Act. One report claims that unions have been obstructionist about representing women who file sex discrimination complaints and in some cases have even retaliated against them (Fleischauer, 1987). The equality ombudsman, an official charged with investigating and resolving charges of sex discrimination, must rely upon complaints in order to take action. Most complaints have concerned gender-based advertising rather than specific acts of sex discrimination in hiring or promotion by employers. Finally, it has been more difficult to enforce compliance in the private sector than in the public sector where opportunities for women have generally been better in the first place (S. Gustafsson, 1984).

Because of the disappointing results of these various measures to achieve equality in the workplace and because of anticipated changes in the labor market including slower growth of the public sector and increased automation of industry, the current emphasis has shifted to the education of female students in order to expose them to a variety of career choices. For example, a summer school program in which about half of Sweden's municipalities are participating, exposes eighth-grade girls to theoretical instruction and hands-on experience in technical areas and manual skills (Ministry of Labor, Secretariat for Equality between Women and Men, n.d.).

The current emphasis on the educational system appears to be well placed, but it is not a novel approach and probably will not be sufficient to overcome traditional occupational choices. An evaluation of curriculum reforms introduced in 1970–1971 and similarly designed to introduce students to studying or training for nontraditional careers shows very few gains in changing sex-segregated study and occupational choices among students (Scott, 1984). Recent government reports show that, although guidance officers in the schools are supposed to challenge conventional stereotypes, the choices girls and boys make in secondary education (where vocational training begins for those not going on to the university) and in universities and colleges remain traditional. For example, in upper secondary schools in 1983, 97 percent of students training for electrotelecommunications were boys whereas 95 percent of those preparing to work in the social services were girls. Similarly, and in the same year, while the majority of first-year college and university students were women, they were only 23 percent of the students studying technical subjects but comprised the overwhelming majority of students in nursing and related subjects (Swedish Institute, 1984b).

Other efforts to achieve greater equality involve integrating equality issues into the labor planning process. Regional Labor Market Boards are now required to submit, along with their annual employment and population forecasts, analyses of the position of women in the labor and education systems. This process forces them to look more thoroughly at ways of dealing with sex imbalances (Ministry of Labor, Secretariat for Equality between Women and Men, n.d.).

However, the long-term picture for expanding occupational choices seems clouded, and the difficulties appear to be largely structural rather than ideological (Scott, 1984). That is, women have served as a labor reserve, and are called upon to fill traditionally male jobs, which are generally more highly skilled and better paying, only when there are labor shortages. This is what happened in the late 1960s and early 1970s. However, with increasing automation, the demand for unskilled blue-collar jobs will decrease. Without highly technical training, women will not be needed in industrial jobs. Instead, they will remain segregated in caretaking and other largely public-sector jobs, receiving lower wages and having restricted job mobility.

DEMOGRAPHIC FACTORS

The contemporary Swedish family is regarded as a somewhat unique phenomenon. Demographers note that there have been dramatic changes in family-related behavior since the early 1960s, or since women started entering the workforce in large numbers. Perhaps the most remarked upon characteristic is the high rate of cohabitation and the corresponding dramatic decline of formal marriages, particularly among young couples. Although precise statistics are not available, most demographers agree that Sweden has the lowest marriage rate and the highest cohabitation rate of any industrialized country (Popenoe, 1986).

In 1984, 45 percent of babies were born to unmarried women, as compared to 20 percent for the United States. However, nearly all these babies were born to cohabiting couples. Indeed, it is a common pattern for Swedish couples to have one or two children before marrying. Births to teenage mothers are very low in Sweden, 16 per 1,000 women aged 15 to 19 as compared to 54 per 1,000 in the United States (Jones et al., 1986). Further, the age at which women bear their first children has been rising and now stands at approximately age 27. Thus, the first child is usually born after a woman has established a position in the labor market, is able to take advantage of job-related maternity rights, and has a permanent labor force attachment (Hoem and Hoem, 1987b). Having two children has emerged as the norm for Swedish women (Hoem and Hoem, 1987a).

Of increasing interest to demographers and of concern to sociologists and social welfare planners is the dissolving of formal marriages and cohabitating relationships. Concurrently, there has been a growth of single-parent families. Precise data are difficult to obtain, but a recent study found that the divorce rate expected for the cohort born in 1945 is 36 percent (compared to 42 percent in the United States). The high divorce rate exists despite the lessening of economic and related stressors that are believed to contribute to divorce and despite the relative freedom with which Swedes experiment with "trial marriages" (Popenoe, 1986). Further, because a high percentage of children are born to consensual unions, because these unions may be increasing, and because they are less stable than marital unions, it is reasonable to conclude that the numbers of single-parent families will continue to grow. At present, 20 percent of all families with children are headed by single parents, one-fourth of all children live with only one parent, and, after divorce, five of six children live with their mothers (Eriksson, 1987).

SOCIAL POLICIES

While labor market policies have not been entirely successful in reducing economic and related inequities for women, various social policies have given the entire Swedish population a very high standard of living. These policies have substantially mitigated the stresses, economic insecurities, and hardships that typically dominate the lives of working class people and, in particular, those households headed by single mothers. Sweden also has a universal health care system and a retirement insurance system that provide a floor of economic and social protection that individuals elsewhere must provide for themselves.

Income supports and family policies assist both the single-parent family and the family in which both parents work. These policies are designed to achieve income stability, promote participation in the labor market, ease the burden of women's dual role, assure familial stability in response to crisis or routine disruption (the birth or illness of a child, for instance), and achieve greater equality in the roles of women and men in the domestic sphere.

Income Supports

A *children's allowance* is paid for all children under 16 years of age. In 1987, this allowance was approximately $78 or 485 Swedish crowns (SEK), per month per child. There are additional supplements for families with more than two children. This allowance is a universal, tax-free benefit and is adjusted yearly to equal about 5 percent of the average wage (Eriksson, 1987; Kahn and Kamerman, 1983; Kamerman and Kahn, 1987).

A *housing allowance* is available, on an income-tested basis, to assist families whose rent is costly. About 30 percent of all families with children receive a housing subsidy, and 60 percent of those with three or more children do so. Eligibility levels are lower for single-parent households, and about 75 percent of these families receive housing allowances (Kamerman and Kahn, 1987; Swedish Institute, 1984d).

Housing needs for low-income families are largely met by local governments that are responsible for development of rental dwellings through public housing corporations. About 45 percent of the housing stock are rental units, and about half of these are owned by public corporations. Insufficient and overcrowded housing conditions that prevailed after World War II have been eliminated through aggressive building programs (Swedish Institute, 1984c).

The *maintenance allowance* is the child support payment that noncustodial parents are obligated to pay. The amount may be set through voluntary agreement, through the social service office, or, in the case of disagreement, by a court ruling. The government assures that children will receive support by providing an *advance maintenance allowance* that is then collected through its debt-collection agency. Most child support is collected and paid through this agency, either through wage withholding or through voluntary payments by the noncustodial parent. The advance maintenance is set at a uniform level, that is, it does not vary according to the father's ability to pay. The amount is equal to 30 to 40 percent of an indexed "base amount," a living allowance computed to cover the basic needs of a single adult. The noncustodial parent's obligation takes into account his or her own maintenance needs and the needs of others with whom he or she may be living, such as a new spouse and children or stepchildren. Payments are also reduced in the case of joint or shared custody arrangements (Eriksson, 1987). As a result, although about 83 percent of support obligations are recovered by the government, these collections cover only 35 percent of the monies paid out as advance maintenance payments (Kamerman and Kahn, 1987). In 1987, the monthly advance maintenance allowance was $130 (SEK 817), while the average amount collected from the noncustodial parent was $72 (SEK 450). Thus, the maintenance advance is really serving as a supplementary grant to the custodial parent and her children.

Social assistance, the closest equivalent to public assistance in the United States, is a means-tested program administered by the municipalities but mandated by national law. According to the Social Services Act of 1980 the assistance "must assure the individual of a reasonable level of living" (Ministry of Health and Social Affairs, 1981). It is calculated by the national social welfare administration (*Socialstyrelsen*) and, like the advance maintenance payment, is set according to the "base amount." The administration produces a model budget, which includes not only food and clothing costs but also such items as newspapers, television licenses, and other leisure expenses. Municipalities must base their assistance grants on the proposed budget. Actual amounts given vary between 80 and 140 percent of the base amount. In August 1988, a single mother with children ages 3 and 6 received $808 (SEK 5050) plus housing costs (Bergittå Akerlind, *Socialstyrelsen*, personal communication, August 8, 1988).

Social assistance, then, can provide income support or supplementation for those whose other sources of income do not total the base amount. Although conceived primarily as a program for childless adults, about 40 percent of single mothers and their children received social assistance in 1985, and the average length of time during which they received this help was four and a half months.

Of all families with children who used social assistance, 53 percent were single-parent families and nearly all of these were headed by women (Nordic Council of Ministers, 1988, p. 97). Since only one-fifth of families with children are headed by single parents, it is clear that there is a disproportionate use of social assistance by single mothers.

Paid employment, coupled with the various grants and allowances cited above, are the primary means by which single parents support their families. The extensive use of social assistance by single parents is an indication that their earnings are inadequate and less stable than the earnings of couples.

Family Policies

Child care has been developed primarily as a means to allow mothers of young children to work and is primarily a municipal responsibility, but parents and the state also pay part of the costs. Most public group care facilities are located in residential areas, and they care for about 29 percent of children under the age of 7, when children enter public school. There are also private group care providers who care for about 18 percent of children in full-time care. Over half of preschool children are cared for by parents, relatives, neighbors, and privately hired help, but by the time they are 6 years old, nearly all children attend either full- or part-time public facilities (Swedish Institute, 1987).

Group care is of a high quality and therefore expensive. Nearly all staff members are trained, and the staff-to-children ratio is very high. Child care settings are seen as places to stimulate and support children's growth and learning (Swedish Institute, 1987). Leisure time centers, also municipally provided, care for school-age children, but they provide places for only a small percentage of these children, mostly those aged 7 to 9 (Swedish Institute, 1987). Professional women appear to make greater use of group care than do blue-collar women (Gustafsson and Stafford, 1988).

Single parents have certain advantages in obtaining child care. They pay lower fees for their children, about 57 percent of the amount paid by two-parent families. Moreover, most communities give priority to children of single parents, so that 70 to 80 percent of single parents who are working or studying use public child care (Eriksson, 1987; S. Gustafsson, 1987). Further, all school children receive a free lunch, and the school day ends at 4 P.M., alleviating parents of some child caring tasks (S. Gustafsson, 1987).

Parental leaves are innovative benefits designed both to compensate parents for time they spend at home with newborns or sick children and to encourage shared parental responsibility. They are financed through the national health insurance system and have replaced maternity benefits of various kinds. Enacted originally in 1975 these benefits have since been expanded and now compensate for 90 percent of the parent's gross earned income for twelve months of full-time leave following the birth or adoption of a child. An additional three months may be taken at a fixed daily rate of about $10 (SEK 60). By mid–1991, parental leave will extend to eighteen months compensated at the full 90-percent rate. At the same time, the employer must hold the worker's job. Fathers are entitled to a ten-day leave at the birth of a child. Therefore, the parental leave must be split between the parents so that only one stays at home at a time. Parental leaves can be spread over a period of four years. In addition, either parent can take time off for the care of a sick child for up to sixty days a year, with the same compensation. Either parent with children under the age of 8 has the right to work six hours a day, but with a corresponding loss of income.

These are policies designed to accommodate the demands of working life and family responsibilities and to reduce the costs of child rearing for working parents. Efforts are made to encourage men to provide child care. For instance, in the summer of 1987, a widely displayed government poster showed a famous athlete holding a child and boasting about taking his parental leave. Nonetheless, these benefits are used primarily by mothers. Thus, while 85 percent of fathers take their ten-day leave at the birth of their children, only 20 percent of them take parental leave. In 1984, for every day a man took parental leave, a women took fifty-two (Statistiska Centralbyran, 1987, table 320). Male industrial workers are much less likely to take parental leave than are professional and public employees, although staying out of work to care for sick children is more evenly shared (Ericsson and Jacobsson, 1985). There is also evidence that employers exert informal pressures to dissuade men from taking parental leaves (Scott, 1982).[1]

The parental leave policy has been quite successful in facilitating the integration of working life with bearing children, and most women postpone having children until they qualify for parental leave. As a measure to induce fathers to take equal responsibility for the care of children, parental leave has been less successful, but it stands as an important social value whose fulfillment is still desired. Parental leave should be seen as an important model for other countries to follow.

FEMINIZATION OF POVERTY?

Abject poverty, homelessness, and social disorganization do not exist in Sweden. There are continuing class differences in material and social amenities available to members of the upper, middle, and working classes, and these issues are frequently discussed. Sweden seems to be without an underclass, indeed without even a concept of it, and it is only recently that Swedish social scientists have begun to talk about a poverty line. Instead, there is a generally high standard of living as demonstrated in a comparative study of levels of living in the Nordic countries (Vogel et al., 1984). Based on 1980 data, the study showed that there is virtually no overcrowded or substandard housing in Sweden. Fully 97 percent of all workers live in dwellings with all modern conveniences, and housing costs consume approximately 20 percent of disposable income. Virtually the entire population owns washing machines and televisions, and there are 348 private cars for each 1,000 inhabitants. Of the entire population, 62 percent had made a trip of at least four days within the year prior to the study. Finally, there was per capita consumption of $4,700, $480 of which was spent on leisure, entertainment, and education.

The most recent analysis of economic resources and their distribution in Sweden compared incomes and consumption patterns in 1967 and 1980 and found that both rose during this period (Åberg, Selen, and Tham, 1987). Pensioners did particularly well, a result of tax and transfer policies, and all classes had at least some disposable surplus income after necessities were met. Families with children fared better than families without, but those with three or more children were economically stressed because transfer programs did not compensate completely for the added expenses of child rearing. Large families fared better after 1983 when children's allowances for the third and subsequent children were increased (Marklund, 1988). Finally, it was found that despite the trend toward equalization of income, "glaring disparities" of wealth and consumption continued without decrease between the economic classes. The working class was still "lagging seriously behind" (Åberg, Selen, and Tham, 1987, p. 150).

Using the social assistance benefit level as a poverty index, two recently published studies deal specifically with the extent of poverty in Sweden (B. Gustafsson, 1988a; 1988b). In 1985, this 'poverty line" was 58 percent of the average adjusted disposable income, and 6 to 8 percent of families with children fell below this index. Slightly more than 20 percent of families with children fell under 125 percent of this poverty line when income from transfer programs was included. Of great interest is the fact that without transfer programs, 42 percent of all families would have been in poverty, including many of the aged and a considerable number of young, single adults (B. Gustafsson, 1988b, pp. 15–20). Björn Gustafsson (1988b) confirms that single-parent households constitute a disproportionate share of families with children who use social assistance. Further, he notes that the numbers of these families grew by one-half in only the four years between 1980 and 1984. In most cases it appears that social assistance is used to supplement other sources of income. Many people eligible for supplemental assistance do not apply for it, so that there is a potential for much greater utilization of social assistance (B. Gustafsson, 1988a).

The overrepresentation of single mothers on social assistance is one indication of their relatively precarious position in the labor market and of their overall poverty. Siv Gustafsson (1987), using different measures of low income as defined in the Swedish tax rules, found that in 1979, 21 percent of single-parent households with one child and 25 percent of those with two children, were living under conditions of economic stress, including many who were living at below subsistence levels. A total of 6 percent of two-parent households were in similar circumstances.

In addition to their relative financial disadvantage, single mothers exert a greater work effort and lead a more arduous life than do women with partners. Thus, single mothers participate in the paid labor force at higher rates than do married mothers (87 percent versus 76 percent), and they work longer hours (34.6 hours versus 26.9 hours per week on the average). Half of all single mothers work full time as compared to about one-fourth of women living with men. These mothers also have longer commuting time and are less likely to take a vacation (S. Gustafsson, 1987). Thus, economic necessity prohibits a single woman from taking full advantage of some of the benefits—particularly the option to work part time if she prefers—which having two incomes allows the more "traditional" family.

These economic difficulties are clearly related to the relatively low wages that many women earn and the clear economic advantages that two-earner households have. A study based on 1985 data shows, in fact, that a typical working-class mother's disposable income, after taxes and transfers, is barely above the social assistance level, even when she works full time (Hedborg and Nelander, 1986).

Heading a household alone in Sweden subjects a woman to clear economic and social disadvantages, and substantial numbers of households headed by single mothers are poor in comparison to other Swedish family units. Nevertheless, tax advantages and transfer programs do assist single parents so that these households are not very much below ones with two earners. Thus, a single mother with one child who works full time has 87 percent of the disposable income per consumption unit of a two-parent household where both parents work full time (S. Gustafsson, 1987). Further, for those families who must rely on social assistance to supplement their earnings or to compensate for lack of earnings, the generosity of the social assistance grant assures that the basic needs of food, clothing, and shelter will be met. Swedish single mothers and their children are virtually assured not to be abjectly destitute.

Compared to similar families in other countries, Swedish lone-parent families are clearly not impoverished. A recent comparative study shows that children in such households are economically better off than children in West Germany, Switzerland, the United Kingdom, Norway, Australia, Canada, and the United States. While 8.6 percent of Swedish children live in single-parent households with an adjusted disposable income below the U.S. poverty line, 51 percent of American children do so (Smeeding, Torrey, and Rein, 1988, p. 102). After taxes and income transfers, 7.5 percent of Swedish single-parent families remain below the poverty line, but 43 percent of similar U.S. families remain impoverished (p. 113).

High labor force participation and, especially, generous transfer programs have succeeded in greatly reducing the poverty rates for single parents and their children in Sweden. In this context, it makes little sense to speak of the feminization of poverty in Sweden, although women's families do have higher rates of poverty than other families.

The population of single mothers and their families is, however, emerging as a subject of some concern to authorities and researchers alike in Sweden. Sune Sunesson and his colleagues at Lund University, for instance, are examining the rather dramatic increase in the percentages of Malmo households utilizing social assistance (10 percent in 1981 rising to 18 percent in 1987), with particular attention to the problem of unemployment and underemployment of women (personal communication, August 12, 1988). A Commission on Single Parents is currently preparing a report on this subject (Sören Kinlund, personal communication, August 16, 1988). Swedish social workers report that there is insufficient day care to accommodate the needs of working mothers, and many women who want to work and would be able to find work in the current economy must resort to social assistance. Communications between the National Labor Market Board (AMS) and the social assistance departments are not always smooth, and thus women family heads who are utilizing social assistance may not be receiving needed job training and referral. Practitioners mention that single mothers often suffer social isolation (personal communications: Gunläg Stenfelt, August 12, 1988; Roy Bjernestedt and Eva Lindberg, August 15, 1988; Calle Waller, August 19, 1988; Peder Uggla, August 19, 1988). In fact, many Swedes appear to regard single mothers as social deviants despite the rather generous benefits for them and despite their relatively large numbers.

In contrast to most other countries, Sweden tries to develop social policies to meet the needs of its entire population as well as specific groups who are identified as having particular disadvantages. Policy recommendations of commissions, such as the Commission on Single Parents, are taken seriously by Swedish politicians and administrators. Clearly, the problems that particularly affect the economic well-being of single mothers and their families and the attention that they are newly receiving provide hope that remedies for this population may soon be forthcoming.

GENDER EQUALITY AND POWER

Sweden has adopted many measures to promote equality between men and women and to encourage the participation of women in public spheres. These measures have been successful, especially insofar as women's participation in employment is concerned. Yet part-time work, occupational segregation, and the reluctance of men to use parental leave point to the conclusion that nearly every observer has reached: equality between the sexes in Sweden has yet to be achieved, and women's continuing responsibility for "reproductive work" is at the same time the cause, the result, and the symbol of that inequality.

Women in Sweden still have the primary responsibility for work in the home. Mothers overwhelmingly retain care and custody of their children in the cases of divorce or separation. One recent study has calculated the number of hours that women and men spend on all work—both paid employment and household work. In families with young children where both parents are employed full time, mothers have a total work week of 74 hours compared to 65 hours for fathers. Where the mother works a typical part-time work week of 24 hours, she works another 38 hours at home for a total of 62 hours; her mate works 41 hours outside the home and 19 hours within it, for a total of 60 hours. While this may appear to be an equal burden, the study pointed out that women's daily household work involves continuing, often unnoticed tasks that allow the household to function, including cooking, cleaning, and laundering. Men are responsible for tasks that can be put off, such as gardening and house and car maintenance. When one looks at the daily responsibilities, women spend 20.5 hours per week on domestic chores while men devote 5.2 to their household tasks. In addition, women spend an average of 17 hours a week attending to the needs of children, while men devote only 7 hours to them (Ericsson and Jacobsson, 1985, pp. 56–57). There is no indication that these patterns are changing.

Reducing the work week in order to enhance the quality of life and to meet full employment goals has been a topic of discussion and study in Sweden for some time. While most agree that the work week should be shortened, women and men express different views about such a reduction. Women have supported a six-hour day in order to allow for time to manage home responsibilities. Men, on the other hand, advocate a four-day week in order to afford them more concentrated time for leisure activities (Scott, 1982, p. 58, citing Liljeström).

Ultimately, the answer to greater equality lies in obtaining political power, and here, too, is a mixed picture. Women in Sweden are active participants in the electoral process (about 90 percent of both sexes vote). As in much of Scandinavia, women comprise a sizeable percentage of elected officials. In 1984, 28 percent of the seats in the Riksdag (the Swedish parliament) were held by women (Ericsson and Jacobsson, 1985), as compared to 5 percent of seats in the U.S. Congress. The percentage of women elected at different levels of government has been increasing in Sweden. For example, the numbers of women elected to the Riksdag doubled between 1971 and 1982 (Skard and Haavio-Mannila, 1985).

Despite these electoral achievements, there is question about how much real power women hold. The most significant political work in the Riksdag is carried out by standing committees. Women are highly represented on committees that deal with social, cultural, and educational issues, but they are barely present in those dealing with "hard" matters. Thus, in 1982, women comprised 47 percent of the membership of the Social Affairs Committee, but only 2 percent of the Industry and Energy, Finance, Economy and Tax, and Defense Committees. A very similar pattern is found on county and municipal councils, where women comprise about 30 percent of the elected officials and where their responsibilities are mainly in the health, social welfare, cultural, and education arenas (Ericsson and Jacobsson, 1985; Skard and Haavio-Mannila, 1985). While it is understandable that women gravitate to these areas because of their expertise, it is also likely that until women participate directly in decision making in the industrial and financial spheres, traditional divisions of labor will continue.

Scholars who have studied the political system in the Nordic countries emphasize that the real power is exercised not in elected political bodies but in the "corporate system," a system of appointed commissions and planning and administrative boards whose members frequently represent important political sectors in society (Wilensky, 1983). It is in this system that policy recommendations are formulated, and it is in this sphere that women hold only a small fraction of the power (Hernes and Hanninen-Salmelin, 1985). Women are active in political parties, particularly at the lower echelons, and in their separate political organizations, unions, and feminist organizations. However, they are very underrepresented in leadership positions of the major labor and employer organizations from which appointments to the corporate bodies are made (Scott, 1982). Clearly, women will need to assume more power in order to achieve greater equality.

A recent debate about state support for the continued expansion of child care illustrates both the political difficulties confronting a women's issue and the effect that greater political representation by women has on resolving those difficulties. In 1984, it was estimated that approximately 64 percent of preschool children needed public day care while 42 percent actually had places (Swedish Institute, 1987). The following year, national legislation was passed requiring municipalities to provide a place in either a day care center or a family day care facility for all children 18 months and older whose parents are working or are in school or training by 1991. There has been considerable concern that this mandate will not be met. Interestingly, however, a recent study shows that the provision of public child care is substantially greater in municipalities with higher numbers of women elected to the municipal governments (Gustafsson and Stafford, 1988). In this instance, greater representation by women has achieved more benefits for women.

Opposition to the universal child care policy emerged in the 1988 elections when the Conservatives proposed substituting the expansion of child care with a new monetary award to mothers of young children that they could use either to stay at home or to purchase cheaper child care services on the private market. The Social Democrats, who won the majority in the election, identified this proposal as an attack on full employment for women and opposed it in the elections. However, the Social Democrats have themselves been proposing an expanded parental leave policy. Such an expansion would also result in women's staying out of work for longer periods of time. Indeed the issue of parental leave versus child care has emerged as a key political issue in the past, with women who are militant about sex-role equality favoring day care expansion and traditionalists of various stripes preferring longer periods of parental leave (Scott, 1982). Thus, the role of women in the workforce is still the subject of active debate, and the question of gender equality remains a matter of political importance.

CONCLUSIONS

In comparison to most other countries, Sweden has shown a strong commitment to universal social and economic strategies that aim both to provide a high standard of living to the entire population and to provide support for labor market and family responsibilities. Far from fostering an attitude of work-shirking, as the stereotype would have it, the Swedish welfare state has reinforced a strong work ethic by supporting full employment through a variety of measures that involve virtually the entire adult population in paid employment and employment-related activities. In addition, many welfare benefits are tied to work effort, and thus the work ethic is reinforced through the welfare system itself (Marklund, 1988). Equally important, the Swedish welfare state has eliminated abject poverty, even for those who are not able to work.

Publicly supported education, training, job placement, and job creation programs are significant full employment programs that serve to assist sectors of the population who are most vulnerable to instability and marginality in modern industrial countries. Universal income transfer programs have avoided economic hardship for significant portions of the population, especially families with children and the elderly, who are typically vulnerable to poverty. These programs are models that other countries would do well to heed.

Women and children have been the particular beneficiaries of several employment and income policies in Sweden. An exemplary parental leave policy allows all women to take considerable time at home with a new baby or a sick child while maintaining both their positions in the labor market and their standards of living. Public child care programs are of a high quality and are provided for in greater quantity than in other capitalist countries. Universal child care is a policy goal and, if fulfilled, will clearly further assist mothers of young children to participate in the paid labor force.

Single mothers, in Sweden as elsewhere, have a more stressful life than other parents from both the economic and social points of view, but unlike their counterparts elsewhere, they are not impoverished. Here, again, Sweden has developed social policies that other governments might wish to follow. Advance maintenance allowances ensure that support from the absent parent will be forthcoming. Adequate housing is generally available because public housing is a major share of the housing stock, and housing allowances assist all families who are eligible for them. Child allowances help meet some of the costs of raising children. Finally, social assistance is a true safety net, provided at a level that allows for a relatively decent standard of living for families unable to meet their own needs through earnings and other welfare benefits.

Sweden's complex of social policies and programs is clearly admirable for having eliminated poverty and for having produced a basic level of economic security for all its citizens, but it has not succeeded in fully eliminating social and economic disadvantages for women. Sex-role divisions remain rather entrenched despite women's high participation in the workforce and despite specific policies to encourage men to participate more actively in child care tasks. Indeed, separate sex roles have moved into the workplace, where women's work is less well compensated than men's and where the pattern of part-time work has served to perpetuate the idea that women's income is only supplementary. For the single mother, lower wages often translate into a pattern of reliance on supplementary social welfare benefits.

Given Sweden's successful efforts in achieving a full employment economy, it would appear possible to arrive at greater equity for women, and for low earners generally, by raising the wages of those at the bottom. Current indications are, however, that Sweden may be turning away from its redistribution approach without adopting higher wages. Recent news reports note that Sweden plans to cut tax rates sharply in order to stimulate economic growth, increase efficiency, and curtail inflation (Gray, 1988; Greenhouse, 1989). This move is being supported by the Social Democratic government, which acknowledges that the public will no longer tolerate increased taxes (Greenhouse, 1989). A reduction in social welfare benefits could result.

In light of this recent turn away from an expanded public sector, it may be posited that greater equality for women can be achieved only by the assumption of more power in the political arena by women and the use of that power to refocus on questions of role and economic inequality. Women in Sweden have achieved a status of separate and almost equal. It remains to be seen whether they can now move toward full equality.

NOTE

The author wishes to acknowledge the receipt of a Faculty Development Grant from Salem State College, Massachusetts, which assisted her in making a study trip to Sweden in the summer of 1988 and thus greatly facilitated the research for this chapter. The author also thanks the Swedish Institute and Annika Baude for assisting in arranging interviews with social welfare personnel as well as academic researchers in Sweden. The author is grateful to Hilda Scott for her pioneering crossnational work on women and for her kind consultation.

1. Eva Falkenberg at the *Arbetslivscentrum* is currently conducting a study on the question of employer pressure against fathers taking parental leave (personal communication, August 12, 1988).

REFERENCES

Åberg, R. (1987). "Employment and working hours." In R. Erikson and R. Åberg, eds. *Welfare in Transition: A Survey of Living Conditions in Sweden 1968–1981*. Oxford: Clarendon Press.

Åberg, R., J. Selen, and H. Tham (1987). "Economic resources." In R. Erikson and R. Åberg, eds. *Welfare in Transition: A Survey of Living Conditions in Sweden 1968–1981*. Oxford: Clarendon Press.

Acker, J. (August 1988). *A Contradictory Reality: Swedish Women at Work in the 1980s*. Paper presented at the annual meeting of the Society for the Advancement of Scandanavian Studies, Eugene, OR.

Baude, A. (1979). "Public policy and changing family patterns in Sweden 1930–1977." In J. Lipman-Blumen and J. Bernard, eds. *Sex Roles and Social Policy: A Complex Social Science Equation*. London and Beverly Hills, CA: Sage.

———— (August 1986). *Strengthening the Family and the Community—A Swedish Perspective on the Care of Children and the Aged.* Paper presented at the meeting of the International Council on Social Welfare, Tokyo.

Bosworth, B. P., and A. M. Rivlin, eds. (1987). *The Swedish Economy.* Washington, DC: The Brookings Institution.

Eduards, M., B. Halsaa, and H. Skjeie (1985). "Equality: How equal?" In E. Haavio-Mannila et al., eds. *Unfinished Democracy: Women in Nordic Politics.* Oxford: Pergamon.

Ericsson, Y., and R. Jacobsson (1985). *Side by Side: A Report on Equality between Women and Men in Sweden 1985.* Stockholm: Gotab.

Eriksson, I. (1987). *Some Facts on Single Parents in Sweden.* Stockholm: Ministry of Health and Social Affairs.

Flanagan, R. J. (1987). "Efficiency and equality in Swedish labor markets." In B. P. Bosworth and A. M. Rivlin, eds. *The Swedish Economy.* Washington, DC: The Brookings Institution.

Fleischauer, B. (1987). "Is the road to equality a dead end?" *Sweden Now* 21 (5–6): 57–59.

Ginsburg, H. (1983). *Full Employment and Public Policy: The United States and Sweden.* Lexington, MA: Lexington Books.

Gray, D. D. (December 27, 1988). "Sweden to slash income taxes to stimulate savings and economy." *The Christian Science Monitor,* p. 10.

Greenhouse, S. (October 27, 1989). "Sweden's Social Democrats veer toward free market and lower taxes." *The New York Times,* p. A3.

Gustafsson, B. (November 1988a). *The Income Safety Net—Who Falls into It and Why?* Paper prepared for the Welfare Trends in the Nordic Countries Conference, Oslo. Goteborg, Sweden: University of Goteborg, Departments of Economics and Social Work.

———— (November 1988b). *Poverty in Sweden 1975–1985.* Paper prepared for the Welfare Trends in the Nordic Countries Conference, Oslo. Goteborg, Sweden: University of Goteborg, Departments of Economics and Social Work.

Gustafsson, S. (1981). "Male-female lifetime earnings differentials and labor force history." In G. Eliasson, B. Holmlund, and F. P. Stafford, eds. *Studies in Labor Market Behavior: Sweden and the United States: Proceedings of a Symposium at IUI, Stockholm, July 10–11, 1979.* Stockholm: Industrial Institute for Economic and Social Research.

———— (1984). "Equal opportunity policies in Sweden." In G. Schmid and R. Weitzel, eds. *Sex Discrimination and Equal Opportunity: The Labour Market and Employment Policy.* Hampshire, England: Gower.

———— (1987). *The Labor Force Participation and Earnings of Lone Parents: A Review of Swedish Policies and Institutions with some Comparisons to West Germany.* Stockholm: Arbetslivscentrum.

Gustafsson, S., and R. Jacobsson (1985). "Trends in female labor force participation in Sweden." *Journal of Labor Economics* 3 (1, part 2): 256–274.

Gustafsson, S., and F. Stafford (1988). *Daycare Subsidies and Labor Supply in Sweden.* Preliminary draft. Stockholm: Arbetslivscentrum.

Heckscher, G. (1984). *The Welfare State and Beyond: Success and Problems in Scandinavia.* Minneapolis: University of Minnesota.

Heclo, H., and H. Madsen (1987). *Policy and Politics in Sweden: Principled Pragmatism*. Philadelphia: Temple University Press.

Hedborg, A., and S. Nelander (1986). *Heta Siffror och Kalla Fakta (Hot Figures and Cold Facts)*. Stockholm: Landsorganisationen (LO).

Hernes, H. M., and E. Hanninen-Salmelin (1985). "Women in the corporate system." In E. Haavio-Mannila et al., eds. *Unfinished Democracy: Women in Nordic Politics*. Oxford: Pergamon.

Hoem, B., and J. Hoem (1987a). *The Impact of Female Employment on Second and Third Births in Modern Sweden*, Stockholm Research Reports in Demography, No. 36. Stockholm: University of Stockholm.

———— (1987b). *Patterns of Deferment of First Births in Modern Sweden*, Stockholm Research Reports in Demography, No. 42. Stockholm: University of Stockholm.

———— (1987c). *The Swedish Family: Aspects of Contemporary Developments*, Stockholm Research Reports in Demography, No. 43. Stockholm: University of Stockholm.

Jones, E. F., et al. (1986). *Teenage Pregnancy in Industrialized Countries*. New Haven, CT: Yale University Press.

Kahn, A. J., and S. B. Kamerman (1983). *Income Transfers for Families with Children: An Eight-country Study*. Philadelphia: Temple University Press.

Kamerman, S. B., and A. J. Kahn (November 1987). *Mother-only Families in Western Europe: Social Change, Social Problem and Social Response*. Report prepared for the German Marshall Fund of the United States. New York: Columbia University School of Social Work.

Knocke, W. (n.d.). *Migrant Women at Work in Sweden—Structural Marginality and Mechanisms of Marginalization*. Stockholm: Arbetslivscentrum.

Korpi, W. (1978). *The Working Class in Welfare Capitalism: Work, Unions and Politics in Sweden*. London: Routledge & Kegan Paul.

Leiniö, T-L. (1988). "Sex and ethnic segregation in the 1980 Swedish labour market." *Economic and Industrial Democracy: An International Journal* 9 (1): 99–120.

Liljeström, R. (1980). "Integration of family policy and labor market policy in Sweden." In R. S. Ratner, ed. *Equal Employment Policy for Women*. Philadelphia: Temple University Press.

Liljeström, R., G. F. Mellstrom, and G. L. Svensson (1978). *Roles in Transition: Report of an Investigation Made for the Advisory Council on Equality between Men and Women*. Stockholm: Schmidts Boktryckeri A. B.

Marklund, S. (1988). *Paradise Lost? The Nordic Welfare States and the Recession 1975–1985*. Lund: Arkiv.

Ministry of Health and Social Affairs, International Secretariat (1981). *Social Services Act and Care of Young Persons (Special Provisions) Act/LVU*. Stockholm: Ministry of Health and Social Affairs.

Ministry of Labor (1985). *The Swedish Act on Equality between Women and Men at Work*. Stockholm: Ministry of Labor.

Ministry of Labor, Secretariat for Equality between Women and Men (n.d.). *Women, Education, Labour Market*. Stockholm: Ministry of Labor.

Myrdal, A., and G. Myrdal (1934). *Kris i Befolkingsfrägen*. Stockholm: Bonnier; Published in English (1941). *Nation and Family: The Swedish Experiment in Democratic Family and Population Policy*. New York: Harper, 1941.

National Labor Market Board (*Arbetsmarknadsstyrelsen*) (1987). *Statistics: Equality in the Labour Market*. Stockholm: National Labor Market Board.

Nordic Council of Ministers (1988). *Kvinnor och Man i Norden: Fakta om Jamstalldheten 1988 (Women and Men in the Nordic Countries: Facts on Equal Opportunities 1988)*. Copenhagen: Nordic Council of Ministers.

Organization for Economic and Cultural Development (OECD) (September 1988). *Employment Outlook*. Paris: OECD.

Persson-Tanimura, I. (October 1988). "Economic equality for Swedish women—Current situation and trends." *Women and Power: The Swedish Experience in Comparative Perspective*. Conference sponsored by the Swedish Institute and Harvard University, Cambridge, MA.

Popenoe, D. (1986). "What is happening to the family in Sweden?" *Social Change* 36: 1–7. New York: Swedish Information Service.

Rivlin, A. M. (1987). "Overview." In B. P. Bosworth and A. M. Rivlin, eds. *The Swedish Economy*. Washington, DC: The Brookings Institution.

Ruggie, M. (1984). *The State and Working Women: A Comparative Study of Britain and Sweden*. Princeton, NJ: Princeton University Press.

Schirmer, J. C. (1982). *The Limits of Reform: Women, Capital and Welfare*. Cambridge, MA: Schenkman.

Scott, H. (1982). *Sweden's "Right To Be Human": Sex-role Equality: The Goal and the Reality*. Armonk, NY: M. E. Sharpe.

——— (1984). "Sweden's efforts to achieve sex role equality in education." In S. Acker et al., eds. *World Yearbook of Education 1984: Women and Education*. London and New York: Kogan Page/Nichols.

Skard, T., and H. Haavio-Mannila (1985). "Women in parliament." In H. Haavio-Mannila et al., eds. *Unfinished Democracy: Women in Nordic Politics*. Oxford: Pergamon.

Smeeding, T., B. B. Torrey, and M. Rein (1988). "Patterns of income and poverty: The economic status of children and the elderly in eight countries." In J. L. Palmer, T. Smeeding, and B. B. Torrey, eds. *The Vulnerable*. Washington, DC: Urban Institute Press.

Statistics Sweden (1985). *Women and Men in Sweden: Facts and Figures*. Stockholm: Statistiska Centralbyrån.

Statistiska Centralbyrån (1987). *Statistisk Arsbok for Sverige* (Statistical Abstract of Sweden). Stockholm: Statistiska Centralbyrån.

Sundström, M. (1987). *A Study in the Growth of Part-time Work in Sweden*. Stockholm: Arbetslivscentrum.

Swedish Institute (1984a). *Fact Sheets on Sweden: The Economic Situation of Swedish Households*. Stockholm: Swedish Institute.

——— (1984b). *Fact Sheets on Sweden: Equality between Men and Women in Sweden*. Stockholm: Swedish Institute.

——— (1984c). *Fact Sheets on Sweden: Facts and Figures about Youth in Sweden*. Stockholm: Swedish Institute.

——— (1984d). *Fact Sheets on Sweden: Housing and Housing Policy in Sweden*. Stockholm: Swedish Institute.

——— (1986a). *Fact Sheets on Sweden: Immigrants in Sweden*. Stockholm: Swedish Institute.

———— (1986b). *Fact Sheets on Sweden: The Swedish Economy*. Stockholm: Swedish Institute.

———— (1986c). *Fact Sheets on Sweden: Swedish Labor Market Policy*. Stockholm: Swedish Institute.

———— (1987). *Fact Sheets on Sweden: Child Care in Sweden*. Stockholm: Swedish Institute.

Vogel, J., et al. (1984). *Level of Living and Inequality in the Nordic Countries*. Stockholm: Nordic Council and the Nordic Statistical Secretariat.

Wilensky, H. L. (1983). "Political legitimacy and consensus: Missing variables in the assessment of social policy." In S. Spiro and E. Yuchtman-Yaar, eds. *Evaluating the Welfare State*. New York: Academic Press.

Wistrand, B. (1981). *Swedish Women on the Move*. Stockholm: Swedish Institute.

7

Socialism: An Escape from Poverty? Women in European Russia

ELEANOR KREMEN

Almost three-quarters of a century has passed since the Bolshevik revolution of 1917. One of the promises of the revolution was to establish equality between the sexes. This chapter can only suggest the extent to which the utopian ideals of the revolution have been achieved. Our focus instead is to determine the proportion of Soviet women of working/reproductive age who are living below the Soviet poverty standard and to identify trends that may suggest whether poverty is becoming "feminized." In the process of achieving this aim we have tried to provide a view of the lives of women in contemporary Soviet society.

The inclusion of a chapter on the Soviet Union in a crossnational study certainly reflects the change in the political atmosphere that has occurred since the mid–1980s. A study of the Soviet Union presents many challenges and problems. The first is to approach the work in an open-minded fashion so that we can dispel some of the myths and expectations that developed during the long period when very little social information was available or exchanged. Second, the Soviets have not been collecting census data on a regular basis, nor are their data well organized or comprehensive enough to permit definitive analysis. Further, it is believed that some of their findings were not published because they were judged to be too sensitive or too revealing of internal problems (Shabad, 1987, p. A10). Many of these gaps in data are quite basic—such as the proportion of the female population who live below the Soviet defined minimum subsistence level, the relationship between earnings and gender, or trends in the number of single-parent households—and affect our ability to draw conclusions about the feminization of poverty in the U.S.S.R.

Scholars in the United States and in Great Britain have had to supplement limited census data with sector analyses and regional reports prepared by various Soviet institutes, industries, and academicians. Some have studied Soviet emigrés, a statistically biased sample that nevertheless offers interesting insights into Soviet life (Millar, 1986, pp. 26–35). Despite these limitations, such findings seem to be fairly consistent and are used as a main source of our data. Whenever possible, we have also tried to use primary sources from Soviet studies, including interviews with knowledgeable Soviet women. Under the new policy of "glasnost" or openness, the Soviet census bureau has been reorganized, and it is anticipated that more data of the type we are seeking will soon be available for students and scholars. Admittedly our data are incomplete and much of what follows may either be confirmed or questioned. This is a risk, although the greater openness in the Soviet Union is certainly a welcome development. The effect of major political changes and economic restructuring or *perestroika*, begun at the end of the 1980s, will undoubtedly have important consequences for the economic well-being of Soviet women. The question of whether women will have to pay a disproportionate share of the costs of increased automation and rising unemployment that are being proposed will need to be carefully followed and evaluated over time.

Another challenge involved in undertaking a study of the Soviet Union is the difference in cultural beliefs and attitudes, especially those that are so deeply embedded nationally that they are often difficult to recognize or understand without making invidious comparisons. One such example is the positive value placed on the individual's solidarity with the group or collective (Shulman, 1977). This value contrasts with cultural ideals that extol individualism in the United States. Differences in the understanding and interpretation of feminism are of particular importance to our work. The Soviets view their achievement in bringing women into the paid workforce as the fulfillment of a promise toward social equality. Thus Lenin stated that, "In order to achieve the complete emancipation of women and to make them really equal with men, we must have social economy, and the participation of women in general productive labor. Then women will occupy the same position as men" (Lapidus, 1978, p. 74). Further, broad constitutional guarantees of gender equality, including the principle of equal pay for equal work, the creation of equal education for women, the development of a widespread system of child care, the legalization of abortion, and the liberalization of divorce are cited as further evidence of the achievement of social equality.[1] The Soviets see themselves as having already achieved many of the objectives sought by Western feminism, which is viewed as politically intrusive and advancing the particular interests of middle-class women (Hansson and Liden, 1983). Western scholars and feminists, some of whom acknowledge substantial Soviet achievements toward equality, point to the discrepancy between Soviet ideals and the reality of women's lives. Among the examples of inequality that they describe are the burdens and inequity of women's dual role, the concentration of women in sectors of the labor market that are low-paid and arduous, and the reluctance of the Soviet state to confront forthrightly the need for equalization of sex roles (Bridger, 1987; Engel, 1987; Lapidus, 1978; Leahy, 1986; Lovenduski, 1986; Scott, 1974).

There are major differences in the lives of urban and rural women (Bridger, 1987). Rural women, including those living on collective farms or in more traditional cultures, generally have a lower standard of living than urban women. The factors contributing to this difference are historically and culturally complex and are beyond the scope of this study. We plan to restrict our inquiry to an examination of women in the European republics of the Soviet Union. These republics are the most highly industrialized and urbanized areas of the country and, therefore, most appropriate for comparison with the other nations in this study.[2]

The Soviet Union is a very large and diverse country. Composed of 15 republics and 100 different nationalities, the population reached 281.5 million in 1987 (UNICEF, 1989, p. 95). The total productive capacity of the Soviet Union is slightly over one-fourth that of the United States. The per capita GNP, as measured in U.S. dollars in 1986, was $4,550, compared to $17,480 for the U.S. (p. 95).[3] While the relationship between GNP and social welfare expenditures is not a direct one, clearly the current productive capacity of the Soviet Union places limits on its ability to spend for social needs. Nonetheless, decisions are made to allocate resources for overall objectives or for the special needs of certain groups. Historically Marxist theory has not regarded women as a class in the way that workers, peasants, and even some national groups have been regarded. We are interested in examining here the extent to which women, and particularly single-parent women, are an economically vulnerable or "at risk" group, and if this is the case, whether Soviet planners and policymakers have identified their economic status as a problem requiring labor market or social policy intervention. It is possible that actions have been taken to address the economically vulnerable position of women without identifying the problem in the context of gender, thus avoiding conflict with traditional socialist ideology.

THE LABOR MARKET

One of the most dramatic aspects of Soviet life since the revolution has been the entry of women into the labor force. In the decades following the revolution, ideological and pragmatic needs coalesced in the policy of recruiting women into the paid workforce. The key economic objective of increasing industrial production required an expanding workforce. Severe and chronic labor shortages that resulted from the losses and the absence of men during both world wars and during the interim periods of civil strife and foreign invasion also stimulated the demand for women's labor. Gail Warshofsky Lapidus states that, "Today almost 90 percent of able bodied women are employed or engaged in study, virtually all full-time" (1985, p. 16).[4] It is believed that the Soviets have one of the highest rates of female labor force participation in the industrialized world (McAndrew and Peers, 1981; McAuley, 1981).[5] In fact, except for the mothers of very young children, students and older women who can retire at 55 years of age, women are expected to work.

The Soviet Union has had a full employment policy since the 1930s. In fact, there has been no formal provision for unemployment insurance since then. People who lose their jobs are entitled to two weeks severance pay. Retraining allowances are provided only to workers who need to learn new technologies or those who are not able to continue on a job for medical reasons. Paid at the former rate of earnings, retraining allowances can continue for a three-month period (Matthews, 1986, p. 108). These allowances could be masking evidence of frictional or seasonal unemployment, but given the economy's need for an expanding labor force, there was little reported unemployment overall (Ofer and Vinokur, 1985). Women, like men, have a constitutional right to a job and can use the courts to litigate this right. In effect, workers have had what amounts to job tenure (Connor, 1987). In fact, many workers have been retained despite their low productivity, thereby reducing the total number of unemployed.

Soviet women work full time and year round (Lapidus, 1985). Part-time work is rare and is usually carried out by students or retirees who wish to add to their pensions. The part-time work that does exist is not carried out as exclusively by women as is the case in Western Europe, Scandinavia, and, to a lesser degree, in the United States (Seager and Olson, 1986, p. 110). Women do withdraw from the labor market during childbearing years for varying periods, but maternity and other child care leaves maintain the women's right to seniority. Payments continue to be made into her social security "account" and cash allowances are paid for the period of the leave. It seems reasonable to conclude that in the U.S.S.R., interruptions in women's earnings are less prolonged and have less of an impact on current income, on job security, and on pension accumulations than in other industrialized nations.

As described earlier, the Soviet constitution assures equal pay for equal work. When there is a violation of this provision, the woman worker can bring a grievance to her trade union, which then has the responsibility of resolving the issue with the work enterprise. While there is a possible conflict of interest for the trade union representative if the women's complaint interferes with production, violations of the specific regulation are thought to be infrequent (McAuley, 1981, p. 20).

Despite the constitutional guarantee of equal pay for equal work, Soviet women clearly do not earn as much as men. There is an earnings differential; women are generally estimated to earn between 65 and 70 percent of what men earn (Lapidus, 1978; McAuley, 1981; Ofer and Vinokur, 1985; Swafford, 1978). Leahy (1986, pp. 79–80) seems to have found a higher ratio, explaining that, "Overall, women's remuneration as compared with men's has advanced towards greater parity since a major effort began in the early 1970s to devote more attention to those areas of the economy in which women predominated—light industry, consumer goods and the service sector" (p. 79). She adds that "whereas in the late 1960s women's average salaries were only 75% of men's, by 1974, a Western study of Soviet wages estimated that per capita female income was roughly 87 percent that of males" (p. 79). The disparity between these estimates can be attributed to the lack of national data, including the absence of wage data by gender, and the consequent need to rely on sample studies drawn from sources and times that are not strictly comparable. Overall it can be concluded that the earnings gap in the Soviet Union is somewhat larger than in Scandinavia but somewhat smaller than in North America or Japan.

There are also differences among our sources as to whether the female-male earnings gap is narrowing over time. Leahy (1986) clearly believes this to be the case as cited above. Gur Ofer and Aron Vinokur believe the gap to be narrowing although they acknowledge that no hard systematic evidence supports their view (1985, p. 337). Alastair McAuley (1981) and Lapidus (1978) point to the marked and continuing vertical and horizontal concentration of women in the low-paid, low-skill sectors of the labor force as evidence that the earnings gap has remained static. Nevertheless, in the Soviet Union, women have penetrated into what were heretofore exclusively male occupational preserves, and they are also found in a range of managerial and executive positions that women tend not to occupy in the West (Dodge, 1966, p. 247; Lapidus, 1978, p. 183; Leahy, 1986, p. 78; McAuley, 1981, p. 87).

In examining the factors that can account for the earnings gap, Lapidus suggests that the "male-female income gap is more the result of differential distribution of men and women in the occupational structure than of wage discrimination" (1978, p. 127). In the U.S.S.R., women predominate in trade and catering (83 percent), health and social security (82 percent), education (75 percent), and culture (74 percent)—the occupational sectors that are the lower paid branches of the Soviet economy (Matthews, 1986, p. 39). Conversely, they are underrepresented in heavy industry where wages are relatively high.

Protective labor legislation was introduced soon after the revolution to guard women from work in occupations that were considered hazardous to their health or harmful during pregnancy (Leahy, 1986, p. 76). This exclusion has not fully protected women from the arduous, unskilled work that the majority of women do. Further, exclusion from these hazardous industries has removed women from jobs that are in the highest paid sectors of the economy. In fact, Soviet law recently expanded the number of hazardous industries from which women are excluded (Peers, 1985, p. 135). Whereas the individual woman who loses her job as a result of these new exclusions will be compensated so that she suffers no loss of income in her new replacement job, the overall effect of protective legislation has been to maintain or even increase earning differentials (Leahy, 1986, p. 76).

Despite their rising level of education, women are employed in jobs that are below their level of skill and that, in turn, result in lower rates of pay (McAndrew and Peers, 1981, p. 13; Morgan, 1984, p. 677). Further, family responsibilities keep women from supplementing their earnings through overtime pay or bonuses. Moreover, the type of enterprises in which women are employed often do not provide these kinds of additions to income (McAndrew and Peers, 1981, p. 13; McAuley, 1981, p. 28). Finally, women generally occupy the lower end of the management structure (Dodge, 1966; Lapidus, 1978; McAuley, 1981; Swafford, 1978). Even in industries and occupations in which women predominate, they do not hold top administrative posts. For example, in the textile industry in which women constitute 80 percent of the workforce (Lapidus, 1985, p. 18), only 21 percent of the top management positions were held by women (Pukhova, 1988a, p. 8).

The U.S.S.R. has made significant progress in moving women into technical and scientific work (Dodge, 1966; Lapidus, 1978; Leahy, 1986; McAuley, 1981). During the 1950s and 1960s, women were actively recruited into professional specializations, particularly engineering and medicine. The proportion of women in these fields increased dramatically as a result of what we would term affirmative action strategies. Norton T. Dodge notes that, "Initially, minimum quotas were set for women to encourage their enrollment, and other efforts were made to increase female matriculation especially in scientific and technical disciplines" (1966, p. 242). Subsequently, the high proportion of women declined in medicine and other professional fields because of a shift in admission policies that sought "a more desirable balance of sexes" (p. 243). In comparison with the West, women are highly represented in the professions. They comprise 82 percent of Soviet economists and planners, 77 percent of dentists, 74 percent of physicians, 57 percent of designers and draftsmen, 40 percent of engineers, 43 percent of teachers in higher education, and 40 percent of scientific research personnel (Unesco, 1983, pp. 18–19). It is worth noting that an engineering degree is a virtual prerequisite for advancement into positions of responsibility in Soviet industry. Entry opportunities in the scientific and technical fields have, however, been more available to women than subsequent professional advancement in these fields. For example, only one woman in twelve is a chief engineer, that is, the deputy director of an industrial enterprise (McAndrew and Peers, 1981, p. 13). The same is true in medicine, health services, and education (Pukhova, 1988a, pp. 7–8).

Wages are set by a national commission in the U.S.S.R. and vary according to economic sector, geographical location and the cost of living (McAuley, 1981; Swafford, 1978). Level of skill and length of service and the particular needs of the enterprise also determine an individual's position on the wage scale (Leahy, 1986, p. 79).

Since the early 1970s there is evidence that Soviet wage policies have been directed toward improving women's remuneration (Leahy, 1986, pp. 79–80). Data indicate that the average wage in the Soviet Union rose substantially during the two decades of the 1960s and 1970s: from 97 rubles in 1965 reaching 169 rubles in 1980 (Matthews, 1986, p. 22). In the period of the Eleventh Five-year Plan (1981–1985), it was expected that the average wage would rise by a further 14.5 percent (International Labour Office, 1984, p. 9).

Further, the minimum wage was increased twice: from 27 to 30 rubles in 1968 and then to 70 rubles in 1977. Since they occupied the lower end of the wage scale, women have been the primary beneficiaries of this 160 percent increase in the minimum wage (Swafford, 1978, p. 669). A third increase of the minimum wage to 80 rubles was scheduled to begin with the production branches of the economy in the mid–1980s (Matthews, 1986, p. 169).

The Soviet government reported that "during the Tenth Five-year Plan (1976–1980), 31 million workers in the service sector (about 70 percent are women) received significant wage increases, mainly in education, health care, culture and other service sectors of the economy" (International Labour Office, 1984, p. 24). Wage increases of 15 to 18 percent were granted in those sectors of the labor market in which women predominate; in industry, construction and transport where men predominate, wages were increased less, or by 10 to 11 percent (p. 9). The rationale for wage policies that favored women was not offered. Apparently responding to the need to improve services, the Twenty-seventh Congress of the Communist Party, held in 1986, raised the salaries of physicians, teachers, and nurses rather sharply, from 25 to 36 percent (Soboleva, 1988). These are, of course, the professions in which women predominate.

An indication of the adequacy of women's wages can be obtained by comparing an estimate of the wage of the average women worker with the Soviet minimum subsistence budget, the equivalent of a poverty standard. Developed in 1967, the budget for an urban family of four, consisting of two adults and two children, amounted to 206 rubles or $339 monthly (Matthews, 1986, pp. 19–21). The figure for one person is 51 rubles or $85. Soviet authorities acknowledge that these figures are outdated now, and "Most agree that around 75 rubles, or $125, a month a person are necessary for what the Government calls minimum material security" (Fein, 1989a, p. A1).

Lacking national wage data by gender, we calculated from the figure of 200 rubles, the national average wage in 1988, that the women's average wage would amount to 165 rubles, 70 percent of the man's average wage.[6] Assuming that this woman is a single parent with one child to support, her earnings would place her just above the poverty level of 150 rubles needed for a family of two (calculated at the proposed higher minimum subsistence standard of 75 rubles per person). Of course, with two or more children, the mother's earnings alone would not be sufficient to maintain her family above the poverty line. Mervyn Matthews, a British social scientist who has studied Soviet social structure and poverty extensively, sees the need for two wage earners to keep a family out of poverty, stating that, "Outside the family situation [women living without a spouse], employed women would be more likely than men to find themselves in a poverty situation" (1986, p. 39).

According to a resolution of the Communist Party of the Soviet Union (CPSU) Central Committee and the U.S.S.R. Council of Ministries in 1979, "Measures for further advancement of training and upgrading of skills of industrial workers focused particular attention on the problems of improving vocational training for women workers" (International Labour Office, 1984, p. 25). As part of the program, women with children under 8 years old have an advantage and can now retrain and upgrade their skills during a break at work paid at their average monthly wage (p. 25). Training is an important route to promotion and it has been recognized that women's responsibilities have kept them from participating in after-work training programs. These training measures appear to have been influenced by training programs for women that are now in place in the German Democratic Republic and that appear to have been successful in upgrading women into higher paid (often traditionally male) occupations (Lovenduski, 1986, p. 288).

It is not clear whether these actions by Soviet policymakers are a deliberate attempt to deal with the female-male earnings gap. Indeed, the problem is often dismissed and the constitutional guarantees of equal pay are cited as evidence that there is no rate discrimination in the workplace (McAndrew and Peers, 1981, p. 13). At the very least, taken cumulatively, these actions do indicate a rec-ognition that women's wages are insufficient to meet socially defined needs.

There is a general agreement among scholars and Western feminists that until now the Soviet state has not addressed the earnings gap directly enough (Bridger, 1987; Lapidus, 1978; Lovenduski, 1986; McAndrew and Peers, 1981; McAuley, 1981; Scott, 1974; Swafford, 1978). The reasons advanced to explain the lack of attention range from the purely economic—that it would be too costly for the Soviet economy to equalize wages and that productivity goals have always superseded women's equality—to the view that Marxist theory fosters the belief in a "naive economic determinism" and therefore has not recognized that desired changes in traditional attitudes and role behavior have to be addressed indepen-dently (McAuley, 1981, p. 213). Lapidus (1978) holds that insufficient attention has been paid to early sex-role socialization and its impact on occupational choice. Further, the acceptance of women's biological appropriateness for certain kinds of work is still a widely held view in the Soviet Union. From a Western feminist perspective, the reluctance to acknowledge or confront the earnings gap and factors that contribute to it is evidence that patriarchal attitudes persist.

THE SOCIAL WELFARE SYSTEM

The range of social welfare programs is very wide in the U.S.S.R., covering many contingencies that women living in many Western industrialized societies, particularly the United States, might well envy. The view of the function and objectives of the social welfare sector in a socialist economy, as set forth by two Soviet authors, does not depart markedly from the objectives of social welfare policy in the advanced welfare states of Western Europe.

In a socialist society, material and cultural benefits are distributed in two main ways— according to labor and through social consumption funds. . . . [T]he main way to increase the people's welfare is to raise wages, on the basis of a rise in labour productivity and the efficiency of social production. . . . The wage fund constitutes the predominant part of the national income to be distributed according to the quantity and quality of each person's work. Distribution according to work cannot, however, ensure that the so-called collective needs of all members of society are satisfied, or those of people who are unable to work. These needs are satisfied by the social consumption funds. In a socialist society, these funds are inevitably created for two major socio-economic reasons: the necessity of (1) providing all members of society with equal opportunities to reveal and develop their capabilities and of (2) eliminating or at least reducing inequality among members of society arising from individual features (different capabilities, marital status, and so on) (Zakharov and Tsvilyov, 1978, pp. 14–15).

The first category of social welfare benefits that will be examined are those that emanate from the workplace and in effect attempt to make the labor market more responsive to the family responsibilities or reproductive role of women. Maternity leaves and allowances, the rights of pregnant women and nursing mothers, and more current proposals for flexi-time, part-time work, and shorter hours fall under this rubric.

Women are entitled to maternity leave after one year of employment or full-time study. The leave now consists of 126 days: 70 before and 56 after birth.[7] The benefit is paid at the rate of the woman's former average wage (Holland and McKevitt, 1985, p. 161). The women's job is retained as are her rights to seniority, annual vacation, and sick leave. Beginning in 1981, an extended leave was introduced to allow the mother to remain at home until the child was a year old. More recent provisions have extended the leave period to eighteen months (Pukhova, 1988a, p. 18). After the first 126 days, through the first year of the leave, the mother receives an allowance amounting to 50 percent of the minimum wage (between 35 and 50 rubles monthly, depending on location) (Buckley, 1985, p. 47).

Women appear to be making use of these extended leaves to care for their infant children at home, as registration in creches (nursery schools) has declined (Motorshilova, 1988). Women generally return to work promptly after the end of the maternity leave not only out of financial need but also because of the satisfactions they derive from employment. Surveys indicate that women want to work and would not remain at home even if their husbands earned the total sum of their combined income (Peers, 1985, p. 140).

Barbara Holland and Teresa McKevitt, who have studied maternity care in the Soviet Union, state that "Soviet legislation to safeguard the health of pregnant women and nursing mothers at work is quite far-reaching" (1985, p. 161). Pregnant women who are employed in strenuous labor must be transferred to lighter work paid at their former average wage (p. 162). They cannot be assigned night work, overtime, or travel in the later months of pregnancy. Women cannot be refused employment because they are pregnant or nursing. After the birth, mothers are allowed time off for nursing, which can be done in day care units attached to industrial work sites, when these are available.

The introduction of flexi-time, part-time employment, and shorter hours as a way of easing the burden of mothers in caring for young children has been a subject of discussion in the Soviet Union for two decades, though probably less than 1 percent of the workforce is now engaged in such arrangements (Peers, 1985, p. 135). However, these proposals appear to be receiving more favorable attention from planners and demographers, particularly those with pronatalist views. Opposition comes from those who fear that these proposals will increase the sexual division of labor and maintain or even increase earning differentials (Buckley, 1985; Lapidus, 1985).

All working mothers are entitled to extended leave with pay if they have a sick or disabled child. Mothers with children under age 12 are entitled to extra days of annual leave and receive priority in timing their vacations to coincide with their children's school vacations (Matthews, 1986, p. 172).

It can be seen that this network of workplace-related benefits that facilitate women's reproductive function addresses many of the unique needs and concerns that plague working mothers throughout the industrialized world. Soviet planners have been careful to retain women's rights to seniority and to other fringe benefits, despite the periods of physical absence from the worksite. Nevertheless these policies reinforce the role of women as exclusively responsible for childrearing, and, ultimately, physical discontinuity in the labor force does interfere with promotion (Pukhova, 1988a, p. 8) and other aspects of full integration into the workplace. Further, the special benefits and protection that women receive may have some negative consequences. For example, managers of local enterprises may be "scared" by the special obligations that women require (p. 10) and that undoubtedly increase the cost of women's labor if this is measured without recognition of the social benefits accrued as a result of women's reproductive and maternal roles.

The second series of benefits that will be examined are those designed to reduce women's family and domestic responsibilities. These include child care and vacations for children; the establishment of communal services to reduce or relieve women of domestic labor, such as prepared meals; and the availability of labor-saving household appliances.

Publicly subsidized child care—including preschool, kindergarten, and after-school programs—was initiated at the time of the 1917 revolution. The growth of the program proceeded slowly in comparison to need, particularly during the rapid drive toward industrialization in the Stalin years. Since 1975, budget allocations have increased markedly, and child care facilities have grown steadily in number and quality, although there are sharp regional differences. Most are located in urban areas, over 50 percent in the republic of Russia alone. In part the location may reflect cultural differences in attitudes toward the use of child care (Lovenduski, 1986, p. 287). By 1980, 14.3 million children, or about 60 percent of the 1 to 6 age group, were registered in nurseries and kindergartens (Matthews, 1986, p. 83).

The Eleventh and Twelfth Five-year Plans (1980–1989) anticipated eliminating the shortage of preschool institutions within the next several years "in regions with a high level of female employment in social production" (Imbrogno and

Imbrogno, 1986, p. 92). New facilities will provide full-week, twenty-four-hour, and holiday care offered by "highly qualified staff." These plans attempt to meet not only current shortages but public criticism of the quality of child care such as poorly trained staff, poor standards of hygiene, low staff-child ratios, and so on. Although child care is publicly supported to about 80 percent of the cost, parents do pay fees according to their income. Many families are, however, entitled to a reduced fee or pay no fee at all; among these beneficiaries are single mothers (and fathers), poor families, large size families, and widows whose husbands died in military action (Matthews, 1986, p. 84). Single mothers also get priority in obtaining child care for their children.

Most children on vacation are sent to summer camps. The arrangements are made by the trade unions. When the mother or family does not have sufficient means, the cost of these vacations can be met by the government or the union. Mothers who are raising children alone (in common with mothers of children under age 12) receive priority in the scheduling of their own vacations so that their holidays coincide with their children's schedule (Soboleva, 1988). Despite the shortages and problems noted, the Soviet child care system is acknowledged to be a significant and costly achievement (McAndrew and Peers, 1981, p. 17; Peers, 1985, p. 123).

In the early days of the revolution, there were plans not only to socialize the provision of child care but also to collectivize all domestic services. Food preparation, laundry, and cleaning services were to be developed to free women from what Lenin described as their "stupefying and humiliating subjugation to the eternal drudgery of the kitchen and nursery" (McAndrew and Peers, 1981, p. 8). These plans were diluted during the Stalin era, when the nuclear family, rather than a new form of communal family, was established as the preferred social unit.

The allocation of national resources to heavy industry delayed not only the widespread provision of child care but the development of consumer goods and services, including labor-saving household appliances. There has been considerable improvement in the quality and availability of consumer "durables" over the past decade (Peers, 1985, p. 123). Nevertheless most women do household work without the advantages of labor-saving devices commonly available in the United States (McAndrew and Peers, 1981, pp. 17–18).

As part of a renewed effort to reduce the burden of women's dual role, food stores and prepared meals (some from Finland) are increasingly being located at the worksite (Peers, 1985, p. 134). The meals can be purchased at low cost. This arrangement can save women precious time and money because it is women who do the shopping and standing on lines. No new policies have been developed that contemplate the assignment or sharing of domestic tasks with men (Buckley, 1985).

The third stream of social welfare benefits to be discussed are those that are directed toward specific types of families. Family allowances, which were introduced following World War II, are only paid to large families with four or more children and only when the children are between 1 and 5 years of age. The amount of the allowance, which is paid regardless of family income, is acknowledged to be small (4 rubles for the fourth child). Most of the families eligible for these allowances live in the Moslem republics of Central Asia and in the Transcaucasus. This program of family allowances has not changed very much since its inception, and it is recognized that the sums do not have a significant impact even on the budgets of rural families (Matthews, 1986, pp. 121–122). It is likely that conflicting public policy objectives have kept this allowance program for large families from being expanded or abandoned. Pronatalist policies are now focused on the women in the Slavic and Baltic republics where most women are having only one child. Maintaining positive ties to diverse national groups is a cornerstone of Soviet policy, and the withdrawal of these allowances would undoubtedly produce a negative reaction among the affected ethnic groups.

In 1974, a separate system of family allowances, specifically targeted to low-income families, was introduced. Families with incomes below the Soviet minimum subsistence level of 50 rubles per person monthly are eligible for this allowance. Entitlement to this program is interpreted broadly, and there is no suggestion that the process of eligibility is designed to act as a deterrent (Matthews, 1986, p. 122). Benefits are set at 12 rubles monthly for each child between the ages of 1 and 8. Matthews calculated that more than one child in seven is eligible for this family allowance program for poor or "underprovisioned" families (1986, p. 47).

There is also a separate allowance for unmarried mothers, paid regardless of need. This was increased in 1981 from the small sum of 5 rubles per month for the first child (the level at which it was introduced in 1947–1948) to 20 rubles per child. This allowance continues from birth until the child reaches age 16, formerly age 12 (Binyon, 1985, p. 51). Such allowances are only for the children of unmarried mothers; presumably children of widowed or divorced parents receive their allowances through the social security system or from child support (Peers, 1985, p. 137).

There are a number of other programs or arrangements that are targeted at special groups or needs. For example, all nursery schools provide three nutritious meals during the day, and the state gives an allotment to schools so that they can distribute clothing to children who appear poorly clothed (Matthews, 1986, p. 85). Others are designed to serve particular policy objectives, such as benefits aimed at increasing the birth rate. For example, one-time lump sum payments are made to mothers to cover the extra cost incurred by the birth of an infant. These have long been paid, but began with the birth of the third child. The new provisions start with payments of 50 rubles for the first child, 100 rubles for the second child, and the same sum for each child after that (p. 171).

An extensive system of universal programs that are provided for all, regardless of income, undergird the network of programs already described. State subsidies are used to bring down the cost of basic foodstuffs, rents, and transportation.

Education is provided at no cost, and medical services were nationalized in 1918 (Matthews, 1986, p. 91).

The problems with many of these universal programs are quite well known. For example, there are recurring food shortages, a faulty distribution system, and the quality of food, when it does arrive, is often poor. Bread, potatoes, and cabbage are mainstays that are generally available in state stores at very nominal prices. Food purchased at collective farm markets is of far better quality but very costly.

There is still a long wait for apartments, and although more housing is becoming available, it is estimated that 20 percent of the urban families are doubled up (Matthews, 1986, p. 71), often with parents. Rents on an average amount only to 5 to 6 percent of the family's income (McAndrew and Peers, 1981, p. 17); they are controlled and have been kept at the same level since 1934 (Matthews, 1986, p. 67).

Transportation costs are minimal as a result of state subsidies. For example, a subway ride in Moscow costs 7 cents as compared to 80 cents in Washington. Airplane fares are also very low, and the policy of subsidizing the cost of transportation is a benefit of special importance to the poor (Matthews, 1986, p. 104).

The Soviet system of health care was also established at the time of the revolution. In the early years, great strides were made in public health, for example, sharp reduction of communicable and infectious diseases and in the rate of infant mortality (Binyon, 1985, p. 53). By the 1970s, however, the system was acknowledged to contain significant flaws such as poor organization (Lisitin and Batygin, 1978, p. 51), poor quality of care, lack of critical materials and indifferent personnel (Binyon, 1985, p. 57). The infant mortality rate declined from 80.7 per 1,000 infants under 1 year old in 1950 to 27.9 per 1,000 in 1974 (Ryan, 1978, p. 131). Subsequently the rate rose again, although this was not officially reported for several years (Schmemann, 1986, p. A7). More current figures put the rate at 27.3 (1980); 25.3 (1983); 25.9 (1984), and 26.0 (1985) (Scherer, 1987, p. 65). The UNICEF figure for 1987 was 25.0 (1989, p. 95).

The U.S.S.R. infant mortality rate, a social indicator that reflects on the general welfare of a society and the health of the female population, is the highest among the industrialized nations in our study.[8] Some factors that have been linked to the high rate in the Soviet Union are the poor quality of prenatal care, food shortages, industrial pollution, poorly managed flu epidemics, alcoholism, and family stress (Worldwatch Institute, 1981, p. 3).

The total social welfare package in the Soviet Union appears to us to be remarkably wide-ranging, and there is a seeming capacity in the system to make modifications as needs are recognized and as policies change. The major question that needs to be answered for our purposes is one of adequacy. Are these programs able to offset the risk of poverty for women who are the sole support of their families?

One measure of the value added to earnings by the social welfare system is the expenditures that are made from the Soviet Social Consumption Funds. In 1986, it was estimated that on average 153 rubles were added to each citizen's income by these funds (Scherer, 1987, p. 291). This average figure does not offer a breakdown of who received these funds, such as single parents or retirees, and it cannot be determined, therefore, whether these funds helped to lift single-parent mothers above the poverty standard.

Many of the allowances in the programs that have been described here were raised at the beginning of the 1980s. Until recently, the rate of inflation in the U.S.S.R. was fairly well contained, so that these increases, many of which were long in coming, may have only kept pace with inflation. Generally benefits alone do not reach the level of the poverty line (Matthews, 1986, p. 175). Lacking needed statistical data, we cannot arrive at a firm conclusion with regard to the adequacy of the total social welfare package in forestalling poverty for single-parent women, especially those caring for more than one child.

DEMOGRAPHIC FACTORS

Virtually since the beginning of the century Soviet women have outnumbered men in the population due to severe losses suffered in the revolution, both world wars, and the period of civil war. While the disproportion has eased since the 1950s, as late as 1982, women constituted 53.2 percent of the population (Peers, 1985, p. 117).

The nuclear family has become the norm in the U.S.S.R. The traditional extended family is still seen in rural areas but rarely in developed regions (McAndrew and Peers, 1981, p. 17). In 1985, the population was almost two-thirds urban (65.6 percent) (United Nations, 1989, p. 59). The 1979 census depicts the size of the urban family as comprising 3.3 persons, compared to 3.8 persons in the family of the countryside (Peers, 1985, p. 128).

Women in the European republics of the Soviet Union appear to be limiting the size of their families as a way of easing their domestic double burden. Limiting their families to one or, at most, two children is also a way of maintaining their current living standards.

While women in the European republics state a preference for larger families, they tend to have few children. In the Russian republic, 56 percent of the couples have only one child; 33 percent have two children; 6 percent have three children. This means that more than 89 percent of the families in the republic of Russia, the most populous of the Soviet republics, have fewer children than the population replacement rate (Binyon, 1985, p. 36).

Divorce rates have been rising steadily since 1965, when Stalin's restrictions on obtaining a divorce were rescinded (Imbrogno and Imbrogno, 1986, p. 95). In the mid–1970s, about one marriage in three ended in a divorce, with the rate being even higher in large cities (Peers, 1985, p. 131). Divorces occur primarily in the early years of marriage, and a high proportion of marriages end during the first year. Surveys describe the husband's alcoholism as the most frequent reason why women seek divorce (Imbrogno and Imbrogno, 1986, p. 96).

Following divorce, men are twice as likely as women to remarry. One study found that ten years after divorce, 50 percent of the men were remarried as compared to only one-fourth of the women (Pukhova, 1988a, p. 27). A survey conducted in an urban area found 7.9 percent of women over age 16 were divorced or separated, compared to only 3.8 percent of the men (Peers, 1985, p. 132). The rising divorce rate clearly adds to the high proportion of women in the Soviet population who are alone or who are raising children by themselves, many of them as the sole support of their families.

Abortions are legally available through the national health system and require only the payment of a small fee. There are some restrictions on when the abortions can be performed, for example, not within six months of a previous birth or abortion and not after the twelfth week of pregnancy (Holland and McKevitt, 1985, p. 152). Nevertheless, abortion is widely used as a method of family planning, and it is believed that four to five abortions per women is not unusual (p. 152). Other higher estimates reflect the fact that women obtain abortions privately (or even illegally) for a variety of reasons, such as secrecy, quicker access to treatment, and quality of care.

Whereas public discussion about sexual behavior and issues like abortion and contraception has been avoided in the past, concern about the impact of multiple abortions on the woman's health and her ability to bear further children has emerged. Some attempts are being made once again to introduce family life education into the schools (Soboleva, 1988) and to disseminate contraceptive information and devices more widely (Holland and McKevitt, 1985, p. 152).

In a study of why abortions were sought, married women replied that they found "jobs and housework too time consuming," that apartments were poorly designed for large families, and that there were shortages of space in day care and after-school programs (Imbrogno and Imbrogno, 1986, p. 96). Despite a move toward a more pronatalist policy, there is no evidence that restrictions on abortions are being considered by Soviet policymakers.

The 1979 census figure for one-parent families was 7.9 million (Matthews, 1986, p. 48). The latest figure for the total number of Soviet families is 70 million (Pukhova, 1988a, p. 27), which would bring the proportion of single-parent families to about 8.9 percent of all families. Maggie McAndrew and Jo Peers (1981, p. 17) cite the percentage as 11 percent, although they do not offer their source.[9] A more accurate and comparable figure for single-parent families in the U.S.S.R. would require data on the total number of families with children.

The high rate of divorce contributes to the figure of "over 700,000 children under 18 who remained without one of the parents" (Pukhova, 1988a, p. 27). Matthews (1986) cited the figure of 500,000 children born to unmarried mothers annually, according to the 1979 census. Salvatore Imbrogno and Nadia Ilyin Imbrogno (1986, pp. 96–97) report that in the Russian republic, the total number of children born to unmarried mothers doubled between 1970 and 1978, but they do not provide the change in the rate of such births.

Following divorce or the acknowledgment of paternity, the father is responsible for paying child support: one-fourth of his wage for one child, one-third for two, and one-half for three or more children, under 18 years of age. After years of frequent complaints in the press and in the courts that payments were not received or that they arrived late, regulations were introduced in the 1960s to require that compulsory deductions be taken from the father's wages. Apparently further changes have been made to assure that women receive needed child support on a regular and timely basis through the establishment of a National Alimony Fund in 1983–1984 (Soboleva, 1988). The mother now can receive child support payments directly from the Fund, which, in turn, can pursue the husband for nonpayment.

In view of the high divorce rate, the low remarriage rate for women, and the large numbers of children identified as living with one parent, it seems safe to conclude that the single parent population in the Soviet Union is large and growing rapidly.

WOMEN AND POVERTY

In general those who have written about the Soviet Union seem to assume that the social welfare system and job security provisions protect the Soviet citizen from poverty (Hollander, 1978, p. 338). For example, Michael Binyon states that, "The system does provide people with much that is essential: with jobs, security, cheap food and housing, a health service, reasonable salaries and a slow but gradual improvement in the standard of living" (1985, p. 5). However Binyon points out that households headed by women "constitute one of the most poorly provided-for groups in Soviet society" (p. 51). Contradicting Binyon's view somewhat, Jill M. Bystydzienski, who has compared women in Poland and the U.S.S.R., reports that when Russian women were interviewed about divorce, they "express confidence that a divorced women and a single parent could manage well in their society" (1989, p. 678). Matthews states, however, that "broken marriages and illegitimacy can be direct causes of poverty if the children have to be maintained on one income" (1986, p. 49). He adds that "in the late seventies, such assistance, except in the case of very high alimony [child support], was far below the per capita poverty threshold. In any case, most maintenance payments terminated at early stages, when the child's needs were still increasing" (p. 48).

One study cited by Matthews (1986) provides evidence of the extent of poverty among single-parent families. This survey of 600 families was conducted in 1978 in Estonia, which has one of the highest standards of living in the U.S.S.R. The survey did not set out to examine poverty specifically, but the findings revealed that 18 percent of "full families with children" and 28 percent of "incomplete" or single-parent families fell below the poverty threshold of 60 rubles per person (pp. 23–24).

The introduction of allowances for children in poor families constituted an official acknowledgment that family poverty exists in the Soviet Union, and it would be fair to assume that many single parents are among the beneficiaries. Mikhail Zakharov and Robert Tsivilyov commented that, "apart from their main purpose to assist families with children, the allowances have become a major socio-economic indicator. They indicate the number of low-income families" (1978, p. 72). These Soviet authors do not provide the total number of such families, nor do they provide a breakdown of the subgroups among the families who are receiving these benefits. Matthews calculated that in 1980, 14.9 percent of children were supported by these allowances (1986, p. 47, table 2.10).

The persistently high infant mortality rate, as described earlier, is another important indicator of poverty among Soviet women. It should be noted that there are wide variations in infant mortality rates between the European republics, where rates are more similar to other industrialized countries, and the Central Asian republics where birth rates are alarmingly high and medical facilities very limited (Binyon, 1985, p. 59; Fein, 1989b, pp. A1, A6; Peers, 1985, pp. 129–130).

On the other hand, Soviet women have a very high degree of attachment to the labor force and do not encounter many of the marginalizing conditions that exaggerate the risk of poverty for women in many of the industrialized countries in our study. Soviet women do not have to face intermittent or prolonged unemployment, the loss of seniority, employment rights, and pension entitlements when they take maternity and other child-related leaves, and they are not part-time workers whose earnings and benefits are often so inadequate. In some capitalist nations, these interruptions in the flow of earnings, coupled with the lack of fringe benefits, help push women, particularly low-wage women, into poverty from which they find it difficult subsequently to rebound.

Women's poverty in the Soviet Union also needs to be examined in the wider context of national poverty. Until very recently, Soviet poverty figures were not publicly available, and discussion of poverty was virtually banned (Matthews, 1986, pp. xi, 176). The estimates of nationwide poverty that we have been able to obtain vary widely. A leading Soviet economist, Leonid E. Kunelsky, the chief of the Economics Department of the State Committee on Labor and Social Issues stated that "more than 43 million people [or 20 percent] are living in families with incomes of less than 75 rubles a month per person" (Fein, 1989a, pp. A1, A9).[10] Matthews concluded that some "two-fifths of the non-peasant labour force earned less than the sum needed to achieve a minimum level of subsistence proposed by Soviet scholars for the small urban families" (1986, p. 176), almost *double* the Soviet estimate. An explanation of this difference will have to await the arrival of more data, some of which have been promised by the Soviet authorities (Keller, 1989a, p. A4).

Women's poverty in the Soviet Union also needs to be seen against a background of generally low living standards, that is, from a relative as well as an absolute perspective. In this vein, Matthews comments that:

Although the condition of the poor is, from a Western perspective, unenviable, they are in some respects less vulnerable than one might suppose. They avoid, it would appear, unemployment. . . . Their diet might be far from satisfactory, but it is well above malnutrition. The clothing situation, though difficult, is not disastrous. Most poor people, by capitalist standards, have moderate housing costs and considerable security of tenure. Many have benefited from the house-building programmes of recent decades. Education and health are free and although the poor do not generally get the best, or even adequate services, the problem of fees does not in itself inhibit access (1986, p. 178).

There are few studies by Western social scientists that can serve as a guide to the extent of female poverty in the Soviet Union. Matthews' (1986) work is an exception although it is not specifically focused on the poverty of women. Bernice Madison (1977) studied the Soviet social welfare system and social services for women some years ago. Based on pre–1975 data, she concluded that "there was a failure of income maintenance programs to lift many eligible individuals and families out of poverty" (p. 329). She also noted that, "There has been a pronounced expansion of social services for women during the Soviet period, and services have become more generous, more diversified and more accessible" (p. 329). Madison went on to deplore the lack of Soviet research, stating, "significant evaluative research in social services simply does not exist— to say nothing of the huge gap in published statistical information" (p. 33). No studies were found that measured the adequacy of benefits, living standards, or living arrangements of beneficiaries, nor was there a single study on the impact of family allowances on the lives of recipients (p. 330).

Based on our review, there are a combination of forces that we believe are currently acting to prevent or ameliorate poverty among women of working/ reproductive age.

First, since the early 1970s, the Soviets have intervened in the labor market to grant general wage increases, to raise the minimum wage, and to increase wages in the labor market sectors and professions in which women predominate. While the specific impact of these increases is not known to us from Soviet data, it is fair to assume that these actions, taken cumulatively, will have the effect of removing a substantial number from poverty. The new training programs for women, particularly useful to those with young children, should help to upgrade women into positions or occupations that are more highly paid than their current jobs.

Secondly, Soviet women, particularly those who live in urban centers and industrialized areas, have engaged in their own personal antipoverty strategy by limiting the size of their families to only one child. The availability of legal abortions has helped make this possible. In combination with wage increases, this has probably proved an effective strategy, although some women have had to override their personal preferences or to withstand social pressure for larger families.

Third, the Soviets have introduced new procedures for obtaining child support. Similar to the Swedish system of advance maintenance, these private income transfers will be paid by the state and should provide women with needed income on a more regular basis than is now the case.

Finally, some of the general characteristics and values of Soviet society and the multitiered Soviet social welfare structure may help women and their children to forestall or avoid poverty; there are a variety of programs to which all women including single mothers can turn; the concept of deterrence is largely absent; family ties remain close; and there is a strong cultural ethos about collective responsibility.

THE ROLE OF WOMEN IN FORMULATING POLICY

Despite their double burden, women have been participating increasingly in public life. In 1979, Soviet women constituted almost half (49 percent) of the representatives to local legislatures; 35 percent at the republic level; and 32 percent at the national level (Browning,1985, p. 208).[11] Women made up almost three-fifths of the membership of trade unions (59.5 percent) in 1982 (Lovenduski, 1986, p. 198) and are now found more frequently in union leadership positions. However the proportion of women in the Communist Party, the major site of political power, is relatively low, with women comprising only 27 percent of the total membership in 1982 (Browning, 1985, p. 209). Women's absence from leadership positions in the Party is rather striking. Only two women have been appointed to the Politburo since the revolution. Aleksandra P. Biryukova, a nonvoting member, began to serve in 1988, the first woman appointed since the departure of Yekaterina Furtseva, over twenty-five years before (Keller, 1989b, p. A6). In the large and influential Central Committee of the Communist Party, women comprised only 3.82 percent of the membership in 1981, a figure which "has not increased during the period of the USSR's existence" (Browning, 1985, p. 207).

Of equal importance to their numerical representation is the degree of influence and independence that women have in defining the terms of political and policy debates. Since the mid–1960s, women have been able to use the press and other public forums to express their dissatisfaction with the double burden, poor working conditions, and the quality of consumer goods. Jerry F. Hough, who reviewed the Soviet press and records of legislative bodies, trade union and Communist Party meetings found that "What seems to be absent from all published Soviet discussion of the position of women is the view that all differences in treatment are wrong and/or that women are subject to systematic discrimination" (1977, p. 364). Women's dissatisfactions are usually formulated as criticisms of a particular enterprise or a specific husband. This often leads to exhortations to husbands to share housework or to the exposure of discriminatory behavior by the staff of a specific workplace. There is no discussion of possible sources of these problems in social and economic policies that have been developed largely without the participation of women. Most observers report that Soviet women accept male party leadership as benevolent and see themselves as part of the general polity rather than as a special interest group in the Western sense. So that while Soviet women are increasing their participation in public life and are more able to voice their discontent, ''male leadership continues to define the terms of women's emancipation'' (Engel, 1987, p. 792).

The history of women's organizations in the Soviet Union—the Zhenodtel of the 1920s and the Zhensovety of the 1960s to 1980s—reveals that Soviet women's organizations do not set policy but rather implement policies that have been developed elsewhere. Historically the Zhenodtel was carefully scrutinized by male Communist Party leaders for separatist or ''feminist tendencies'' (Stites, 1978, pp. 341–342). Typically the task of ''building socialism'' took precedence over women's unique needs and experiences. Genia Browning who studied the Zhensovety concluded that, ''As women, they are presented not only with an *a priori* definition of political priorities but also one that is male oriented'' (1985, p. 220).

The Soviet Women's Committee was transformed in 1987 from an international to an internal women's organization. The stimulus for this change came from Mikhail Gorbachev's call for ''women's support in order to accomplish the task of restructuring [perestroika]'' (Pukhova, 1988a, p. 2). Some of the strategies that have been discussed to implement perestroika—for example, allowing for some unemployment, the loosening of job tenure (Connor, 1986), and the introduction of advanced technology and automation—can have negative economic consequences for women. The Soviet Women's Committee appears to have accepted Gorbachev's charge but has publicly commented that the layoffs proposed in the next two Five-year Plans will affect about 16 million manual laborers, at least 15 million of whom are women (Pukhova, 1988b, p. 23).

It is not only the policy of perestroika that may have short- or long-term negative economic consequences for women. The adoption of a pronatalist policy may be also problematic. Indeed, Mary Buckley (1985) and others (see, for example, Lapidus, 1985, p. 28) share the view that Soviet policy is now moving in a pronatalist direction. Buckley states that, ''In the last two decades, Soviet writings on the family have not been couched in terms of the need to socialize housework and restructure the family, but rather in terms of the need to boost the birthrate through strengthening and stabilizing the nuclear family'' (1985, p. 45). The reasons for this possible shift are thought to be the declining birth rates in the industrialized areas of the European republics and anticipated labor force needs. Already several programs, including the newly extended paid maternity leave, have been put in place. Shorter hours and part-time work for women are receiving serious consideration, despite the fact that in industrial work this might lead to the separation of women part-time workers from the rest of the labor force and further the concentration of women in low-skill and low-wage jobs (Lapidus, 1985, p. 27).

It is likely that many women struggling with the double burden may welcome part-time work, particularly if rights to return to full-time employment, leaves, and seniority are retained. Some Soviet proposals for a shorter workday for women have recommended that there be no loss in pay (Lapidus, 1985, p. 25). Vera Soboleva (1988), of the Soviet Women's Committee, feels confident that part-time work will be offered only as an option or a benefit and will not be forced upon women who do not request it.

In conclusion, the needs of the Soviet economy, as defined by male Communist Party leadership, have led to policies broadly designed to enhance either production or reproduction. Such objectives are formulated without the input of women, despite the fact that it is women who experience the effect of these policies directly, even intimately. Beginning in the 1970s, for example, the Soviets became more active in their efforts to reduce the toll of women's double burden and facilitate women's productive role. Large budgetary allocations for social needs led to increases in child care, housing, the supply of household appliances, and the availability of prepared foods at work sites and other measures. Entering the 1980s, when a more pronatalist policy was defined, maternity and family allowances were increased and extended maternity leaves introduced. Wedded to the women's dual role, Soviet planners have not seriously attempted to reconceptualize the male's role in work and family life. Ideological constraints, moreover, appear to have limited the development of social innovation.

Historically the U.S.S.R. has pioneered among nations in establishing women's equality. Possibly as a result of their pioneering role, their impressive achievements, and their ideological perspective, the Soviets have found it difficult to recognize and confront the changed conditions of women's lives. New sources of economic vulnerability have arisen for women in industrial and postindustrial society, and new policies are needed to respond to the complex interplay of historical, structural, and demographic factors that contribute to the feminization of poverty.

NOTES

1. Article 34 of the Soviet Constitution of 1977 reads: "Citizens of the USSR shall be equal before the law irrespective of origin, social or property status, nationality, race, sex. . . . Equality of the rights of the citizens of the USSR shall be ensured in all fields of economic, political, social and cultural life." Article 35 states:

In the USSR women shall have equal rights with men. Exercise of these rights shall be ensured by according to women equal opportunities for education and professional training, for employment, remuneration and promotion, for social political and cultural activity, and likewise by special measures for the protection of the labour and health of women; by legal protection, material and moral support of mother and child, including paid leave and other benefits to mothers and expectant mothers and state aid to unmarried mothers (McAndrew and Peers, 1981, p. 10).

2. For a full discussion on the status of rural women in the Soviet Union, see Susan Bridger (1987).

3. Central Intelligence Agency (CIA) figures for 1988 describe the total Soviet GNP as 2.5 trillion dollars, compared to 4.9 trillion dollars for the United States—the Soviet total being closer to one-half rather than one-fourth of the United States GNP (Protzman, 1989, pp. 1, 14). We have used the 1986 GNP per capita figure, obtained from the UNICEF publication *The State of the World's Children* (1989, p. 95).

4. Margaret E. Leahy (1986), however, using 1980 data, states that 71 percent of women between the ages of 15 and 64 were employed. Her figures do not include students, and the age classification used, while comparable to that in most Western countries, does not reflect the 55-year retirement age for women in the Soviet Union. If that were used, the percentage of employed would, of course, be much higher, although the earlier retirement age can also inflate the labor force participation figure by removing potentially unemployed women workers from the labor market.

5. The labor participation rate in the Soviet Union in 1985 for women 15 to 64 years old was 70.0 percent. This was exceeded in the ECE region and in North America only by Sweden (77.3 percent) and East Germany (77.5 percent) (Turgeon, 1989, p. 57). National Soviet figures reflect lower labor force participation rates among women in the more traditional republics of Central Asia and the Transcaucasus. Further, the proportion of women working part-time in both Sweden and East Germany is considerably higher than in the U.S.S.R.

6. The figure of 200 rubles for the national average wage (for both sexes combined) was obtained in an interview with N. Rimashevskaya (1988).

7. The total number of days for pregnancy leave, taken before birth, was increased to seventy days in legislation passed in 1981 (Matthews, 1986, p. 171).

8. UNICEF figures for other countries in this study, for the year 1987, are: Poland, 18; United States, 10; France, 8; Canada, 8; Sweden, 6; and Japan, 6 (1989, p. 95).

9. The lack of consistent national statistical data presents a real obstacle to understanding trends in the size of the single-parent population. No statistical breakdown is provided to distinguish between subgroups of single parents, that is, widows, divorced and separated, and the unmarried. Aggravating these difficulties is the fact that some authors apply the term "single-parent family" only to unmarried mothers, whereas others use the term to apply to all women who are raising children without a spouse or partner. As elsewhere, women are overwhelmingly the custodial parents in the Soviet Union.

10. As indicated earlier, the 75 ruble figure is the proposed new poverty standard, which is not yet in use. It is anticipated that when the results of the current census become available, the present figure of 51 rubles will have been raised to 75 rubles.

11. By way of comparison, the highest rates of women's representation in national legislative bodies in 1985 were: Finland, 31 percent; Sweden, 29 percent; Denmark, 26 percent; and Norway, 26 percent (Seager and Olson, 1986, p. 115). The figure for the United States (House and Senate combined) was 5.2 percent in 1989 (Dionne, 1989, p. A12).

REFERENCES

Binyon, M. (1985). *Life in Russia*. New York: Berkley Books.

Bridger, S. (1987). *Women in the Soviet Countryside*. Cambridge: Cambridge University Press.

Browning, G. (1985)."Soviet politics—Where are the women?" In B. Holland, ed. *Soviet Sisterhood*. Bloomington: Indiana University Press.

Buckley, M. (1985). "Soviet interpretations of the woman question." In B. Holland, ed. *Soviet Sisterhood*. Bloomington: Indiana University Press.

Bystydzienski, J. M. (1989). "Women and socialism: A comparative study of women in Poland and the USSR." *SIGNS* 14: 668–684.

Connor, W. D. (1986). "Social policy under Gorbachev." *Problems of Communism* 35: 31–46.

———. (June 2, 1987). "Soviet society and social policy." *The Soviet Union in the Gorbachev Era*. Remarks at Third Annual P.A.W.S.S. Summer Faculty Institute on the Soviet Union and U.S.-Soviet Relations, Hampshire College, Amherst, MA.

Dionne, E. J., Jr. (August 8, 1989). "Women make gains in attaining office." *New York Times*, p. A12.

Dodge, N. T. (1966). *Women in the Soviet Economy*. Baltimore, MD: Johns Hopkins University Press.

Engel, B. A. (1987). "Women in Russia and the Soviet Union." *SIGNS* 12: 781–796.

Fein, E. B. (1989a, January 20). "Soviet openness brings poverty out of the shadows." *New York Times*, pp. A1, A9.

———. (1989b, August 14). "In Soviet Asia backwater, infancy's a rite of survival." *New York Times*, pp. A1, A6.

Hansson, C., and K. Liden (1983). *Moscow Women: Thirteen Interviews*. New York: Pantheon Books.

Holland, B., and T. McKevitt (1985). "Maternity care in the Soviet Union." In B. Holland, ed. *Soviet Sisterhood*. Bloomington: Indiana University Press.

Hollander, P. (1978). *Soviet and American Society: A Comparison*. Chicago: The University of Chicago Press.

Hough, J. F. (1977). "Women and women's issues in Soviet policy debates." In D. Atkinson, A. Dallin, and G. W. Lapidus, eds. *Women in Russia*. Stanford, CA: Stanford University Press.

Imbrogno, S., and N. I. Imbrogno (1986). "Marriage and family in the USSR: Changes are emerging." *Social Casework* 67: 90–100.

International Labour Office (ILO) (1984). *Women at Work: Employment for Women (1975–1985)*. Geneva: ILO.

Keller, B. (1989a, January 19). "Prying where it counts: Into the Soviet census." *New York Times*, p. A4.

———. (1989b, January 24). "A Soviet women's point of view." *New York Times*, p. A6.

Lapidus, G. W. (1978). *Women in Soviet Society*. Berkeley: University of California Press.

———. (1985). "The Soviet Union." In J. Farley, ed. *Women Workers in Fifteen Countries*. Ithaca, NY: ILR Press.

Leahy, M. E. (1986). *Development Strategies and the Status of Women: A Comparative Study of the United States, Mexico, the Soviet Union and Cuba*. Boulder, CO: Lynne Rienner Publishers.

Lisitin, Y., and K. Batygin (1978). *The USSR: Public Health and Social Security*. Moscow: Progress Publishers.

180   The Feminization of Poverty

Lovenduski, J. (1986). *Women in European Politics*. Brighton, Sussex: Wheatsheaf Books.

Madison, B. (1977). "Social services for women: Problems and priorities." In D. Atkinson, A. Dallin, and G. S. Lapidus, eds. *Women in Russia*. Stanford, CA: Stanford University Press.

Matthews, M. (1986). *Poverty in the Soviet Union*. Cambridge: Cambridge University Press.

McAndrew, M., and J. Peers (January 1981). "The new Soviet woman—Model or myth?" *CHANGE*. International Reports: Women and Society. London.

McAuley, A. (1981). *Women's Work and Wages in the Soviet Union*. London: George Allen and Unwin.

Millar, J. R. (July 1986). *The Soviet Interview Project: History, Method and the Problem of Bias*. Soviet Interview Project, Working Paper #27. Urbana-Champaign: University of Illinois at Urbana-Champaign.

Morgan, R. (1984). *Sisterhood is Global*. Garden City, NY: Anchor Press/Doubleday.

Motorshilova, N. (August 1988). Interview. Institute of Philosophy, Moscow.

Ofer, G. and A. Vinokur (1985). "Work and family roles of Soviet women." *Journal of Labor Economics* 3, Part 2: 328–354.

Peers, J. (1985). "Workers by hand and womb—Soviet women and the demographic crisis." In B. Holland, ed. *Soviet Sisterhood*. Bloomington: Indiana University Press.

Protzman, F. (November, 20, 1989). "The Germanys as an economic giant." *New York Times*, pp. 1, 14.

Pukhova, Z. (1988a). *For a Better Life and More Good Will*. Moscow: Novosti Press Agency Publishing House.

———. (1988b). "Remarks at the Plenary Session of the Soviet Women's Committee." *The Current Digest of the Soviet Press* XL, p. 23.

Rimashevskaya, N. (August 1988). Interview. Center for Social Matters and Population, Moscow.

Ryan, M. (1978). *The Organization of Soviet Medical Care*. London: Basil Blackwell and Mott Ltd.

Scherer, J. L., ed. (1987). *USSR: Facts and Figures Annual* 11. Gulf Breeze, FL: Academic International Press.

Schmemann, S. (October 28, 1986). "Kremlin resumes issuing key data." *New York Times*, p. A7.

Scott, H. (1974). *Does Socialism Liberate Women?* Boston: Beacon Press.

Seager, J., and A. Olson (1986). *Women in the World: An International Atlas*. New York: Simon & Schuster/Touchstone Books.

Shabad, T. (February 20, 1987). "Soviet sociologist candid about official disregard for her science." *New York Times*, p. A10.

Shulman, C. (1977). "The individual and the collective." In D. Atkinson, A. Dallin, and G. W. Lapidus, eds. *Women in Russia*. Stanford, CA: Stanford University Press.

Soboleva, V. (August 1988). Interview. Soviet Committee on Women, Moscow.

Stites, R. (1978). *The Women's Liberation Movement in Russia*. Princeton, NJ: Princeton University Press.

Swafford, M. (1978). "Sex differences in Soviet earnings." *American Sociological Review* 43: 657–673.

Turgeon, L. (1989). *State and Discrimination: The Other Side of the Cold War*. Armonk, NY: M. E. Sharpe.

Unesco (United Nations Educational and Scientific Organization) (1983). *Research on the Status of Women. Development and Population Trends in Eastern Europe: An Annotated Bibliography by Barbara Tryfan*. New York: Bowker/UNIPUB.

UNICEF (United Nations Children's Fund) (1989). *The State of the World's Children*. New York: Oxford University Press.

United Nations (UN) (1989). *Compendium of Statistics and Indicators on the Situation of Women in 1986*. Series K, No. 5. New York: United Nations.

Worldwatch Institute (December 12, 1981). "Infant mortality and the health of societies." News release, Worldwatch Institute, 1776 Massachusetts Avenue, N.W., Washington, DC 20036.

Zakharov, M., and R. Tsivilyov (1978). *Social Security in the USSR*. Moscow: Progress Publishers.

8

Poland: A Country of Conflicts

SOPHIE WOJCIECHOWSKI

Contemporary Poland is a country of 37 million people located in the heart of Europe between the East and West. For many centuries, Poland's political and cultural links were with the West. After World War II in 1945, the Yalta agreement reached by the victorious allied powers brought Poland, the largest country in eastern Europe, directly under the political influence of the Soviet Union. Many Poles never accepted this agreement because it deprived Poland of its political independence. The new borders created by the Yalta agreement changed Poland's population as well as its frontiers, making it a much more homogeneous country with few minority groups and a population that is over 90 percent Catholic.

During the years 1945–1949, Poland became, in effect, a one-party state with the communist-dominated United Polish Workers Party being the majority in the Polish Parliament (*Sejm*) with 450 seats. Other parties in the Polish Parliament were never able to form an effective opposition. Following the Soviet political model, the Act of Land Reform and the Act of Nationalization of Industry were passed, and the economy was nationalized through the process of expropriation without any compensation to the former owners.

The new system based on the national ownership of property became the base of a centrally planned economy. There was some opposition to this by a few outstanding Polish economists, members of the State Economic Council, who were critical of such an excessive growth of the state apparatus. Oscar Lange, an economist, well known in the West, warned that such a plan was not suited to Poland's economic conditions and that it would harm "the initiative of the masses" (Hunter, 1986). Some successful opposition to total nationalization, however, was accomplished in the field of agriculture. State agriculture units were created, but only from the land confiscated from large land owners, the aristocracy, and the church. Private ownership of small farms (two to ten hectares) was retained with the result that Polish peasants became a unique, independent social class in eastern Europe. Some nonsocialized small industry was also permitted.

For more than forty years, Poles have been the recipients of various universal social benefits provided by the "welfare state" of the socialist government. These benefits include universal health services, free education on all levels, low-cost public housing, free or low-paid vacations, especially for families with children and older people, low-cost public transportation, and government-subsidized prices for basic food items. In addition to these social policies, the government has guaranteed full employment.

Despite these universal programs, many Poles have believed that the Western type of market economy and the American style of "rugged individualism" would be much better for their country. In fact, it is said that, "there can be few countries in the world where the system of government is held in greater disrepute than it is in Poland"(Davies, 1986, p. 1). The general feeling in Poland has been animosity toward external domination. The intensity of the disrepute in which the government was held fluctuated. Attempts to work out some compromise between the ruling United Polish Workers Party and the majority of the people had emerged in every decade since 1945, although the compromises had been of short duration.

In 1980, conflicts between the ruling party and Solidarity, a union of working people, aroused all of Polish society. This led to a declaration of martial law in December 1981, taken as a preventive measure against the possible invasion of Poland by Soviet troops. Concurrently, Solidarity was declared illegal. These events had serious consequences for the Polish economy. As a result of the imposition of martial law, Poland's privileged trade status with the United States was cancelled. By the end of the 1980s, troubled by strikes and inflation, the Polish economy had deteriorated drastically, reaching its worst economic crisis since the end of World War II.

Faced with disaster, Poles from all social groups—industrial workers, academics, professionals, and so on—mobilized to search for a solution to their country's severely ailing political and economic system. In 1989, a compromise was reached at a round table meeting among the various political parties, the Catholic Church, and the United Polish Workers Party. Following this meeting, Solidarity regained its status as a legal union. While all the round table results have not been publicized, it is known that democratization of the political system will be synchronized with the introduction of features of a market economy such as private initiative, which can help attract foreign capital. Attempts were made to retain central control of the economy and the system of broad social welfare provisions.

The forty-five-year experience of the Polish People's Republic was a period of dynamic change, which can be divided into several phases. During the first phase, the war-torn country was rebuilt. In the second phase, the wealth and income were redistributed in an attempt to build an egalitarian welfare society. There was a very modest standard of living for most social groups during this period. The next phase of the national economy was the growing industrialization of the country, which produced a higher standard of living for most people.

In the late 1970s, however, Poland became dependent on the world economy by accepting extensive financial loans from the West. These loans were made to accelerate industrialization and the modernization of the Polish economy, but they may have contributed in part to Poland's subsequent economic distress. Internal economic mismanagement and the worldwide economic crisis of the early 1980s had a major negative effect on Poland's trade balance and on the condition of the national economy.

This chapter was written during a time when Poland's economy was being rapidly transformed. The impact of these changes on the status of women is difficult to predict. Questions have been raised, for example, as to whether women will be able to retain the workplace-related government benefits they now receive (especially those provided in the public sector) in the new private sectors of the economy. In this period of drastic change and inflation, statistical data clearly cannot keep up with the day-to-day changes that are occurring. Events in Poland will need to be followed very carefully in order to identify the impact of the current economic and political transformation on the economic vulnerability of women.

Mobilization of the diverse social constituencies in Poland will, of course, be an important element in a successful revival of the economy. There is a historical precedent for this. During the years 1945 to 1949, the reconstruction of war-torn Poland was accomplished despite the loss of over 6 million of its citizens and about 60 percent of its prewar assets. Poland experienced an amazing recovery and showed in those years an 18 to 29 percent increase in economic growth (Hunter, 1986). This surpassed the levels of growth in any other postwar period. During this period of reconstruction, all of Poland's people were mobilized, and the contribution of women to this effort was unstinting.

In the current crisis, the effort of all Poles will be needed once again to achieve successful reform. While in the past, women provided much of the leadership for economic reconstruction, they were not proportionately represented in the critical round table discussions of 1989. Among the fifty-six participants, only one was a woman, a professor in sociology at Warsaw University. Despite the socialist government's rhetoric and Solidarity's democratic idealism, women have not been offered proportionate leadership roles in the current period of economic and political change. They have provided mainly technical help and support. There seems to have been a strong reaction to their absence, however, especially in the women's press. An editorial in the weekly magazine *Woman and Life* said, ''Decisions are made about us without us'' (Kaszuba, 1989).

A HISTORICAL OVERVIEW OF THE ROLE OF WOMEN

From its very beginning, Poland has had a turbulent relationship with its neighbors. Various aggressive actions from countries to the east and the west have demanded constant vigilance. During the long period of partition of Poland by Russia, Germany, and Austria (1795–1918), the population was involved in numerous national uprisings, and the human sacrifice was great. Poles were not only killed, but thousands were deported to Siberia or emigrated abroad.

During the thousand years of Polish history, women have played a very special role. When left alone, women had to assume responsibility for the survival of the family and for bringing up children in the Polish tradition. When, in certain parts of the country, schools were closed and teaching of the Polish langauge was forbidden, women developed an underground system for teaching the Polish language, history, and literature. These activities were undertaken at great risk, and they demanded a great deal of courage.

More recent Polish history reveals the same pattern of women's roles and sacrifices. During the German occupation (1939–1945), women were actively involved in the underground army as liaison officers and couriers.[1] They were responsible for contacts with prisoners of war in concentration camps. Women transported money and ammunition. In the Warsaw uprising of 1944, women faced exactly the same danger as male soldiers, although their contribution was not fully recognized.

The front line is a great equalizer. Men and women were in equal measure heroic and afraid. There are many stories of women's heroism. However, women were always overworked. Often they received neither rank nor honors for their heroism. Their sacrifices were the greatest, and their contributions the least recorded (Steven, 1982, p. 352).

Polish women, who are the survivors of many wars and revolutions, have developed a perspective different from that of most women in America and western Europe. Polish women feel they have already won their formal equality with men. In the first Polish constitution of 1921 and in all subsequent formulations, women are accorded equal rights with men in all spheres: political, economic, social, and cultural.

WOMEN IN THE LABOR MARKET

From the beginning of the post–World War II reconstruction of Poland, it was evident that the success of the highly labor-intensive rebuilding of the country would depend on the participation of women. During the years from 1945 to 1949, men and women were equally involved in rebuilding the country. Economic remuneration seemed to be secondary at that time; volunteer efforts were primary. In the subsequent Six-year Plans, quantitative goals were set for women's participation in the labor market as an essential condition for Poland's economic growth.

An increase in women's participation in the labor force must be considered one of the most significant events in postwar Poland. In 1985, 60 percent of women 15 years old or older were in the labor force. Along with the Soviet

Union, Poland has the highest labor force participation rate among the countries in our study (United Nations, 1989, pp. 176–197).

The following figures were obtained from *Glowny Urzad Statystycny* (GUS), the Central Statistical Office of Poland (1988a, pp. 49–51).[2] They describe the increase of women as a proportion of the labor force in Poland from 1950 to 1985:

Year	Percent
1950	31.0%
1955	31.9%
1960	33.7%
1965	36.8%
1970	39.6%
1975	42.9%
1980	44.2%
1985	45.0%

During periods of high economic growth (1970–1975), women's participation in the labor force increased; in periods of economic stagnation (1975–1980), the increase continued but at a somewhat lower rate. Since the national economy demands a certain stability in women's participation in the labor force, many Polish economists called for measures to maintain women's labor force participation on a more stable basis without abrupt shifts related to short-run political objectives.

At present, women are working in all fields in Poland. In theory at least, no type of work is reserved for men only, except for that work considered harmful for women of reproductive age. Women comprise almost half of the workers in science and technology. Increasingly women are becoming the majority of the workers in education, health and welfare services, administration, law, finance, and insurance. In making educational choices, women tend to enter programs leading to occupations in these fields. Despite the fact that education and jobs are widely open to them in other fields, most women choose people-oriented professions, such as those listed below, as described in material published for the United Nations Decade on Women (Glowny Urzad Statystycny, 1985):

Proportion of Workforce
Who Are Women

Education	79%
Health	81%

Administration/Jurisprudence	63%
Finance/Insurance	85%

Legally there are no sex differences in pay for the same type of work in Poland. This principle appears to work, but data indicate that women's average earnings are about 70 percent of men's earnings (Kurzynowski, 1986, p. 303). Some explanations that have been offered for this apparent inconsistency are:

1. Women are concentrated in low-paid professions.

2. Only a small percentage of women are found in skilled, blue-collar jobs that tend to be higher paid than service jobs.

3. Since supervisory and leadership positions are very hard to combine with the basic roles of mother and housewife, women remain in the less personally taxing positions.

4. Until recently women were less well-educated, academically and vocationally, than men.

5. Polish men appear to have a difficult time accepting women as equal working partners. Women are in demand as auxiliary or supportive personnel but rarely accepted in positions of authority. In Poland, the patriarchal type of family persists and influences labor market relations.

The government's social policy is, in general, guided by pronatalist forces but with a strong emphasis on the need for mothers to participate in the labor force. This policy seems to be an amalgam of the conflicting pressures in the society, which come from various sectors including the church, academicians, and economists.

Of the working women in Poland, a great majority (75 percent) are married; only 13 percent are single; 4 percent are widowed; and about 8 percent are separated or divorced (Les, forthcoming). While there is no legal requirement for women to work, there is significant social pressure that they do so especially if they are professionally trained or not responsible for the care of children. In fact, according to the results of a survey conducted by GUS (1988b), most Polish women believe that they should participate in the labor force but that they should also be provided with time that can be devoted to raising a family. Further, those surveyed feel that they should not be penalized for this interruption of their economic services.[3] Legislation in Poland does provide up to three years of maternity leave, both paid and unpaid, all of which counts toward retirement (Turgeon, 1989, p. 76).

Despite the national economy's need for workers, women in Poland can choose between work or study. Married women who are better educated, whether through professional or vocational education, usually want to enter the labor force and return there soon after the end of their maternity leave. However, the more children a woman has, the less likely she is to return to the labor force. In the current economic crisis situation in Poland, most women are eager to work to supplement their husband's earnings because, in fact, two incomes are necessary for survival.

Poland has had a full employment economy, and all workers, especially those working in the socialized sectors of the economy, have had a sense of job security. Workers have never been fired even when their productivity is low. The government has assumed responsibility for retraining, if needed. The increasing participation of women in various enterprises seems to have improved the general level of efficiency, especially in reducing absenteeism. The original reluctance to hire women, who were considered to be more expensive employees because of work-related benefits, has been reduced as women have demonstrated a high level of productivity (Kurzynowski, 1986).

Most Polish women work full time. Statistical data indicate that of the women who work in the public sector, only 9.6 percent are employed part time (Strzeminska, 1989, pp. 1, 2, 5). Jobs in the private sector provide more opportunities for part-time work, often in trade or in small businesses, such as dressmaking or beauty culture. Many older women take part-time jobs to supplement their pensions.

WOMEN IN THE COUNTRYSIDE

Poland is unique among the countries in this study in that a high proportion of its economy is devoted to agriculture. Women are heavily engaged in work in both the private and public sectors of the agricultural economy. For this reason, despite the focus of this book on women in industrial economies, some discussion of women working in the agricultural sector can serve to deepen our understanding of the lives of Polish women.

Between the two world wars, Poland was a country with a strong agricultural sector. Before 1946, about 70 percent of the population earned its livelihood from agriculture. By 1984, only about 30 percent of the population depended on agriculture, although this figure is far higher than in the capitalist countries in this study (see chapter 1, table 1.1). Due to the intensive industrialization of the country, two trends have emerged: there has been a large scale exodus from rural to urban communities, and a new group of predominantly male workers has emerged who combine agricultural and industrial jobs.

There are two types of private farms: the larger agricultural enterprises that require the use of machinery, and smaller units that are located near urban industrialized communities. Men have left these smaller farm units to seek better paying industrial jobs. The exodus of men from private agricultural units has left women in charge of this farming sector. It is estimated that about 70 percent of small private farms are run by women (Tryfan, 1987). Among the women who run small farms, many are unmarried, widowed, or divorced. Married women, whose husbands work in industry, have not legally owned these farms and have faced legal problems when they become widows or seek to divorce. In 1977, when the social security system was extended to cover rural families, men were covered on the basis of their employment. Women also wanted to be covered for their work but often encountered legal difficulties because the ownership of the farm was in the name of the husband. As a result of many complaints, the law was finally adjusted in 1982 so that women could be included for coverage.

Because of their better housing and the greater availability of modern appliances, cars, and motorcycles, most women in charge of private farms seem to be better off economically than urban women. However, according to Barbara Tryfan (1987), an expert in rural problems, the situation of women in the countryside is not that privileged. Isolation, lack of leisure time, and the exodus of the younger generation to the urban centers affect the lives of women running small farms, especially elderly women. Most complain bitterly that they are overworked and that they have little time for themselves, no vacations, and long working hours. Many mothers in the Polish countryside encourage their daughters to seek better opportunities in the cities.

THE SOCIAL WELFARE STRUCTURE

According to Eva Les (1985), the Polish social welfare system has three major sectors: the governmental or public sector, voluntary associations, and the "informal sector." The range and types of service in each of these sectors vary considerably. The governmental sector, financed and operated by the state, directs the social security system and some basic social services. The nongovernmental sector, comprised of voluntary associations like Caritas, works jointly with public authorities to provide state-subsidized services. The informal sector is partially funded by the public sector and operates through a variety of grassroots groups, operated by volunteers.

Cash benefits are predominantly offered by the governmental sector, while in-kind services predominate in the voluntary and informal sectors. The voluntary sector, comprised of sectarian and nonsectarian associations, foundations, and charitable committees, provides some rehabilitation, special education, health care services, and some supplemental income. In general, voluntary associations are considered complementary to the public sector.

The informal sector is a growing social service sector aimed at addressing unmet needs. Presently there are several hundred mutual aid and self-help organizations in the fields of child welfare and family problems. Now the most vulnerable groups and individuals in the population are attempting to use self-help strategies aimed at meeting their own needs. The informal social welfare sector is attempting to bridge the gap in service delivery between the governmental and voluntary sectors and to monitor and advocate for services at the grassroots level.

Both the voluntary and the informal sectors of social welfare structure are very much concerned with the situation of families and children. Women play a considerable role in the management of these services and are also the majority of the recipients. Volunteer counselors (about 30,000) work under the guidance of professional social workers, numbering about 11,000. Social workers and volunteers are responsible for the "case finding" of individuals and families in need of social services. They are responsible for referral of these individuals and families to the local government authorities or voluntary organizations.[4]

The informal sector helps to provide a sense of security for older women, single mothers with small children, and women with severe handicaps. It also gives them a sense of assurance that they have not been forgotten.

GOVERNMENT TRANSFERS

Many Polish academicians argue that in order to stimulate economic growth in a socialist country, investment in human services is as important as technical and capital input. Following this reasoning, despite modest financial resources, the government made a considerable investment in building a "welfare society" during the first decades of its existence. Subsequently, striking achievements were made in eliminating illiteracy, especially among the rural female population. A free educational system was organized on all levels, and the children of the working class and the rural population were encouraged to attend school. As already noted, all restrictions on the education of women in special fields were eliminated.

Free access to health services was established for all, including compulsory medical examinations and necessary immunizations for children. Free prenatal care and maternity services became available for both urban and rural women. Substantial public housing was built, and free or low-paid vacations for working people and retired seniors were organized and became very popular. Access to cultural events has been greatly facilitated. Summer camps for children and adolescents were made available for the majority of youth. Children with special health problems (e.g., respiratory problems and diabetes) were given the opportunity for intensive treatment in government-sponsored health resorts. For example, in Rabka, a famous spa primarily for children, about 30,000 youngsters receive free intensive treatment every year. Yet Poland needs many more facilities like Rabka for children.

Day care facilities and nurseries are now available for working mothers, although there are widespread shortages. Working women obtain priority in securing a place for their children in public day care facilities, and single mothers who are employed are accorded the highest priority for these slots. There has been a deterioration in the quality of public facilities due to the budget crisis. Increasingly there have been efforts to organize private day care centers. The modest cost of public transportation and government-subsidized prices for basic food items along with these other benefits created a society where about 40 percent of the family budget was covered by government transfers (Rutkowski, 1988).

There were limits, however, to building a "welfare society." All of these public transfers could not satisfy the rapidly growing expectations of the Polish people. Many men and women who received public transfers complained at the same time about the limited supply of health and social services, especially in periods of economic downturn. One of the reasons for this may be that in Poland's centrally planned, highly bureaucratic system, decisions were not the subject of democratic debate. Recipients of services were never actively involved in planning or decision making.[5]

Government transfers in relation to women's participation in the labor force were influenced by two factors: the rate of the country's economic development and pronatalist considerations. In the first Six-year Plan (1950–1955), goals were set to increase the proportion of women in the labor force. During this period, the government encouraged women's education and enforced antidiscrimination legislation in the workplace. In the 1960s, however, due to the very low level of fertility, the government introduced some pronatalist measures, such as family allowances and one year's leave without pay for mothers of children under the age of 4.

During the 1970s, changes were enacted that compensated women for their childbearing and childrearing roles. According to the International Labor Organization (ILO) publication *Poland (Polish People's Republic): Working Women in Specialist Countries* (Titkow, 1985, pp. 132–133), the following are the most important child care and maternity leave provisions that were enacted during the 1970s and the early 1980s in Poland:

—Paid maternity leave was extended from twelve to sixteen weeks for the first birth and eighteen weeks for the second and subsequent births (July 1, 1972).

—Maternity leave for multiple births was extended from eighteen to twenty-six weeks (January 1, 1975).

—Leave with pay for the care of small children was extended from one to three years. At the same time it was decided to count this leave toward the period necessary to obtain a pension (January 28, 1972).

—A benefit for disabled children of 500 zlotys per month was introduced to be paid independently of the normal family allowance for this child (August 1974).

—Fully paid leave for the care of sick children under age 14 was extended from thirty to sixty days per year (January 1, 1982).

—Childbirth benefits were raised for manual workers from 30 to 50 percent of salary and depending on family situation up to 100 percent, thus ending one of the greatest differences in benefits between manual and nonmanual workers (July 1, 1972).

—The first stage of an increase in family allowances was introduced (August 1, 1974).

—The second stage of the increase in family allowances was introduced. This raised benefits for the first, second, and third child in families with incomes below 1,400 zlotys per person per month (August 1, 1975).

—A maternity grant of 2,000 zlotys for every child born was introduced, available irrespective of income and other benefits received (May 1, 1978).

—An alimony fund was established. Persons with an income below 1,400 zlotys per month, unable to obtain child support, received up to 500 zlotys monthly from the state (January 1, 1975).

In the 1980s, mounting inflation, declining productivity, public indebtedness, and low public morale seriously affected the standard of living of the entire Polish population. Those who were most seriously affected were workers on low wages, salaries, and pensions—men and women alike. Investment in building the welfare society was virtually eliminated, with no new monies devoted to public housing, hospital beds, nurseries, and so on. Government subsidies, however, were retained to help the poor and people on the threshold of poverty.

Since 1985, several cost-of-living adjustments were made by the Cabinet to increase the lowest earnings and pension levels in order to keep pace with inflation. Substantial changes in wages, salaries, and family allowances are currently under consideration in Poland.

FAMILY POLICY

The 1964 Family and Custodian Code was enacted in response to the entry of women into the paid labor force. The Family Code stipulated equal rights for spouses, equality of children, and equal cooperation between spouses for the good of the family. The nuclear family was established as the basic social unit. Despite the intentions of the Code, it is believed that women are still relegated to a traditional and often subordinate position in marriage, and the church in Poland has continued to support a traditional patriarchal family structure. Over 75 percent of Polish women are practicing Catholics who tend to follow the Church's views about marriage and contraception. There are, nevertheless, an increasing number of separations, which are not finalized in legal divorces. In the majority of cases, women initiate these separations on the grounds of alcoholism or infidelity. Despite the fact that abortion became legal in Poland in 1956, many women seek out-of-hospital abortions. Women are reluctant to register in public hospitals where they have to reveal their identities.

There is a great need in Poland to provide young people with better education about family life and sex. Yet when a group of well-known teachers and psychologists prepared such a textbook for teenagers, its distribution encountered strong opposition in Catholic circles.

The new Polish Parliament is now considering antiabortion legislation, which appears to have limited support; indeed the proposal aroused protests among the younger generation. There is evidence, too, of a growing movement among young urban women who are demanding greater equality of the sexes and a more equitable division of labor among husbands, wives, and children within the family.

There is also some evidence of a new, more egalitarian family emerging among young families. Young husbands are more willing to play an active part in various household duties (such as shopping, cleaning the house, and taking responsibility for young children) than their fathers were a few decades ago. This is especially evident in urban communities.

EFFORTS TO INCREASE WOMEN'S EQUALITY

For over forty years, the official policy of the Polish People's Republic was to ensure women's full equality in the labor market and in family life. In order to make it possible for women to play an equal role with men in the workplace, many opportunities were opened to women. They not only gained full access to education in all fields and on all levels, but some educational and vocational programs were especially adapted to women's double responsibility. For example, some educational programs are now offered during weekends, and women, even more than men, have taken advantage of this arrangement that allows them to improve their education or to meet various professional requirements. This innovation is especially popular among teachers, social workers, and other white-collar workers.

Poland introduced protective labor legislation for working women in 1924, an accomplishment of the first democratic government. Women were forbidden to work night shifts or in heavy industry in tasks which might endanger their health. All establishments employing more than 100 women were obliged to provide nurseries. Governmental labor inspection was initiated. This nearly seventy-five-year-old tradition of protective labor legislation was reinforced by new legislation in 1974 and 1979 to further protect working women in Poland.

The reality of the labor market—the fact that riskier work is higher paid—means that protective labor legislation can create problems and inequities for women. At the time of the postwar reconstruction or in times of economic hardship, women often have taken "dangerous" jobs, which are usually better paid. The press has reported the protests of skilled women workers who were transferred to lower paying jobs because of the danger posed to their health in the manufacture of thermometers. Also, despite the fact that night shifts for women are discouraged by law, many women request these shifts. They are more highly paid than day shifts, and some women find it easier to combine the night shift with the care of their children.

Despite the original intent of protective labor laws, the need for well-trained labor inspectors to enforce full safety for women in the workplace continues. An editorial in the Polish publication *Kobieta i Zycie* (*Women and Life*) (1989a) describes working conditions in Lodz, the textile center of Poland, which has a predominantly female labor force. Century-old machines that are obsolete, hazardous, and harmful to women's health have not been improved for decades. The article concludes that the absence of protest by women and their lack of political influence are the main reasons for this neglect.

There is continuing evidence of women's failure to advance in academic and scientific work. On the basis of a survey conducted in 1983 (Iwaszczyn, 1987), it was found that more than half of the persons who complete higher education in Poland are women. Whereas the proportion of women taking part in the work of Polish scientific societies is considerable, only a small group of women are given the opportunity to take part in international conferences. In the universities, women occupy only 11 percent of the posts of associate professor. About 60 percent of the administrative posts in universities are occupied by women, but only rarely are they promoted to the higher levels of dean or rector. There is not a single female university president. Often women are supervised by men with lower scientific degrees. Most respondents in this survey were convinced that if they were men, scientific advancement would have been achieved more easily, requiring less sacrifice in their private lives.

DEMOGRAPHIC FACTORS

Since World War II, the population of Poland has increased by 57 percent. In 1946, the population of the country was 23.4 million. In the 1987 census, 37 million people were recorded. This increase was accompanied by pronounced rural-urban population changes. In 1946, the urban population was estimated at 31 percent and by 1987 it had climbed to 57 percent. In 1985, the average life span for women was 74 years and for men 66.5 years. This was a decline from the 1975–1976 census when women lived to an average age of 75 and men to 67.3. At the same time a considerable growth in the elderly population has been noted, and it has been projected that the most rapid increase will be in the 85 and over age group (Glowny Urzad Statystycny, 1988a).

In Poland, people marry young and have children early in life. Only a small number of women in their productive years (18–50) are single. According to GUS data (1988a), the number of divorces is growing, particularly in urban communities. These divorces usually occur in the first ten years of married life. With easy access to gainful employment, contemporary Polish women are apparently not as long suffering as their mothers were. A large proportion of divorcing couples have children, and women most often gain custody of the children. In 1984, there were 1,242,000 divorced mothers (12 percent of all families) who had custody of their children. There were only 153,000 divorced fathers (1.5 percent of all families) who had custody of their children (Rosset, 1986).

During the last forty years, the provision of free prenatal care and maternity services provided by the government has resulted in a continuing decline in the infant mortality rate. According to GUS data (1988a), for every 1,000 births, the mortality rate of children under the age of 1 was 54.8 in 1960, 33.4 in 1970, 24.5 in 1977, 22.5 in 1978, and 18.2 in 1985. Despite the fact that the infant mortality rate has declined continuously in Poland, it is still quite high in comparison with other European countries.

ECONOMIC DEPRIVATION

Until 1980, the term "poverty" was rarely used in Poland. However, the concept of "social minimum" was widely discussed. The Institute of Labor and Social Affairs, an official government agency, was in charge of the development and computation of the social minimum. Attempts were made to include representatives of the unions in this task, but no agreement could be reached on what should be included in the "market basket" items. Two different computations were developed, the union's being the higher one, although the differences were not very great. The market basket includes items that are needed for basic survival plus items related to the cultural and leisure time activities of the individual and the family. Because of rising inflation affecting the prices of basic items, the social minimum has had to be readjusted constantly. In the economic crisis of the late 1980s, it was very difficult to estimate how many people and which particular groups were forced to exist below the social minimum. The official weekly *Polityka* (Hemler, 1988) estimated the figure at about 6 million, which means that about 16 percent of the general population lived below the minimum subsistence level. The government, concerned about the situation, periodically had to raise the level of the lowest wages, pensions, and social welfare benefits.

In response to the current crisis, the Minister of Labor and Social Policy called a conference in May 1988 devoted to the problem of how to estimate the level of poverty at which governmental help becomes essential. It was noted at this conference that an increasing number of Poles were not able to live on the earnings of their labor or solely from their pensions (Rutkowski, 1988).

Families and individuals who live in public housing and have well-equipped households (refrigerators, washing machines, television sets, and so on) are much better off than those who struggle for living quarters or who lack household appliances. Large groups of the population receive help from families and friends who live or work abroad. (In 1987–1988, only $10 sent from the United States provided the equivalent of one month's salary.) An increasing number of families send one of their members to work abroad. Even for a short time, this can considerably improve the economic situation of the family. Part-time work in the private sector of the economy is another means of increasing family income, and women especially have been adding to their income in this way.

When these additional sources of income are combined, many persons or families with only minimum earnings do not have to make use of the limited public resources available from the government. On the other hand, many needy people may be deprived of governmental help because their earnings are just above the social minimum.

Although no precise figures are available on the number of single-parent families who live below the poverty standard, single mothers who rely solely on family assistance checks may be among the most vulnerable groups in the current skyrocketing inflationary economy. This may be the case despite frequent adjustments that have been made in the cost of living since 1985. Employed single mothers can receive family allowances and have priority in access to a variety of social services. In financial need, they can turn to voluntary organizations, such as Caritas or Lutheran Services, for in-kind help such as clothing, medicine, and coal for heating. Many of these goods are obtained from abroad and are of adequate quality. The women who appear to be most vulnerable and at risk of poverty are those who are not in the labor force. They are often mothers of large families who have to contend with the economic and emotional instability of alcoholic husbands. This appears to be one of the most important and widely experienced social problems in Poland.

PARTICIPATION OF WOMEN IN GOVERNMENT

The feminist movement has never gained popularity in Poland. In the Polish People's Republic, feminism, as a theory to explain inequality, has always been overshadowed by the Marxist concept of class struggle. It is believed that the resolution of the class struggle will automatically provide a solution to gender discrimination or even prevent the feminization of poverty. At the present time, Marxist concepts are undergoing reexamination in Poland, and women are asserting their desire to be included in the decision-making process of the country.

In Poland, women have long been very active in trade unions, political parties, and various charitable organizations. Until the mid–1980s, there was, however, only one women's organization, the League of Women, that represented women's rights and interests (although in an apolitical way, similar to the League of Women Voters in the United States). Women's participation in the government is still limited. In 1988, there were 93 women in a 460-member Parliament. A woman was appointed to represent women's issues in the Ministry of Labor; however this position is not of ministerial rank. Women are more adequately represented at the lower levels of government. Rural women play a more significant role on the local political level and are also active in various agricultural cooperatives (Tryfan, 1987).

Thus while women represent a large proportion of the persons working in government administration, jurisprudence, insurance, and finance, they predominantly hold supportive positions, rarely reaching leadership roles. The history of women's role in the Solidarity movement is still to be written. There is evidence of women's strong and enthusiastic participation in the rank and file of this movement, but as yet there is no evidence of women's participation in leadership. At this point, women do not have a strong political base, but according to Anna Titkow (1985), there is evidence of a new trend toward a women's movement in Poland.

CONCLUSION

Despite extensive government transfers and a profamily policy, women are heavily burdened by their life situation in Poland. ''Men have too much power and women too much work'' (Danecki, 1988). Women in Poland are confronting the following issues:

1. There are a growing number of separations and divorces in Poland, and these are creating hardships for women, especially those who are single parents, not solely in economic terms (Marynowicz, 1985).
2. The great majority of married women combine two jobs—in the workplace and at home. The greatest complaint of women both in rural and urban situations is that of being overworked. There is no such thing as leisure time for women.
3. The very slow process of democratization in family life and roles is another source of difficulty. The need for all members, including husbands and children, to share family tasks is now being discussed publicly. However, implementation of change is slow because of the patriarchal traditions that persist.

In conclusion, Polish women currently make up about 45 percent of the Polish labor force. They also play an important domestic role in the home, which poses stress and hardship, especially in the present economic situation. Despite the growing number of women receiving higher education, women still play a minimal role in governing the country. Thus Poland does not differ much from capitalist nations with regard to the status of women, despite its socialist rhetoric.

NOTES

1. Participation in the very dangerous activities of the Polish underground army was subsequently recognized by the Polish People's Republic through conferring of honors and monetary rewards.

2. GUS predates the Polish People's Republic. GUS has achieved an international reputation and is recognized (with some dissenters) to have produced reliable data over time. GUS is operated by professional demographers, conducts the national census, and has issued statistical yearbooks in several languages. It has published special statistical material on women, such as *Kobieta w Polsce* (*Women in Poland*, 1985), in preparation for the United Nations decade on women, and a more recent publication, *Sytuacja spo-leczno-zawodowa kobiet w 1978R* (Social situation of working women in 1987) (1988b).

During the 1980s, Solidarity sponsored the collection of data about existing social and economic conditions, which were reported in underground publications. Much of these data were anecdotal, however.

3. This survey conducted by GUS was stimulated by the earlier events of the United Nations Decade for Women. Several leading Polish women academics attended the Nairobi conference and recognized the need to obtain more information about the status of Polish women. A sample was developed by GUS representing 90 percent of Polish women between the ages of 15 and 55. Mailed questionnaires were sent to 4,817 respondents to investigate the situation of women in the family, in agriculture (both private and public), and in education. Women who were engaged neither in work nor school were also represented in the sample.

4. During 1979–1980, the author and Narayan Viswanathan of the Adelphi University School of Social Work, studied the use of volunteer counselors in the informal sector of

the Polish social welfare system. The results of their study were summarized in an unpublished report to the American Academy of Sciences in 1980. The informal sector of the social welfare structure continues to function despite the severe economic crisis now facing Poland.

5. Solidarity, the free trade union, originally developed, at least in part, as a response to Polish society's strong negative reaction to their lack of involvement in the creation of social welfare policies and their absence from overall political decision making.

REFERENCES

Danecki, Jan (November 1988). Interview, Professor of Sociology, Warsaw University.

Davies, N. (1986). *The Heart of Europe: A Short History of Poland*. Oxford: Oxford University Press.

Glowny Urzad Statystycny (GUS) (1979). *Maly Rocznik Statystycny (Pocket Statistical Yearbook)*. Warsaw: GUS.

––––––– (1985). *Kobieta w Polsce (Women in Poland)*. Warsaw: United Nations Decade of Women.

––––––– (1987). *Maly Rocznik Statystycny (Pocket Statistical Yearbook)*. Warsaw: GUS.

––––––– (1988a). *Maly Rocznik Statystycny (Pocket Statistical Yearbook)*. Warsaw: GUS.

––––––– (1988b). *Sytuacja Spoleczno-zawodowa Kobiet w 1987R (Social Situation of Working Women in 1987)*. Materialy Statystczne 55. Warsaw: GUS.

Hemler, J. (November 13, 1988). *Polityka*. Warsaw.

Hunter, R. (1986). "The management perspective on Poland's economy: Crises and recent attempts at reform." *The Polish Review* 31 (4): 301–304.

Iwaszczyn, K. (1987). *Modern Women in Polish Science*. Unpublished paper. Warsaw: Polish Academy of Science, Study Center of the Committee—Poland 2000.

Kaszuba, K. (1989). "O nosbez nas (About us without us)." *Kobieta i Zycie (Women and Life)* 12 (14): 2–3.

Kobieta i Zycie (Women and Life) (1989a, May 17). Editorial.

––––––– (1989b, October 11). Editorial.

Kurzynowski, A. (1986). "A ktywnosc zawadowa kobiet w 40—leciu PRL (Professional activity of women in 40 years of the Polish People's Republic)." In *Kobiety Polskie (Polish Women)*. Warsaw: Ksiaka i Wiedza.

Les, E. (1985). "Swiadczenia spoleczne na rzecz osob zyjacych w niedostatku (Government transfers for people in poverty)." In *Polityka Spoleczna w Okresie Przemian (Social Policy in a Period of Change)*. Warsaw: Panstwowe Wydawnictwo Ekonomiczne.

––––––– (forthcoming). "Social welfare in Poland." In J. Dixon and D. Macarov, eds. *Social Welfare in Socialist Countries*. London: Croom Helm.

Marynowicz, E. (1985). *Praca Socjalno-wychowawczayz Rodzina Niepetna (Social-educational Work with Single-parent Families)*. Warsaw: Instytut Wydaniczy Zwiazkow Zawadowych.

Rosset, E. (1986). *Rozwody (Divorce)*. Warsaw: Panstowe Wydownictwo Ekonomiczne.

Rutkowski, J. (1988). *Polityka spoleczna (Social Policy)*, volume 16. Warsaw: Instytut Pracy i Spraw Sojacnych.

Steven, S. (1982). *The Poles*. New York: McMillan.

Strzeminska, H. (1989). *Part-time Work in Poland*. Unpublished paper. Warsaw: Polish Academy of Science, Study Center of the Committee—Poland 2000, Poland.

Titkow, Anna (1985). *Poland (Polish People's Republic): Working Women in Socialist Countries*. Geneva: International Labor Organization.

Tryfan, Barbara (1987). *Kwestia Kobieca na Wsi (Situation of Rural Women)*. Warsaw: Panstwowe Wydawnicto Naukowe.

Turgeon, L. (1989). *State and Discrimination: The Other Side of the Cold War*. Armonk, NY: M. E. Sharpe.

United Nations (1989). *Compendium of Statistics and Indicators on the Situation of Women in 1986*. New York: United Nations.

9

The Feminization of Poverty: Not Only in America

GERTRUDE SCHAFFNER GOLDBERG
AND ELEANOR KREMEN

This study began with the assumption that the economic inequality of women is a global phenomenon but asked whether the feminization of poverty exists in industrialized societies other than the United States. Industrialized societies were chosen because the trend toward the feminization of poverty was first identified in one of the world's most advanced industrialized nations and because in that country at least the great resources and great promise of prosperity that industrialism makes possible were evidently bypassing many women, even at a time when they were asserting their rights to economic and social independence. Was this paradox of feminized poverty peculiar to American life or a phenomenon characteristic of industrialized society itself?

Looking carefully at labor market, equalization policy, social welfare, and demographic factors in seven industrialized nations—five capitalist and two socialist—the study found that the feminization of poverty, though not uniquely American, is most pronounced in the United States where it was first identified. However, without very strenuous and sustained efforts aimed at both the labor market and the social welfare system, the feminization of poverty could occur in most, if not all, advanced industrialized societies. Economic inequality is, as we anticipated, the lot of women in all seven countries; indeed we found striking similarities in the experience and condition of women wherever we looked.

UNDER WHAT CONDITIONS DOES THE FEMINIZATION OF POVERTY OCCUR?

The feminization of poverty occurs wherever there are insufficient efforts to reduce poverty either through labor market or social welfare policies and where single motherhood is sufficiently widespread. Both these conditions have been met in the United States. The rate of single motherhood has risen to nearly one-fifth of all families with children, and women are assured neither a fair market wage nor a decent social wage. In fact, nearly half of single-mother families are poor, and they comprise three-fifths of all poor families, more than meeting our definition of the feminization of poverty.

In the United States it has long been assumed that there is a direct link between poverty and family composition or single motherhood. However, Sweden has gone far toward breaking this link—a notable achievement. Single motherhood is about as prevalent in Sweden as it is in the United States. By using a combination of labor market and social policies, developed and pursued for at least four decades, Sweden has achieved a relatively low rate of poverty for single-parent families. In the only study for which there are standardized figures on poverty, American single parents were shown to be nearly six times as likely to be poor as their Swedish counterparts (Smeeding, Torrey, and Rein, 1988, p. 113). Nonetheless the Swedish poverty rate of 7.5 percent, twice the overall rate for families with children, does not indicate the absence of poverty for single-parent families.

Japan is the other country in the sample where the feminization of poverty is not in evidence. Japan presents a very different picture from Sweden, however, in that women are extremely disadvantaged in the labor market. Their labor force participation rates are relatively low and their employment careers interrupted not only for motherhood but often a second time for elder care. In a system that rewards seniority, women are at a severe disadvantage. They are rarely hired by the large firms that provide such enviable wages, fringe benefits, and job security. The wage gap between Japanese women and men is even wider than it is in North America. In order to offset these disadvantages in the labor market, the state would need to provide a very generous system of income transfers. At present Japan has a very minimal social assistance program, and its other benefits—such as health insurance and means-tested family allowances—do not lift the single mother out of poverty.

What prevents the feminization of poverty in Japan is a very low rate of single motherhood—about one-fourth the rate found in Sweden and the United States. It appears that the economic prospects of Japanese women are so bleak that relatively few of them can risk the economic independence that divorce entails. Those few women who do support themselves in Japan are probably at greater risk of poverty than in any of the other countries studied. While single motherhood does not appear to be on the increase at this time, social and economic policies in Japan are ill-prepared to cope with increases in the rate of divorce and separation that characteristically occur in most industrialized societies. It should be noted that the U.S. rate of single motherhood in 1960 was not much greater than that of Japan in the 1980s. Between 1960 and 1987, however, the U.S. rate almost tripled.

While the feminization of poverty may be a distant prospect in Japan, it is a distinct possibility in Canada. Single motherhood is still not as prevalent there as it is in the United States and Sweden, but it is 13 percent and growing. Single-mother families already comprise over 40 percent of all poor families in Canada.

If divorce rates continue to rise, so, we believe, will the feminization of poverty. Canadian women have relatively high rates of unemployment, a wage gap about equal to that of American women, and little progress has been made in overcoming occupational segregation. Canada however differs from its North American neighbor in having a wider range of social welfare programs, although these benefits are not sufficient to offset the disadvantages of a single wage and a woman's wage. Canada now appears to be moving toward more restrictive social policies that could result in even less protection against the economic liabilities of single motherhood.

It has been more difficult to state with confidence whether France, Poland, and the Soviet Union are experiencing a trend toward the feminization of poverty. In all three countries there is an absence of national data on family poverty. What we do know about the combination of market and social welfare income in France leads us to be guardedly optimistic about the prevention of poverty there. Compared to Canada, Japan, and the United States, France is clearly the more generous welfare state. The range of benefits for families is comparable to Sweden, although the adequacy of these benefits is lower. Available studies suggest that the antipoverty impact of French social programs is considerable. In any case, single parenthood, though it has increased measurably in France since the 1960s, is still relatively low. Even with increasing rates of single parenthood, it is less likely that feminization of poverty will occur in France than in Japan or Canada. One area of concern, however, is persistently high unemployment rates for French women. Since French social policy assumes that single mothers earn part of their income through employment, the high unemployment rate poses a threat to the adequacy of their income.

We are also uncertain about the feminization of poverty in the two socialist countries in our study—Poland and the Soviet Union. Like the capitalist nations, there are both similarities and differences in labor market and social policies in these two socialist countries. In Poland, conditions are in such a state of both crisis and flux that assessment is complicated. Perestroika is effecting changes in the Soviet Union, which, like Solidarity's program in Poland, may have a deleterious impact on the work and welfare of women, at least in the short run.

On the basis of the data presented in the chapters on Poland and the U.S.S.R., we have nonetheless drawn some tentative conclusions. Single motherhood is relatively prevalent in the Soviet Union, particularly in the European republics where divorce rates are nearly as high as in the United States. It is difficult to arrive at a firm estimate of the number of single-parent families in the Soviet Union because of the absence of nationwide data. The rate for Poland is lower, akin to that of Canada and France.

In both socialist countries, but to a greater extent in the Soviet Union, women tend to work full time and to have high rates of labor force participation. Despite paid maternity leave in the U.S.S.R., there is probably less interruption of employment due to motherhood than in the other six countries. Yet, women still pursue their careers less ambitiously in order to carry out their substantial family

responsibilities. Despite their presence in occupations and professions traditionally held by males in the West, women are still largely employed in unskilled
and low-paid occupations. The wage gap in these two socialist countries is wider
than the wage gap for full-time workers in Sweden and France although somewhat
lower than in North America. This comparison is somewhat misleading. Wage
gap figures for the socialist countries encompass virtually the whole workforce.
In the capitalist countries a substantial proportion of part-time workers, largely
female, are not included. This tends to underestimate the differences between
women's and men's earnings in the capitalist countries. In recent decades Soviet
authorities, for reasons that are probably mixed but not entirely clear, have
pursued policies that have increased the wages of women and have had the effect
of comparable worth or pay equity approaches in the West. There is thus reason
to believe that the female/male wage gap may be narrowing even though the
occupational segregation of the sexes remains. In the Soviet Union and in Poland
as well, two wages are necessary to achieve what is considered a social minimum
for families, and a single wage, particularly a woman's wage, is therefore unlikely
to be an adequate family wage.

A wide range of benefits has existed in the two socialist countries—subsidization of basic goods and services for all, allowances to ease the costs of parenthood, and special provisions for single parents including priorities and lower
fees for services as well as allowances. Overall economic resources, which are
low in both countries, set limits on the amount that can be spent on social
welfare. The Soviet Union has about one-fourth the GNP per capita of the United
States,[1] and Poland is even poorer. It is thought that there are substantial numbers
of families below the social minimum in both countries—at least one-fifth in the
Soviet Union. Social welfare benefits are not sufficient to remove large numbers
of these families from poverty, but it is not clear that families supported by a
single woman suffer disproportionately. Subsidies for housing, health, food, and
transportation do appear to prevent the type of grinding poverty—homelessness
and hunger—that is currently found in the United States. The market mechanisms
that are being introduced by the Solidarity government in Poland and through
perestroika in the Soviet Union are designed to increase productivity and to
achieve higher living standards. However, these reforms may result in reductions
in the extensive, though rather thin, safety net of social welfare programs in
these two socialist countries.

THE FOUR FACTORS: A CROSSNATIONAL PERSPECTIVE

In her crossnational study, Hilda Scott found "that the position of women in
the industrialized countries is more alike than it is different" (1984, p. viii).
Although there are differences in the extent to which feminization of poverty is
developing, we too found remarkable similarities in the condition of women
across our seven-country sample, capitalist and socialist countries alike. Whether
we observed labor market, equalization policy, social welfare, or demographic

factors, this was clearly the case. We identified the following common conditions:

- large-scale entry of women into the labor force
- significant educational gains for women
- emergence of the dual role for employed women
- occupational concentration of women in low-wage sectors of the economy
- persisting female/male earnings differentials
- insufficient governmental commitment to equalization policies
- insufficient publicly supported child care
- irregular and insufficient paternal child support
- underrepresentation of women in governmental and policymaking bodies

We found there is an increase in single motherhood and divorce in all of the countries studied but Japan.[2]

With the sole exception of the United States, there are social programs that are common to the countries studied in this book. These programs include paid maternity leave, national health care, and family allowances.

Child support is a means of retaining a portion of the second income of an absent parent. However, since fathers so often fail to pay, governments have adopted a variety of measures to assure that this private income transfer is made. Some governments, notably the advanced welfare states and socialist countries, have begun to guarantee child support whether or not it can be collected from the absent parent.

Thus far, we have identified common conditions experienced by women in both capitalist and socialist countries. However, we also found differences in the condition of women living in these contrasting economic systems. For example, in the capitalist countries, the vast majority of part-time workers are women. In some of these countries, as many as one-third or two-fifths of women workers are employed part-time. This part-time work entails different degrees of economic disadvantage depending on the extent of the wage differential between full- and part-time workers and the availability of fringe benefits. By way of contrast, few women work part time in the socialist countries. Protective labor legislation is still prevalent in the socialist countries, but it is being reduced in the capitalist countries.[3] Socialist countries guarantee full employment for both sexes, while the capitalist countries vary in this respect, some maintaining a commitment to full employment and others allowing unemployment to exceed 10 percent for one or both sexes.[4] Moreover, in capitalist countries, full employment, as conventionally defined, has not meant a fully employed female population of working age. In Japan and Sweden, two capitalist countries with full-employment policies, women either have relatively low labor force participation rates or, if in the labor market, high part-time employment rates.

THE DUAL ROLE

None of the societies in this sample has raised the question that would arise in a more egalitarian, less patriarchal context: Should women who are employed outside the home be expected to maintain their household roles and their primary responsibility for the care of children? At the most, some societies recognize the burdens that the dual role entails and attempt to mitigate them. Others accord little or no recognition to the fact that most women are in the labor market, and as a result women are obliged to devise private solutions.

From a policy perspective, there are a number of ways in which the burdens of the dual role can be alleviated. Among these are part-time work, workplace adjustments to parental roles, subsidized child care, communal or market mechanisms to reduce household work, and the equalization of family roles. Our study of these seven industrialized countries has identified various combinations of these approaches, although it must be acknowledged that the equalization of family roles is more theoretical than real. For the single mother, moreover, equalization of family roles is scarcely an alternative, and she requires these other approaches.

Public policy in the socialist countries acknowledges that women are performing both roles. In the Soviet Union the two roles are roughly equal, while in Poland the maternal role seems to be valued somewhat more than the employment role. The socialist countries have made subsidized child care a cornerstone of their approach to the dual role. While the responsibility for the care of children has been lightened, shortages of consumer goods, the poor quality of household appliances, and an inefficient system of distribution add to the burden of women's domestic responsibilities. Indeed, it is widely recognized that women in the socialist countries are overworked. The early socialist objective of communal provision of domestic services has not been realized, although new attempts in this direction have been made through such devices as provision of food at the worksite. In both socialist countries the workplace has shown flexibility in responding to the needs of working mothers through vacation priorities, leave to stay home with sick children, and, most significantly, paid maternity leave. In these ways the economic penalty for performance of the maternal role is mitigated. Part-time work as an option for mothers of young children is being considered in the Soviet Union, although full-time work remains the overwhelming pattern.

The socialist experience suggests that despite a wide range of measures to reduce the burden of the dual role, nevertheless women are overworked and at a disadvantage in the workplace. The equalization of male and female roles in the family has not been seriously addressed by public policy in either of the two socialist countries.

The Swedish or social democratic approach offers women a variety of options for combining employment and family roles. This approach makes extensive use of subsidized child care and of part-time work that retains workplace benefits.

Part-time work certainly leaves women less strained but at the same time can interfere with their advancement in the workplace. The immediate loss of earnings for Swedish women is cushioned by an extensive system of social welfare benefits and policies to reduce the wage gap. The Swedish government has encouraged equalization of family roles through its policy of paid parental leave. However, implementation has faltered partly because the private sector releases male workers only reluctantly. The policy of a parental leave is clearly a laudable social innovation. Yet there are difficulties implementing this policy, including the reluctance of some men to leave the labor market to care for their children. In France, where leave is unpaid, men, whose incomes are generally higher, seldom take it. In most other respects France's approach to the dual role is similar to that of Sweden.

The North American governments have done very little to recognize or ease the unfair dual role that women have assumed. Indeed, North American women tend to lack the advantage of either the socialist or social democratic approaches. In Canada particularly, but also in the United States, many women work part time, but, unlike their counterparts in Sweden, they are not assured fringe benefits. Part-time workers tend to be paid at lower rates than full-time workers. Particularly in the United States the social welfare system does not offset the economic losses from part-time work or other labor market penalties incurred as a result of the woman's reproductive role. While Canada provides paid maternity leave and family allowances, its overall effort to offset the costs of parenthood is relatively modest. The passage of parental leave in Canada appears to be imminent, and it is now joining the more advanced welfare states in this step toward the equalization of family roles. Publicly supported child care, however, is not yet a universal policy in either North American country, although recent developments suggest increased federal support in the United States. Labor-saving devices and privately purchased domestic and child care services do reduce household burdens. They are widely available in these two countries but are not as affordable for the poor. In short, Canadian as well as American women have moved into the labor market with scant help from their governments, and they are obliged to find private solutions to the dual role at great cost to themselves and their families.

Women in Japan have a dual role, but they are clearly expected to give priority to their very considerable family or domestic duties. These include not only complete responsibility for the household and infant and child care but intensive supervision of their children's education and, in some cases, care of elderly relatives. Moreover, small homes with limited storage space necessitate frequent shopping in an economy where daytime hours are still the norm for food markets. The solution for Japanese women is to interrupt their careers, to work part-time when their children are young, and after child care responsibilities are over, to return to a labor market where discontinuity imposes severe penalties on workers. Child care facilities are often too expensive for poorer women and perhaps more importantly, not open long enough hours to permit full-time work. The term

"part-time" is somewhat of a misnomer because many women on part-time
schedules work longer than thirty-five hours a week. The more appropriate term
would be marginal work, since it is paid at lower wages than full-time work,
lacks fringe benefits, and is without advancement opportunities. Nor does the
social welfare system, despite the paid maternity leave and family allowances
for the poor and single mothers, attempt to offset the economic hardships of
discontinuous and "part-time" work. For the Japanese woman, employment is
not viewed as a career but as an extension of her family role—one that is expected
to yield to family responsibilities when they beckon.

TOWARD A POLICY FOR WOMEN

The feminization of poverty is a possibility in all industrialized societies. To
the best of our knowledge it is only the most advanced welfare states such as
Sweden that have succeeded in inhibiting this troubling trend. Yet, even Swedish
women do not escape the common conditions of inequality that women experience throughout the industrialized world. While the measures taken by the
Swedish state through labor market and social policies might be considered a
model for the prevention of poverty, it is necessary to develop a policy perspective
that focuses on the inequality of women. This would have the advantage of
encouraging a gender-oriented analysis of existing and proposed labor market
and social welfare policies. Through the lens of such an analysis, we could more
clearly perceive the effects on women of apparently gender-neutral policies like
the minimum wage, social insurance, welfare reform, and national health coverage. A women's policy perspective can stimulate the search for and coordination of strategies to deal with chronic labor market inequities and the dual
role. It can also lead to the development of an institutional response to the risk
of poverty that women and particularly the single-mother family confronts the
world over.

Women's Policy and the Dual Role

The solution to the problem of the dual role must begin with the societal
recognition that it exists. Through entry into the labor market, women have
begun the process of emancipation, a process that clearly should continue. The
retention of family responsibilities is a more complex issue since both significant
benefits and significant burdens are involved.[5] One approach to policy is for
women to retain their dual role but to reduce its most burdensome aspects.
Within the context of retaining the dual role, this study has identified a variety
of measures such as subsidized and widely available child care, paid maternity
leave, parental leave, and part-time work, providing that it assures fringe benefits
and is paid at a rate equivalent to full-time employment.[6]

Another alternative would, in effect, obviate the dual role by treating child
care as paid employment in the labor market and compensating either the mother

or the father for this work. By way of comparison, maternity or parental leave only compensates for the loss of income while parents are outside the labor market. This alternative, which has not been tried in any of the countries studied, could expand choices for women and men and also reduce the artificial distinction between reproductive and productive work.

While we see little evidence that societies are inclined to equalize family roles, it is our belief that this strategy would come closest to eliminating the unjust division of labor that exists everywhere. Further, it would offer men and women greater satisfaction in their parental roles and permit some relief from pressures in the workplace. Just as the combination of primary nurturer and secondary earner restricts women's careers in the labor market, so the combination of primary earner and secondary nurturer attenuates men from their families. In a society that facilitates equalization of family and labor market roles, single parenthood itself might cease to be an almost exclusively female phenomenon. Equalization of family roles would require a deep commitment to affirmative action in the broadest sense—not only in the labor market but in the political arena and the educational system as well as in the home.

Despite our view, it is not clear how women feel about the dual role, nor do we know which combination of measures women would find most compatible with their culture or most helpful at different stages of their lives. These questions require research informed by a women's perspective on social policy.

Women's Policy and the Single-Mother Family

The findings of our crossnational study suggest some measures to reduce the poverty and inequality that single-mother families experience. Our first inclination would be to adopt a labor market approach that would enable the female breadwinner to support herself and her family. However, we cannot avoid the recognition that the single breadwinner, even if male, is a vanishing breed. We must continue to seek parity for women in the labor market through enlarging opportunities for them to enter higher paying jobs, eliminating discriminatory practices, stimulating employment through macroeconomic interventions, and assuring more equitable pay through minimum wage and comparable worth policies. In Sweden where most of these labor market policies have had a fair trial, social welfare benefits, including public assistance, must be used extensively to forestall poverty for single-parent families.[7] One important conclusion that we draw is that it is necessary to pursue a combination of work and social welfare policies to prevent the poverty of women. We want to distinguish our proposal from current welfare reform in the United States, which restricts the right to relief for mothers with young children and forces them into a labor market with limited jobs and low wages. Although we favor expansion of social welfare benefits and a minimum standard beneath which no person should fall, we believe that every effort should be made to remove inevitably stigmatized and usually inadequate social assistance from the repertoire of social welfare policy.

Social welfare benefits need not be directed solely to the single-parent family. As we discussed in the chapters on the United States and Canada, it is useful to think of four levels of provisions, only one of which is specifically for the single-parent family. These are:

1. subsidies or benefits to help all citizens pay for the costs of basic goods and services such as housing or health care;

2. benefits that protect against threats to income security arising from unemployment or underemployment;

3. benefits that reduce the costs of parenthood such as family allowances and paid parental leave; and

4. benefits specifically geared to single parenthood such as government-assured child support, special income maintenance measures, and priorities for services.

There are severe deficiencies in the adequacy and scope of U.S. social welfare programs at all four levels of provision. The absence of national health insurance, the failure to treat housing as an entitlement, restricted coverage and low replacement of earnings in unemployment insurance, and the lack of paid maternity leaves and family allowances create hardships for single-parent families. One U.S. program, the Earned Income Tax Credit (EITC), attempts to compensate both for low wages and the costs of parenthood through a tax reduction or rebate. Although benefits are low and do not reflect the number of children in a family, Congress is considering measures that would both raise benefits for all recipients and provide higher credits for families with two and three or more children. With modifications, the EITC could be a substantial aid to all employed parents, including single mothers. An advantage would be the use of the relatively neutral tax system to determine income eligibility.

Although programs that aid all individuals and families reduce the economic deprivation of single-mother families, the experience of other countries suggests that programs targeted specifically to single parents are also necessary. Government-assured child support, a program adopted by both advanced welfare states in this study, France and Sweden, provides a minimum child support payment in advance of collecting the support from the noncustodial parent. One inference drawn from the Swedish experience is that the father's contribution, even when it is obtained, is often not sufficient to provide minimally adequate child support and must be subsidized by the state.

In view of the increased incidence of single parenthood, the consequent risks to the welfare of children and the need to resort to the use of public or social assistance for single parent families, it seems prudent to reconsider the proposal for fatherless child insurance made years ago by Alvin Schorr (1966). His proposal would extend social insurance to children who are "socially orphaned"— fatherless as a result of divorce, separation, or nonmarriage of parents.

In the United States the approach to the poverty of single mothers has tended to focus on demographic factors and on the attempt to restrict the growth of single parenthood. We recognize that rising rates of single parenthood occur in nearly all industrialized societies and that efforts to combat this complex phenomenon, short of restoring women's total economic dependence on men, are likely to be futile. There is, however, a form of single parenthood that is itself born of poverty, the result of limited employment opportunities and low earnings of both women and men. Such economic deprivation strains marriages or prevents them from forming in the first place. The prevention of this form of single parenthood is within the legitimate purview of social policy.

GENDER AND RACE

It was hoped that by including ethnically heterogeneous countries we would gain a better understanding of the relative importance of gender and race in the feminization of poverty. With the exception of the United States, data were generally lacking. Further, the minority populations of other countries are not comparable to those in the United States because of differences in size, history, and permanence. In our chapter on Canada, however, we did suggest that gender seems to be a more important contributor to the trend toward the feminization of poverty than minority status. In the United States race and gender were shown to contribute significantly to the feminization of poverty. Ruth Sidel (1986, p. 22), in fact, refers to both the "minoritization" and the feminization of poverty in the United States. Women of color in the United States do experience greater labor market inequities than white women. This is particularly true of young black women whose high unemployment rates and low rates of labor force participation may leave them few career alternatives other than premature motherhood. Furthermore, black men, owing to chronically high rates of unemployment, are thought to be less "marriageable" than white men (Wilson, 1987). The same can be said of young black women, two incomes being particularly important among low-wage-earning parents. The high rate of single motherhood among women of color contributes to their disadvantage by exposing them to a social welfare system that is inadequate, punitive, and that in no way compensates for the inequities in the labor market.

POLITICAL RESOURCES FOR PREVENTING THE FEMINIZATION OF POVERTY

This book has been largely directed to the definition and description of the feminization of poverty in industrialized countries and to the identification of promising policies for the prevention and reduction of this problem. Our ultimate objective is the adoption of policies that would reduce the feminization of poverty in the United States. We therefore conclude with a discussion of the political resources that could contribute to the requisite policy changes.

The labor market, equalization, and social welfare policies that appear to prevent and reduce the feminization of poverty in other countries will not be easy to achieve. In the United States, as elsewhere, long-term trends in the labor market are creating more contingent work, less steady and secure employment, and fewer jobs with full fringe benefits for women (for most men as well). Affirmative action and antidiscrimination policies have lost the support of the federal government, and some recent Supreme Court decisions have reversed earlier rulings that furthered desegregation, both gender and racial. Pay equity strategies have had some success at the state level among public and unionized employees, although the lower courts have tended to regard comparable worth settlements as counter to free market principles. Minimum wage policies benefit the lowest paid workers and have been used to reduce the wage gap in other countries. Yet, during the 1980s, the federal government did not increase the statutory minimum wage for nine years.

Crossnational comparison, however, indicates that it is in social welfare policies that the United States is particularly deficient. Unfortunately, antipathy to the welfare state runs deep, expressing the value American society still places on individualism and economic self-reliance. Fueling and reflecting these attitudes are journalistic misrepresentations and distortions of welfare programs and their recipients. Inadequate, inequitable, and punitive, American welfare programs are unlikely to inspire support, even among prospective beneficiaries. Further, the United States still lacks programs for people of working age that could aid and draw the allegiance of the nonpoor—programs such as paid maternity leave, children's allowances, and national health insurance.

There is another reason why women of various social classes may be wary of the welfare state. It has been argued that the English poor law and its successors—particularly the very reluctant American welfare state—have been geared to "regulating the lives of women," with the state's role being primarily one of social control rather than social provision (Abramovitz, 1988; Ursel, 1986). Yet, it is possible to envision a more benign, dependable, and less controlling welfare state. Reflecting their more positive experience, Scandinavian women regard government benefits as creating an "alliance" between women and the state, a relationship that offers them more choice and more freedom than the traditional patriarchal family (Siim, 1988; Hernes, 1987).

Despite the overwhelmingly negative perception of welfare in the United States, there is historical evidence of an attempt by women to expand the welfare state. In the 1960s, poor women, with allies in civil rights, religious, labor, academic, and antipoverty organizations, mobilized to defend and redefine their rights as recipients of public assistance. Through vigorous protest and demonstration strategies, they pressed local authorities to reduce restrictive requirements and to expand benefits. Ultimately the proponents of welfare rights, many of them black as well as poor, lobbied for a guaranteed national income (West, 1981; Piven and Cloward, 1977; Steiner, 1971). Although a few welfare rights groups continue to function, the welfare rights movement lasted less than a decade. In the 1980s, when the federal government was conducting a virtual "war on welfare," recipients, lacking some of their former resources and allies, were in no position to mount an effective resistance.

The second wave of the movement for women's equality that began in the 1960s has accomplished significant changes in public policy, fostered political participation of women, and deepened women's understanding of their role in society.[8] However, the American women's movement, in contrast to its Canadian counterpart, has, on the whole, distanced itself from the struggle to defend and expand the welfare state. This may be related to the fact that American feminism, though it has tried to unite women on the basis of common gender oppression, has not yet been able to transcend the divisions of class and race (Degler, 1980).[9] Yet, it is apparent from our crossnational study that women, particularly those who support themselves, need the welfare state both to escape poverty and to achieve greater equality. Even in Sweden, with its full employment and solidarity wage policies, one-third of single-parent families would be poor without government transfers (Smeeding, Torrey, and Rein, 1988, p. 113).

Since the 1960s increasing numbers of American women of all strata have faced the risk of single parenthood, which, in turn, has exposed them to the full force of their inequities in the labor market. Although social insurance has taken firm, if belated, root on American soil, growing incrementally and adding risk upon risk, it has not addressed the new economic vicissitudes that confront women. Widespread recognition of their common economic vulnerability and of the consequent need for a decent social as well as economic wage could be the basis for a new mobilization of American women. Perhaps the organization of women on the basis of the risk of single parenthood that so many will face at some time during their adult lives could contribute to such a mobilization.

To change the position of the federal government in the United States, particularly one that has become more adversary than advocate of disadvantaged constituencies, women would need to mobilize themselves and join with potential allies who are already advocating for workplace, labor market, social welfare, and equalization policies. There is no dearth of such allies, but there are obstacles to coalescing with each of them. Although inequities overlap, there is potential for conflict of interest among those who press for the reduction of gender, class, or racial inequities.

However weakened and unresponsive, even resistant, to the needs of women in the past, organized labor is a potential ally of women in the workplace. There is indeed evidence of successful drives by labor to organize women workers and of union support for issues such as pay equity. A number of trade unions, in fact, are represented on the board of the National Committee on Pay Equity. An increasing number of women in trade unions, moreover, can be a force for exerting pressure from within. In addition to the labor movement itself, there are independent organizations of and for working women such as Wider Opportunities for Women and 9 to 5: National Organization of Working Women (Gelb, 1990, p. 281). These organizations can be allies in supporting a broad range of labor market and equalization policies.

Although we favor expansion and improvement of the welfare state, the task in the 1980s was largely to prevent its dismantling, particularly to save programs that reach the very poor. A diverse group of human needs advocates has struggled to preserve the social safety net and to build some foundation for future expansion. These organizations include the Children's Defense Fund, the Center on Budget and Policy Priorities, the Coalition on Human Needs, the National Association of Social Workers, and other lobbies, task forces, or coalitions concerned with such critical problems as hunger and homelessness. As women recognize the extent to which their interests are linked to government programs or the welfare state, these human needs advocates will be their potential allies.

Another potential ally for women is the civil rights movement whose gains have certainly benefited women as well as people of color. Sometimes forced to compete for scarce resources, these two constituencies have had an uneasy relationship. Some political leaders are achieving moderate success in creating coalitions that encompass civil rights and women's organizations.[10] Separate organizations may well permit women of color to define and give voice to their "double disadvantage."

A potential and largely untapped ally is the elderly, predominantly women, who may have organized effectively to protect and expand social security. Many older women have direct experience with labor market inequities and social welfare inadequacies. A recent study by the Older Women's League (OWL) found that despite the mass entry of women into the labor market, many younger women may be not better protected by social security than their mothers (Loeb, 1990). This warning by an organization of older women identifies a welfare-state issue that could be pursued by both younger and older women. To an even greater degree than younger women, the elderly face the risk of being single. A movement based on this common risk could unite and mobilize women of all ages.

Obviously the electoral process is a means to advancing economic justice for women. Nowhere are women fully integrated into the central decision-making apparatus of their governments so that labor market, social welfare policies, and certainly major economic and strategic decisions are made without them. In the United States, the underrepresentation of women in the national legislature is especially egregious, although there has been more progress at the state and local levels of government. One of the organizations that seeks to achieve an equal voice and role for women in government is the National Women's Political Caucus whose stated purpose is to oppose "racism, sexism, institutional violence, and poverty through the election and appointment of women to public office" (Mueller, 1990, p. 97, citing Feit, 1979).[11] Voter registration drives geared to extending the franchise to poor people, including the many women who are public welfare clients, are an attempt to change the composition of the

American electorate and to elect government officials who are more responsive to the needs of disadvantaged groups (Piven and Cloward, 1988).

The unexpected and profound political and economic changes that have reduced the tensions between the United States and the Soviet Union offer an opportunity to utilize some of the vast resources formerly appropriated for armaments to address the enormous social deficits that have developed. As we write, a ''peace dividend'' network comprised of a very wide range of interest groups is forming. Whether women disadvantaged by social class, race, or family composition do collect a much-deserved peace dividend depends in large measure upon the extent to which women recognize both the economic and social risks they face and take action to achieve a just economic and social wage, in their own right.

NOTES

1. There is a discrepancy between the estimates of the size of the Soviet gross national product. The U.S. Central Intelligence Agency estimate (Protzman, 1989) is considerably higher than that of the World Bank (1988) or the United Nations (UNICEF, 1989).

2. In her study of family trends in ten developed countries Constance Sorrentino (1990) also found that the only country not experiencing accelerating rates of single parenthood is Japan. However, in contrast to Axinn (chapter 4), Sorrentino found that divorce rates, while still low in Japan, rose between 1960 and 1986. Axinn, using a different measure of divorce rates than Sorrentino (number per 1,000 women in the population rather than per 1,000 married women), found that divorce rates peaked in 1983 but fell between then and 1986.

3. It should be noted that in the capitalist countries the term ''protective labor legislation'' is restricted to measures that exclude women from jobs deemed dangerous or injurious to their health. In the socialist countries the term appears to be more embracing and apparently can refer to measures that compensate or facilitate women in their reproductive function.

4. In Canada, men's and women's unemployment rates exceeded 10 percent in 1983 and 1984. The rates of unemployment for French women ranged from 11.1 percent to 13.7 percent between 1983 and 1987, while the rates for men were lower but still considerable, 6.6 to 8.7 percent. During the 1983–1987 period, unemployment in the United States was lower than in Canada and France; nonetheless, the rates for both sexes exceeded 9 percent in 1983. During this five-year interval, unemployment rates in Japan, which is thought to have full employment, were either 2.7 or 2.8 percent for both sexes. The range in Sweden was from 3.7 percent for women in 1983 to 1.9 percent for both sexes in 1987 (OECD, 1988, p. 143).

5. The assumption that a multiplicity of roles produces a strong tendency toward role strain or overload is challenged by a theory that emphasizes the benefits of role accumulation, such as increased resources for satisfaction and ego gratification (Sieber, 1974).

6. According to Marianne Sundstrom (1989), part-time work in Sweden encourages women's labor force continuity. It has not grown at the expense of full-time work and is an alternative to women's dropping out of the labor market to care for their young children. Swedish part-timers apparently have little difficulty shifting to full-time work when their children reach school age, and the great majority work long part-time schedules (twenty to thirty-four hours). This analysis, however, does not take into account issues

of income loss resulting from part-time work, particularly for the single mother, and its effect on occupational mobility. It also overlooks the existence of involuntary part-time work, a form of unemployment in all of the capitalist countries.

7. About 40 percent of single-mother families in Sweden received social assistance in 1985, and the average length of time during which they received this help was four and a half months (Nordic Council of Ministers, 1988, p. 97).

8. There is little doubt in our minds that this book owes a debt to the women's movement and the intellectual ferment that it created.

9. Referring to the "first wave" of American feminism, historian William L. O'Neill writes that organized women "shared the dominant values of their class and failed to see that, unlike bourgeois men, they stood to benefit directly from the welfare state" (1971, p. 166).

10. Jesse Jackson, former presidential candidate, formed the Rainbow Coalition during his election campaign, an attempt to include all economically depressed groups across racial and ethnic lines. He has also been a speaker at rallies for abortion rights.

11. Former Representative Bella Abzug, one of the founders of the National Women's Political Caucus (NWPC), was not interested in "getting just any woman elected." The main goal, she felt, should be "to build a political movement of women for social change that would simultaneously help elect more women, minorities, and other underrepresented groups and build an electoral bloc strong enough to influence male politicians to support our programs" (1984, p. 21). In this regard she claims to have differed from Betty Friedan, another founder of NWPC and author of *The Feminine Mystique*, who was primarily interested in electing women to political office "with fairly minimal guidelines" (1984, p. 21).

REFERENCES

Abramovitz, M. (1988). *Regulating the Lives of Women: Social Welfare Policy from Colonial Times to the Present*. Boston: South End Press.

Abzug, B., with M. Kelber (1984). *Gender Gap: Bella Abzug's Guide to Political Power for American Women*. Boston: Houghton Mifflin.

Degler, C. N. (1980). *At Odds: Women and the Family in America from the Revolution to the Present*. New York: Oxford University Press.

Feit, R. F. (1979). "Organizing for political power: The National Women's Political Caucus." In B. Cummings and V. Schuck, eds. *Women Organizing*. Metuchen, NJ: Scarecrow Press.

Gelb, J. (1990). "Social movement 'success': A comparative analysis of feminism in the United States and the United Kingdom." In M. F. Katzenstein and C. M. Mueller, eds. *The Women's Movements of the United States and Western Europe*. Philadelphia: Temple University Press.

Hernes, H. (1987). *Welfare State and Woman Power*. Oslo: Norwegian University Press.

Lewis, D. K. (1983). "A response to inequality: Black women, racism, and sexism." In E. Abel and E. K. Abel, eds. *The Signs Reader: Women, Gender, and Scholarship*. Chicago: University of Chicago Press.

Loeb, L. (1990). *Heading for Hardship: Retirement Income for American Women in the Next Century*. Washington, DC: Older Women's League.

Milwaukee County Welfare Rights Organization (1972). *Welfare Mothers Speak Out: We Ain't Gonna Shuffle Anymore*. New York: W. W. Norton & Company, Inc.

Mueller, C. M. (1990). "Collective consciousness, identity transformation, and the rise of women in public office in the United States." In M. F. Katzenstein and C. M. Mueller, eds. *The Women's Movements of the United States and Western Europe*. Philadelphia: Temple University Press.

Nordic Council of Ministers (1988). *Kvinnor och Man i Norden: Fakta om Jamstalldheten 1988 (Women and Men in the Nordic Countries: Facts on Equal Opportunities 1988)*. Copenhagen: Nordic Council of Ministers.

O'Neill, W. L. (1971). *Everyone Was Brave: A History of Feminism in America*. New York: Quadrangle/The New York Times Book Co.

Organisation for Economic Co-operation and Development (OECD). (September 1988). *Employment Outlook*. Paris: OECD.

Piven, F. F., and R. A. Cloward (1977). *Poor People's Movements: Why They Succeed, How They Fail*. New York: Pantheon Books.

——— (1988). "New prospects for voter registration reform." *Social Policy* 18 (3): 2–15.

Protzman, F. (November 20, 1989). "The Germanys as an economic giant." *New York Times*, pp. 1, 14.

Schorr, A. L. (1966). *Poor Kids*. New York: Basic Books, Inc.

Scott, H. (1984). *Working Your Way to the Bottom: The Feminization of Poverty*. London: Pandora Press.

Sidel, R. (1986). *Women and Children Last. The Plight of Poor Women in Affluent America*. New York: Viking.

Sieber, S. D. (1974). "Toward a theory of role accumulation." *American Sociological Review* 39 (August): 567–578.

Siim, B. (September 1988). *Reproductive Politics, Gender Politics, and the Political Mobilization of Women*. Paper presented at the Conference on Public Policies and Gender Policies, Social Science Research Council and Wagner Institute, City University of New York.

Smeeding, T., B. B. Torrey, and M. Rein (1988). "Patterns of income and poverty: The economic status of children and the elderly in eight countries." In J. L. Palmer, T. Smeeding, and B. B. Torrey, eds. *The Vulnerable*. Washington, DC: The Urban Institute Press.

Sorrentino, C. (1990). "The changing family in international perspective." *Monthly Labor Review* 103 (3): 41–58.

Steiner, G. Y. (1971). *The State of Welfare*. Washington, DC: The Brookings Institution.

Sundström, M. (August/September 1989). *Part-time Work: Trends and Equality Effects in Sweden and EEC*. Paper presented at the 9th World Congress of the International Economics Association, Athens.

UNICEF (United Nations Children's Fund) (1989). *The State of the World's Children*. New York: Oxford University Press.

Ursel, J. (1986). "The state and the maintenance of patriarchy. A case study of family, labour, and welfare legislation in Canada." In B. Russell and J. Dickinson, eds. *Family, Economy, and State: The Social Reproductive Process under Capitalism*. New York: St. Martin's Press.

West, G. (1981). *The National Welfare Rights Movement: The Social Protest of Poor Women*. New York: Praeger.

Wilson, W. J. (1987). *The Truly Disadvantaged: The Inner City, the Underclass, and Public Policy*. Chicago: University of Chicago Press.

World Bank (1988). *World Development Report 1988*. New York: Oxford University Press.

Index

About the Editors and Contributors

GERTRUDE SCHAFFNER GOLDBERG is associate professor and director of the Center for Social Policy, Adelphi University School of Social Work. She received her doctorate in social policy from Columbia University. Goldberg began her career as a social worker and program planner at Mobilization for Youth, the delinquency prevention program on the Lower East Side of New York that became a model for programs in the War on Poverty. Combining scholarship and social activism, she has been involved in the establishment and leadership of New Initiatives for Full Employment and in efforts to reorder national priorities through the vehicle of a "peace dividend." Her articles on organizational change, the education of socially disadvantaged children, and socially and economically vulnerable groups of women have appeared in a number of books and in such journals as *Social Service Review* and *Social Policy*. Goldberg is author of *Government Money for Everyday People* (4th ed., 1990). She is currently engaged in research on the unionization of women clerical workers and on strategies for preventing the spread of AIDS.

ELEANOR KREMEN is a member of the faculty and education director of the Center for Social Services of the Adelphi University School of Social Work. Her dissertation at Columbia University was a study of counseling and shelter services for battered women. Kremen has been a leader in the development of services for rape victims, battered women, and women with midlife problems and has trained many graduate students and community service providers in these areas of service. In addition she has written articles for journals and books and delivered numerous papers on women's issues, drug abuse, and poverty. Kremen's articles have appeared in such journals as *Social Work*, *Social Policy*, and the *International Journal of Addictions*.

JUNE AXINN is professor of social welfare at the University of Pennsylvania School of Social Work. She received her doctorate in economics from the University of Pennsylvania. The coauthor of *Social Welfare: A History of the American Response to Need* (2nd ed., 1982), *The Century of the Child* (1973), and *Dependency and Poverty: Old Problems in a New World* (1988), her articles on family policy, social security, poverty, and aging have appeared in a wide variety of books and journals, including *Social Work, Milbank Memorial Fund Quarterly/Health and Society, the History of Education Quarterly,* and *The Family Coordinator.* She is book review editor of *Administration in Social Work* and is on the editorial board of a number of leading journals in the field. During 1987–1988 she was a visiting professor of economics at Temple University Japan. Axinn is currently engaged in research related to productive uses of the Social Security Trust Funds.

JANE JENSON is a professor of political science at Carleton University, where she has taught since 1971. She has also held a research appointment as an affiliate of the Center of European Studies, Harvard University since 1980. In 1988, she was the W. L. Mackenzie King Professor of Canadian Studies at Harvard. She is coauthor of, among others, *The View from Inside: A French Communist Cell in Crisis* (1984); *Crisis, Challenge and Change: Party and Class in Canada* (1980; 2d ed., 1988); and *Absent Mandate: The Politics of Discontent in Canada* (1984; 2d ed., 1990). Jenson has also coedited two books on gender relations and has written numerous articles in journals and books in the fields of Canadian and comparative politics. In 1989, Jenson became a Fellow of the Royal Society of Canada.

RUTH KANTROW was Professor Emerita at the Adelphi University School of Social Work where she had taught since 1959 and had taken leadership in the development of research curricula at both masters and doctoral levels of study. Kantrow had master's degrees in psychology and social work from Columbia University and New York University and a doctorate in psychology from Iowa State University. Her earlier publications were in the area of evaluative research. In recent years, Kantrow, in addition to continuing her work in the supervision of doctoral dissertations, participated in the planning, execution, and publication of research related to vulnerable groups of women at the Center for Social Policy of the Adelphi University School of Social Work. At the time of her death in April 1990, she was at work on the evaluation of a training program for the treatment of AIDS.

MARGUERITE G. ROSENTHAL is associate professor of social work at Salem State College in Massachusetts where she teaches courses in social welfare history, social policy, social work and the law, and child welfare. Prior to beginning an academic career in 1984, she worked for over a decade as a child advocate, assisting children and adolescents involved in legal proceedings, many of whom were the victims of economic and social maldistribution and their attendant stresses. Rosenthal previously taught at the Adelphi University School of Social Work where she participated in the planning of the research on which this book is based. Rosenthal is now pursuing research on the condition of single mothers in Cuba, a developing country with a commitment to social planning. In her study of Cuba she has used an approach to studying single mothers similar to that employed in this study of the feminization of poverty in the developed world. Some of the material for her chapter in this book was gathered during a study visit to Sweden in the summer of 1988.

SOPHIE WOJCIECHOWSKI was born and educated in Poland. She left her birthplace in September 1939 and is currently Professor Emerita at the Adelphi University School of Social Work. Since the end of World War II, she has returned to Poland repeatedly for lengthy visits. On several occasions she was invited by the Polish Academy of Sciences (PAN) to lecture at schools of social work throughout the country. She has had continuing contact with leading officials, academicians, and authors in the field of social services. In her extensive travels Wojciechowski has also interviewed scores of working women, students, and housewives to gather information about the lives of women in contemporary Poland.